THE GRETSCH
ELECTRIC GUITAR BOOK

GRETSCH

THE GRETSCH

ELECTRIC GUITAR BOOK
60 YEARS OF WHITE FALCONS, 6120s, JETS, GENTS, AND MORE

TONY BACON

THE GRETSCH ELECTRIC GUITAR BOOK
60 YEARS OF WHITE FALCONS, 6120s, JETS, GENTS, AND MORE
TONY BACON

A BACKBEAT BOOK
First edition 2015
Published by Backbeat Books
An Imprint of Hal Leonard Corporation
7777 West Bluemound Road,
Milwaukee, WI 53213
www.backbeatbooks.com

Devised and produced for Backbeat Books by
Outline Press Ltd
2A Union Court, 20-22 Union Road,
London SW4 6JP, England
www.jawbonepress.com

ISBN: 978-1-4803-9924-2

Text copyright © 2015 by Tony Bacon. Volume copyright © 2015 by Outline Press Ltd. All rights reserved. No part of this book may be reproduced in any form without written permission, except by a reviewer quoting brief passages in a review. For more information you must contact the publisher.

DESIGN: Paul Cooper Design
EDITOR: Siobhan Pascoe

Printed by Everbest Printing Co. Ltd, China

15 16 17 18 19 5 4 3 2 1

CONTENTS

THE GRETSCH ELECTRICS STORY

EARLY YEARS	8
NEW YORK CLASSICS	11
BALDWIN & BOONEVILLE	77
FRED & FENDER	100
ENDNOTES	122

THE REFERENCE LISTING

INTRODUCTION	125
MODELS A-TO-Z	126
MODEL TIMELINE	151
DATING & SERIALS	153

INDEX	156
ACKNOWLEDGEMENTS	158

"Until you have actually had one of these guitars in your own hands, until you have really played one, you can't begin to appreciate what truly magnificent instruments they are."

GRETSCH PROMOTIONAL MATERIAL, 1940

THE GRETSCH ELECTRICS STORY

IF YOU WERE ANYWHERE NEAR ELLIS ISLAND in New York City during the middle decades of the 19th century, you would have seen a mass of European-born immigrants arriving with the hope of a new life in the United States. Germany was the main source of this new blood, but people also came from Italy, Ireland, Russia, and Scandinavia. You might even have spotted one particular middle-class émigré, the man who begins our story. He was Friedrich Gretsch, the son of a grocer from Mannheim in central Germany.

Friedrich Gretsch was only 17 when he sailed to America in May 1873. He settled in New York City and took a job with a drum and banjo manufacturer, Albert Houdlett & Son – despite the fact that his Uncle William, with whom he lived in Brooklyn, had a successful wine business there. Friedrich, it seems, was already determined to go his own way. He further staked his independence by anglicising his forename, and in 1883 he left Houdlett to set up his own business, calling it the Fred Gretsch Manufacturing Company. He was soon producing drums, banjos, tambourines, and toy instruments at the firm's small premises on Middleton Street in Brooklyn and selling them to local instrument wholesalers such as Bruno or Wurlitzer.

Friedrich's son Fred, the eldest of seven children, was born in 1880, and when he was 15 he had an unexpectedly swift introduction to his father's music business. Friedrich returned to Germany in April 1895 for the first time since his emigration, and in Hamburg, on the way to a meeting with a half-brother in Heidelberg, he died suddenly after contracting cholera. He was just 38 years old. Another son, Louis, later recalled the shock of this unexpected news. "The first word the family received after he sailed for Europe," Louis said, "was a cable reporting his death and burial."[1]

Friedrich's widow Rosa told Fred to leave his studies at Wright's Business College and go straight into the real world of commerce. The teenage Fred found himself heading up a still modest operation with about a dozen employees, based since 1894 in a converted wooden stable on South 4th Street. Family members liked to tell a story that whenever Fred took a customer to lunch in a nearby Brooklyn bar, the waiter would take one look at the youngster and say that whatever he ordered, he was drinking milk.

Fred channelled his youthful enthusiasm into the growth and expansion of the Fred Gretsch Manufacturing Company, and apparently he would regularly venture out on to the roof of the building to help tan the hides used for drum skins. By 1900, he'd added mandolins to the company's drums and banjos, and Gretsch's original cable address, Drumjolin, neatly encapsulated the company's trio of merchandise. Fred was importing instruments from Europe and elsewhere, too: he introduced K Zildjian cymbals from Turkey to the American market, for example.

Two of Fred's brothers joined him in the business soon after the turn of the century. Louis Gretsch went on the road selling instruments for a year before giving up his one-third interest and becoming a real-estate agent. Walter Gretsch lasted longer, leaving in

EARLY YEARS

1924 with a salesman to establish Gretsch & Brenner, importing musical instruments and lasting into the mid 50s.

Fred continued his successful expansion of the business into the early years of the 1900s. In '02, he bought out R.H. Benary, a New York manufacturer of guitars, mandolins, and banjos, and the following year the Gretsch company was incorporated with capital of $50,000. The directors were named as Rosa, Walter, and Frederick Gretsch. A trade report described the firm as "successors" to Benary and characterised Fred as "a young, hustling, up-to-date business man".[2] In 1905, the company was based in a new six-floor building at the 104–111 South 4th Street site.

Just over ten years later, in 1916, Gretsch completed construction on a new ten-floor building at 60 Broadway, Brooklyn, after many years work. The Gretsch Building was set alongside the approach to the Williamsburg Bridge, which had opened in 1903, crossing the East River to connect Brooklyn to Manhattan in New York City, and it was just a few blocks south of the old 4th Street premises. The Fred Gretsch Mfg Co had gradually moved into the new building, beginning in 1910, and the large, imposing premises would house the factory and offices for many years to come – as well as at least 15 other businesses that rented space from Gretsch, including a print works. Gretsch ads proudly claimed the company's own space at 60 Broadway as "the largest musical instrument factory in the United States".

By 1920, Gretsch was selling a large and flourishing line of instruments, most with either the Rex brand (string instruments) or the 20th Century brand (band instruments). Banjos headed the list, as the most popular stringed instruments of the time, but there were also mandolins, guitars, violins, wind instruments, drums, bells, accordions, harmonicas, and gramophones, as well as accessories such as strings, cases, and stands. Gretsch also owned the Eagle Tannery, which produced its skins and leathers.

In 1925, Gretsch's vice president, Phil Nash, said that the ukulele had now pushed the tenor banjo into second place in popularity, and Emerson Strong, the company secretary, said Gretsch employed more than 150 workers in the plant and was increasing production year on year.[3]

At the end of the 20s and into the early 30s, the guitar began to replace the banjo and uke as a more versatile and appealing instrument. The company first used "Gretsch" as part of a brandname on guitars in 1927, introducing four new Gretsch-American small-body flat-top six-strings (models 125, 130, 135, and 150) and a couple of tenor four-strings (220 and 230), most with mahogany back and sides and spruce tops.[4] The Gretsch Broadkaster flat-top was added to the line in 1931, and Gretsch-American Orchestra archtop models joined a little later (models 25, 35, 50, and 65 six-strings, plus a 42 tenor).[5]

These guitars weren't especially notable, and they weren't particularly meant to be. It wasn't until 1939, when the Synchromatic line replaced the earlier instruments, that professional musicians had an opportunity to take Gretsch acoustics seriously. The

Synchromatic archtops (models 75, 100, 160, 200, 300, and 400) were bigger and louder, had distinctive styling, including cat's-eye soundholes, and during the 40s they brought Gretsch a fair reputation alongside the better-rated instruments of the market leaders, Gibson and Epiphone.

Gretsch offered the new acoustics among a continuing wholesale list of other brandnames, including guitars made for Gretsch by the "big two" Chicago manufacturers, Kay and Harmony. Gretsch itself made instruments for other outlets, including some mail-order catalogue companies such as Montgomery Ward and Sears, Roebuck. In 1930, the company spread its distribution still wider across the USA by opening a Midwest office and warehouse in Chicago, headed by vice president Phil Nash. In combination with the factory and office in New York City, this provided an efficient and profitable network right across the country: the New York office covered the area from the East Coast to Ohio, the Chicago office from Ohio to the West Coast.

The company sold its first Gretsch-brand Spanish electric in 1939. ("Spanish" here means a regular guitar, as opposed to a lap-steel Hawaiian type.) It was called the Electromatic Spanish and was made by Kay in Chicago; Gretsch simply added a headstock veneer with its own logo. It was virtually identical to a Valencia model sold by the Oahu company of Cleveland and made by Kay at the same time. The Gretsch had a non-cutaway laminated archtop body with f-holes and checkerboard binding, with coloured position dots on the fingerboard. It had a simple single-coil pickup near the neck and, unusually, the volume and tone knobs were mounted on opposite sides of the upper body, either side of the neck. It was not the last time that Gretsch would use an unconventional control layout.

The Electromatic Spanish came complete with an amplifier for $110, but it made little impact on the market – if it was actually sold in any quantity at all. During the 30s, Rickenbacker, National, Gibson, and Epiphone had also taken regular Spanish-type archtop hollowbody f-hole acoustic guitars and built electric pickups and associated controls into the tops. Aside from a handful of notable exceptions, however, most guitar-makers and guitarists did not see much use for these unusual new instruments.

When the United States entered World War II in 1942, Gretsch quietly dropped its Spanish electric guitar. Changes were happening elsewhere in the company. Fred was still nominally president but had effectively retired from active management in the early 30s to devote himself entirely to banking, the business he really loved. He officially retired from Gretsch in 1942, and he died ten years later. Fred was replaced as company president in '42 by his third son, William Walter Gretsch – generally known as Bill – who had taken over the Chicago office in the mid 30s. Bill headed the business until his premature death at the age of 41 in 1948. His brother Fred Gretsch Jr, already the company treasurer, then took over as president. It was Fred Jr who would steer Gretsch through its glory years in the 50s and 60s. During the war, Gretsch continued to make some musical instruments alongside government war contracts, making among other things the circular wooden hoops used in gas-masks. Of course, many Gretsch people were called up for active service, but the company was able to return to full instrument production during the years from 1946, gradually re-organising itself into a firm ready for whatever the 50s might bring. Charles "Duke" Kramer was an important new recruit. He'd started working for the Midwest office in Chicago in 1935, first as a purchasing agent and later as a salesman. After a wartime stint in the army, Kramer returned to his job with Gretsch in Chicago, and he started to run the branch when Bill Gretsch died in 1948.

Kramer said that when everyone came back from the services, there was a meeting at the New York HQ in 1946 to decide how the company would develop its business. "Up to that time, we had been making drums and guitars mostly for other people," Kramer recalled. "We decided we wanted to go major line, selling product under the Gretsch logo. It was shortly after that we started to make our first electric model guitars."[6]

Gretsch needed new people to promote this new direction and hired Phil Grant to look after drums and Jimmie Webster for the guitars. Grant was a professional drummer who played with the Pittsburgh Symphony and the Edwin Franko Goldman band. Gretsch pioneered and developed the plywood drum shell, introduced smaller-size bass drums and decent hardware, and went on to produce some superb drums in the 50s and 60s that are still revered by players today. Webster was a professional piano-tuner, pianist, and guitarist who, as we'll discover, would have a far-reaching and profound influence on the development of Gretsch's electric guitar lines.

Grant talked about his first years at Gretsch and the changes following the war. "The Gretsch company did carry on as a jobber – that is, a wholesaler who sells miscellaneous things to retail stores – and so that part of the business never really changed for us: Monopole band instruments, LaTosca accordions, Eagle strings, that kind of thing. What changed was that, on the drums and guitars, we stopped selling to catalogue-houses and people like that, who were only interested in low-price merchandise. We decided to go and shoot for the big stuff, so the low-price items sort of faded into the background."[7]

■

In the early 50s, Gretsch issued an 18-page booklet called *Your Gretsch Guitar Guide* that talked up a fresh emphasis on guitars for professionals. Also it publicised the firm's new and generous three-year guitar guarantee, which covered any defects caused by faulty workmanship or defective materials. "The guitar you play is a definite factor in the quality of the music you produce," Fred Gretsch Jr wrote from his office in the Gretsch Building at 60 Broadway, Brooklyn. And he couldn't resist adding a final flourish: "A Gretsch guitar truly glorifies the talents of the artist who commands it."[8] Over the top, certainly – but it showed a company serious and fired up about its new guitar models.

The first post-war Gretsch electric guitar revived the Electromatic Spanish name and had debuted in 1949 alongside a number of Synchromatic acoustics. The new electric had a non-cutaway archtop body with f-holes, at first finished in sunburst and later also in natural. It had a single-coil pickup, described in the catalogue as a "built-in Gretsch mike". In fact, it was Gretsch's DeArmond pickup, made by Rowe Industries of Toledo, Ohio, a company run by Harry DeArmond. Despite a listing in a 1951 catalogue that called it the "Gretsch-DeArmond Fidelatone", a few years later the pickup was officially given its more familiar Gretsch name, the DynaSonic. The company would use it on all its electric guitars until the late 50s.

The 1949 Electromatic Spanish sold for $110, and it competed with other basic electric instruments of the time, including Gibson's $137 ES-150. Both had non-cutaway bodies – a design that already seemed old fashioned. Gibson had led the way in cutaway-body electrics since its ES-350 Premier model of 1947, and with more guitarists now playing electric instruments, a cutaway body was becoming a necessity. There was little point in playing high up the fingerboard on an acoustic because the results were unlikely to be heard. On an instrument equipped with a pickup and suitably amplified, however, a cutaway offered easier access to the audible and useful upper reaches of the board.

Gretsch issued two Electro II models in 1951 – the 6187 (sunburst) or 6188 (natural), with 16-inch-wide bodies, or the 17-inch 6192. These models were effectively a public statement by Gretsch that it was serious about the new electric guitar business. "Electric guitar at its peak!" proclaimed an ad for the 6192 ($355 sunburst; $20 more for a natural-finish version), which came with gold-plated hardware. It was Gretsch's first cutaway electric, and again it was aimed to compete with the market leader, Gibson, whose similarly upscale ES-350 sold at the time for $385 ($15 more in natural). A few years later, the 6192 Electro II would morph into the Country Club model.

Gretsch first presented its new hollowbody electrics to professional guitarists and music dealers in January 1951 at a three-day promotional show at New York's Park Sheraton Hotel. *The Music Trades* magazine reported that Gretsch's event enjoyed excellent attendance by "many top-flight guitarists" and described it as "an exciting forerunner of the important position the new Gretsch [models] will hold". Jimmie Webster demonstrated the latest electrics as well as a number of acoustic models at the hotel launch, and he was described in the report as Gretsch's "special representative".[9]

Jimmie Webster was born in 1908 in Van Wert, Ohio, and later he moved to Long Island, New York. He played piano and guitar and worked during the 30s as a musician in nearby New York City. He also made money as a qualified piano tuner, and at one stage he ran a music store, just like his piano-playing father, Harry. Webster's mother, Kathryn, also played and taught piano, and sometimes when money was tight she accompanied silent movies at the local cinema.

Webster was casually involved with Gretsch before the war – as early as 1941 he was visiting music stores to promote Gretsch guitars and showcase "the guitar technique of tomorrow for the artist of today"[10] – but from 1946 he began to work regularly for the company. His daughter, Jennifer Cohen, who was born in 1948, recalls that he was always busy with different things, and when she was growing up he started to work more for Gretsch. "He began to travel a lot for them," Cohen says, "promoting the guitars. I don't think he was ever exclusively a Gretsch employee, he just regularly billed them for his services, more like a freelance. He wanted to call his own shots and run his own life, and he always said he never wanted to be tied to them – that was his personality."

Webster worked three days a week for Gretsch, and on alternate days he tuned pianos. "Monday, Wednesday, and Friday he would go into Gretsch in Brooklyn; Tuesdays and Thursdays he would tune pianos around the small town we lived in on Long Island," Cohen recalls. "He was very much in demand as a piano tuner, very popular." Webster would drive in to New York City from his home at Northport, Long Island, and on the way he'd pick up the boss, Fred Gretsch Jr, who lived further along Long Island at Manhasset. "My father would pick him up and they would go to work, and they were always talking in the car," Cohen says.[11] Webster seems to have been popular with his colleagues at Gretsch: Phil Grant described him as "a wonderful guy, and very smart," a typical view among his co-workers.[12]

Webster became Gretsch's main ideas-man for guitars, bombarding management and production people with all manner of models and add-on gadgets in an effort to distinguish Gretsch's instruments from the growing competition. He travelled around the country, and occasionally abroad, to promote the latest items at trade fairs and public shows. Today we'd probably describe the sort of show that Webster put on as a clinic; Gretsch's name for the event was a Guitarama. A typical local-paper ad from the time announced: "Meet Jimmie Webster, famous Gretsch guitar stylist and teacher. See the sensational 'Miracle Neck', the Gretsch innovation that makes this the easiest, fastest-playing guitar. Jimmie appears as our guest under the sponsorship of the Fred Gretsch Manufacturing Co. Come and see him at 8:00pm this Friday!"[13]

Webster was a great find for Gretsch: a musician, an inventor, and a salesman, all wrapped up in one likeable and outgoing personality. He probably did more than anyone else at the time to spread the word about Gretsch guitars, and he became a travelling ambassador for Gretsch, for electric guitars, and for guitar playing in general.

His own playing style was unusual, and the company made a plus of this, too, often using space in catalogues and brochures – and in ads for those music-store appearances – to explain about the Touch System. This was also a peg on which Gretsch could artfully hang general publicity for its guitars: a 1952 ad, for example, mentioned appearances by Webster on a couple of television shows where he would show off what it called "his amazing Touch System of guitar playing".

What was the Touch System? You probably know about the tapping technique that Eddie Van Halen popularised in the 80s: Webster employed a similar idea back in the 40s and 50s. He produced chordal rhythms with his left hand using a sort of rapid hammering-on motion and, without a pick, he would simultaneously play the melody by tapping the strings against the upper fingerboard with his right-hand fingers, adding a

1953 ELECTRO II 6192-3

1954 CORVETTE 6182-3

BROOKLYN BEGINNINGS

Gretsch was founded in the 1880s after Friedrich Gretsch emigrated to the USA from Germany. Following Friedrich's death in 1895, his son Fred Sr (top right) took over. In 1916 he opened the impressive Gretsch Building (right; 1923 ad, top) in Brooklyn, New York City. One of Gretsch's first electric models was the non-cutaway Corvette (left), while the Electro II (top, left) was its first cutaway electric. Jimmie Webster was the main ideas-man behind many Gretsch instruments, and he's pictured (above right) with an Electro II and (above left) with Fred Gretsch Jr, Fred Sr's son and the man who would guide Gretsch through its golden years during the 50s and into the 60s.

THE GRETSCH ELECTRIC GUITAR BOOK

bassline with his thumb. "It's like patting your head and rubbing your stomach at the same time," Webster joked.[14]

He probably drew on his abilities as a piano player for the Touch System. Several people recalled that Webster was a better pianist than guitarist, and so maybe it seemed natural when he played the guitar that he should use both hands in a somewhat similar manner to the way he would on the piano. Many of those who heard him play said at first they couldn't believe that all the sounds were coming from one person playing one guitar, that it seemed as if they were hearing two guitarists.

"Credit for the discovery of the Touch System belongs to Harry DeArmond," Webster admitted in an early 50s Gretsch brochure, "whose name you probably recognise since he manufactures the popular and powerful DeArmond pickups." Harry DeArmond may have developed the system in order to demonstrate his pickups – which, as we've already learned, Gretsch used on its electric guitars in the 50s. Webster insisted: "Professional players like the Touch System because it gives them a whole new field of solo possibilities. People who play for their own amusement and for their friends find the guitar now more complete within itself than ever before."[15] This was an optimistic view. The style did not catch on at the time, although Webster continued to use it happily and effectively for decades. It wasn't until that high-volume application of a similar concept by Van Halen in the 80s – by which time Webster had been dead for a number of years – that tapping techniques had their moment of fame.

During the first few years of the 50s, Gretsch was content to offer a selection of four electric hollowbody models, but naturally it was keeping an eye on other manufacturers and the development of a new idea, the solidbody electric instrument. During 1950, Fender in California was the first to bring a commercial product of this type to market. Gretsch certainly noticed this, because Fender called its new guitar the Broadcaster, a name that Gretsch still used (spelled Broadkaster) for some drum products. Fender salesman Dale Hyatt recalled the reaction from Gretsch. "There was a camaraderie between the manufacturers in the early days, and no one was trying to beat the other to a patent or anything like that," Hyatt explained later. "So Gretsch just pointed it out and we agreed to change it."[16] At Gretsch's request, Fender dropped the name of its innovative Broadcaster, and from 1951 it became the Fender Telecaster. At first, most guitar makers considered Fender's electric solidbody to be a small-fry manufacturer's oddity that probably would not last. But that attitude soon changed.

Gretsch was certainly surprised when its chief rival, Gibson, produced a solidbody electric in 1952, the Les Paul Model. Fred Gretsch Jr told Ted McCarty, Gibson's president at the time, that he was amazed that such a traditional company as Gibson could be bothered to be involved in this modern nonsense. "When we introduced the Les Paul at the trade show," McCarty recalled in 1992, "Fred Gretsch, who was a personal friend of mine, said how could you do this? Why and how could you do that for Gibson? We were good friends, and I said Fred, somebody's got to stop this guy Fender, he's just about trying to take over. Fred said, but Ted, anybody with a bandsaw and a router can make a solidbody guitar, and I just can't believe that Gibson would do it."[17]

The businessman in Fred Gretsch Jr soon took over when he noticed that Fender and Gibson were actually selling quite a few of these new-style electrics. In 1953, Gretsch launched its first solidbody-style guitar, the $230 Duo Jet. The new guitar may have looked like a solid, recalling the general outline and visuals of the $225 Gibson Les Paul, but it was made differently, drawing on the hollowbody styles that Gretsch understood.

At the time, Gibson used a sturdy sandwich of carved maple glued to a solid mahogany base for its Les Paul, while Fender used solid ash for its Telecaster. For the Duo Jet, however, Gretsch routed out the mahogany base to make a sort of sectioned box, where the cables and electric components went, to which it added a pressed laminated maple lid. The lid joined the base only where the box was not routed, primarily at the sides and around and under the bridge. The pickups were then mounted on the top.

Gretsch's new "solid" guitar was technically semi-solid. As a result, it was light and had a particular sound, qualities that would attract many players to this type of Gretsch over the years. In terms of its look, catalogue description, and intended place in the market, however, the Duo Jet was in effect Gretsch's first solidbody electric guitar, as Duke Kramer confirmed. "A lot of people called it a semi-solid, because we routed out an awful lot of space in the wood for the electronics," Kramer said. "But basically we considered it a solidbody guitar."[18]

Unusually, during its early years, the front of the new Duo Jet had a black plastic covering, the same that Gretsch used on some of its drums. The company was well used to adding a plastic "skin" as the top layer of its laminated drum shells, so it was no great stretch to apply the same technique for the laminated top of the new guitar. Another interesting feature was Gretsch's unique two-piece strap buttons, an early take on the idea of locking strap buttons. One part of the button was screwed into the body so that the hole in the strap could be placed over the protruding threaded peg, and then a knurled knob was screwed down to hold the strap securely in place.

The control layout of the Duo Jet marked the start of Gretsch's fondness for positioning a master volume knob down on the cutaway bout rather than with the other controls (the Electro II also gained one of these around the same time). Early Gretsches with two DeArmond pickups almost always had a layout of four knobs and one switch. At the bottom of the body were three knobs: nearest to you, a volume for the neck pickup; then a bridge-pickup volume; and, below, an overall tone knob. On the cutaway bout was the master volume knob, and on the top bout there was a three-way both-or-either pickup switch for a two-pickup guitar.

The Duo Jet also had a Melita Synchro-Sonic bridge, which had first appeared on some Gretsch electrics the previous year. The Melita Synchro-Sonic was the first bridge to offer independent intonation adjustment for each string. This meant that, potentially, you could get the guitar more in-tune with itself than a regular bridge allowed. It beat

1955 *ROUND UP* 6130

■ The first two Gretsch semi-solid guitars were the Duo Jet, launched in 1953, and the Round Up, which appeared the following year. This Round Up (above; side view, left) shows well the Western decoration that Gretsch lavished on the guitar, including a G-brand on the body, a steer's head on the pickguard, a belt-buckle with a wagon-train scene on the tailpiece, and metal-studded leather attached to the sides. "Masculine beauty in real Western finish," said Gretsch. In a '55 ad (opposite) session man Thumbs Carllile, who played a regular electric in an unusual lap style, praised the Round Up's "wonderful tone". Singing star Conway Twitty went so far as to have a personalised leather cover made for his Round Up (pictured opposite).

18 **THE GRETSCH ELECTRIC GUITAR BOOK**

SEMI-SOLID SYNCHRO-SONIC

1954 DUO JET 6128

■ The Duo Jet (above) had DeArmond pickups and a Melita bridge (ad, below centre). Gretsch's semi-solid chambered body set it apart from other early solidbody electrics, such as the Fender Telecaster and the Gibson Les Paul, which were genuinely solid. Gretsch's construction was typically idiosyncratic, and Hank Garland promoted the Duo Jet in a 50s Spotlight ad (below left), saying that it "gives a performance like you've never heard before".

CONWAY TWITTY'S c.1957 ROUND UP 6130

(Advertisement)

Gretsch Spotlight
How nimble-fingered can you get?
Hank Garland on Duo-Jet's the answer

Hank "Sugar Foot" Garland and his Gretsch Guitar

Big, Big Favorite Hank "Sugar Foot" Garland plays in smart modern style on the one guitar that's ideal for his flying fingers. Here's how he talks about his new love of his: "It's called the 'Duo Jet' and man it really lets you go like one! Solid body, all-electric, and gives a performance like you've never heard before!" Hank has worked toward his present top-rank position since his start at 15, has thrilled audiences playing with Red Foley, Hank Williams, Eddy Arnold and on Grand Ole Opry. Hank recommends a Gretsch to everybody who wants to play fast and easy. The secret is in the exclusive "Miracle Neck" that makes tough chords a cinch, keeps fingers from tiring. Want to try one? Write us. We'll tell you where — and send you a FREE Gretsch Guitar Guide as well. Address: FRED. GRETSCH, Dept. 11453, 60 Broadway, Brooklyn 11, N. Y.

Electric Guitarists!
GET PERFECT TUNING, CLEARER HIGH NOTES
with spectacular new bridge for arched top guitars!

Now for the first time, you can tune perfectly at every fret, regardless of string gauge. And, hear those highs come out with a brilliance you've never enjoyed before!
Melita "Synchro-Sonic" Universal Guitar Bridge has separate adjustable saddle for each string; permits split-hair tuning from nut through to bottom fret. No special tools needed! SAVES MONEY. Brings old strings back to perfect pitch. Fits any arched top guitar.

Order from your dealer or use this coupon. **SEND NO MONEY!**

The FRED. GRETSCH Mfg. Co. DB-6
60 Broadway, Brooklyn 11, N. Y.
☐ Send Melita Guitar Bridge C.O.D. at $15.00. Money-back guarantee.
☐ Send more facts on Melita. No obligation.

Name_____
Address_____
City_____Zone____State____

Play a slim, fast-playing GRETSCH the guitar of the stars

Missouri-born guitarist, "THUMBS" CARLILE, smiling, earned his nickname — and a big following of admirers — with his unusual playing style. He actually uses his fast-flying thumbs to play his Gretsch guitar. You've heard this new prairie star with Jimmy Dickens and The Country Boys at WSN, Nashville, and on Grand Ole Opry.

"THUMBS" PLAYS THE GRETSCH ROUNDUP GUITAR, a cutaway model with a solid body and Western-style finish. Says Thumbs, "That twin pickup sure gives a wonderful tone, and the slim Miracle Neck is just what every guitarist needs for easy playin'." Try it yourself. See your Gretsch dealer or write us.

FREE! Send for the Gretsch Guitar Album with pictures of the guitars played by top Western artists.

THE FRED. GRETSCH MFG. CO.
Dept. J755, 60 Broadway, Brooklyn 11, N.Y. • Makers of guitars for the stars

THE GRETSCH ELECTRIC GUITAR BOOK

Gibson's Tune-o-matic version by at least a year. Sebastiano "Johnny" Melita brought the design to Gretsch and subsequently manufactured the units in his own shop.

The Melita's complex mass of chrome-plated metal might have looked more at home on a saxophone, but Gretsch immediately recognised its potential to provide the more accurate intonation required on electric guitars. Loosening one of the easily accessible row of six top-mounted screws allowed the guitarist to move the attached Bakelite saddle back or forward and set optimum intonation for that string. In a June 1952 ad, Gretsch promoted the Melita as "for the first time" offering "perfect tuning and clearer high notes" thanks to its "separate adjustable saddle for each string [that] permits split-hair tuning".[19]

At first, the Duo Jet had Gretsch's old-style brand logo on the headstock, known to collectors now as the script logo thanks to its flowing handwritten look. But during 1954, the Jet acquired a new logo, known today as the T-roof. The crude lower-case look of the script logo gave way to a brandname rendered entirely in capitals, a style that Gretsch had used elsewhere since the 30s. The signature touch came with the horizontal stroke on top of the central T, which was stretched (like a kind of roof) across the other letters to meet the extended height of the G and the H at each end. This distinctive T-roof logo has remained in use on the headstock of virtually every Gretsch guitar to this day.

Early in 1954, two further "solidbody" electric models in the style of the Duo Jet were added to the line: the country-flavoured Round Up and the sparkle-finished Silver Jet. Country & Western music was spreading in popularity – Hank Williams even had hits on the pop charts in 1953 – and Gretsch aimed the Round Up squarely at the rising number of country players, adorning the guitar with unrelenting Western decoration. It had a steer's-head logo on the headstock and pickguard, plus steer's heads and cacti engraved into the block-shape fingerboard markers. A belt buckle with a homely wagon-train scene was attached to the tailpiece, and there was even a big "G" for Gretsch actually branded into the front of the Western orange-finish body. The body was often made from pine, with real knots in the wood, and had metal-studded leather stuck around its sides, embossed with yet more cacti and steer's heads. To hang all this from the shoulders of the adoring owner, the guitar came with a leather strap encrusted with rhinestones and the obligatory steers and cacti. Subtle it was not. Gretsch described the Round Up as having "masculine beauty". The country singer Conway Twitty went further still: he had a leather body-cover made for his Round Up, complete with his name on the front.

Almost equally unsubtle was the Silver Jet, also launched in 1954, this time a Duo Jet with a silver sparkle finish on the body front – another by-product of Gretsch's drum department. Drum boss Phil Grant recalled that it was Jimmie Webster's idea to use drum coverings on some of the guitars, just as Gretsch had done with the black finish of early Duo Jets. "We would buy our plain, pearl, and sparkle drum covering in plastic sheets from a local company called Monsanto, and Jimmie went into the factory one day and could see we were making drums with it. He said well, why can't we make guitars with it? So we did! We would glue the plastic covering to the body, just like you do on a drum shell. Maybe the acceptance wasn't a hundred percent out there in the field, but they were good looking guitars."[20]

In a busy time for the inventive guitar department, Gretsch was also revising its line of hollowbody electrics during 1953 and '54. The non-cutaway Electro IIs were dropped, while the three other models were renamed and in some cases subtly altered. The non-cutaway 16-inch-body Electromatic Spanish turned into the Corvette and the cutaway 17-inch Electro II became the Country Club in '53, and the 16-inch Electromatic became the Streamliner in '54. Unusually, Gretsch revealed some of its thinking to choose the new names by prematurely announcing the renamed Electro II as the "Country Song" model in an ad published in October 1953.

The Country Club had a body seventeen inches wide and three-and-a-quarter inches deep, with laminated maple back and sides and a pressed laminated maple top. It had a three-piece maple neck with bound ebony fingerboard, at first with block markers and then from about 1955 with Gretsch's fancy hump-top blocks. It had a Melita bridge and what's become known as the G-cutout tailpiece, a simple string-retainer with a G for Gretsch cut into the sheet of shaped metal. Two DynaSonic single-coils were linked to the contemporary two-pickup control layout of four knobs and one selector.

Gretsch made another significant addition at this time to the way it marketed its guitars. In 1954, a new option was offered of flamboyant coloured finishes for some models, beyond the regular sunburst or natural-wood varieties. The car industry had a growing influence on guitar manufacturers in the early 50s, and the theme was especially evident in Gretsch's colourful new campaign. It announced a Cadillac Green option for the Country Club and a Jaguar Tan finish (a sort of dark gold) for the Streamliner and as an option for the Corvette. The paints came from DuPont, which also supplied most of the car companies (and later Fender, too). We've seen how Gretsch used laminated drum-style coverings on the sparkly Silver Jet and the early black Duo Jet, and for these new paints the company drew again on its experience of finishing and lacquering drums in different colours, applying the knowledge and skills that already existed within the company to help its guitars stand out in the marketplace.

Not many makers had tried to sell colourful electric guitars before. There was Gibson's gold ES-295 and Les Paul of 1952, and Fender's infrequent custom colours, soon to be spurred to official status by Gretsch's influence. For a few years, Gretsch's use of colour was a marketing bonus almost entirely its own, and one that also probably prompted the wild visuals of Harmony's Colorama guitars, introduced in '55. Through the middle 50s, Gretsch added a number of pleasant two-tone options – yellows, coppers, ivories – by contrasting a darker body back and sides against a lighter-coloured front, mimicking the style of natural-wood flat-top acoustics. This was yet another idea that came from long-standing techniques that Gretsch used in its drum department. With an eye on the TV boom of the 50s, Gretsch vice president Emerson Strong told a reporter: "These colour combinations are likely to become even more effective as colour television

■ The Silver Jet, Gretsch's first sparkly-finished guitar, debuted in 1954. Like the earlier Duo Jet, the body was topped with laminated plastic, an idea borrowed from the Gretsch drum department. The other three semi-solids are pictured in the '55 catalogue (opposite), left to right: red Jet Fire Bird, black Duo Jet, and "Western finish" Round Up.

1956 *JET FIRE BIRD* 6131

22 THE GRETSCH ELECTRIC GUITAR BOOK

JET POWER & THE JAGUAR TANS

1956 SILVER JET 6129

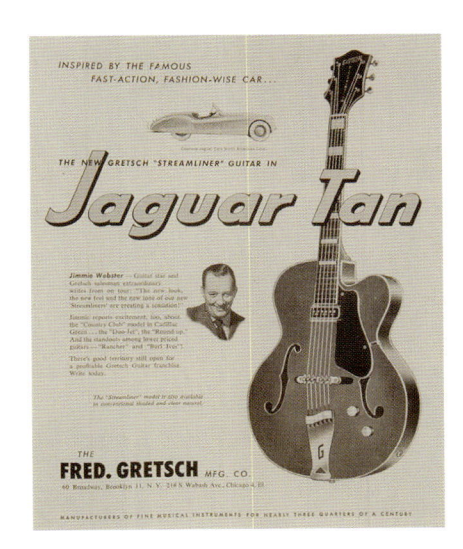

- Gretsch completed its Jet line with the red Jet Fire Bird, launched in 1955. The example shown here has the block markers, DeArmond pickups, Melita bridge, and four-knobs-plus-selector control layout of the period. Another colourful addition to the finishes that Gretsch made available at this time was Jaguar Tan, akin to Gibson's goldtop look, seen in a 1955 ad (above) that featured the Streamliner. Session man Al Caiola, meanwhile, said in this 50s ad (right) that his Electro II helped to "cut down the tension" of his heavy schedule.

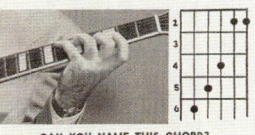

THE GRETSCH ELECTRIC GUITAR BOOK

23

receivers are installed and the public grows increasingly accustomed to the bright hues they will see on their screens every day."[21]

By March 1954, Gretsch's guitar pricelist boasted a respectable line-up of six electrics (alongside eight acoustics from $52.50 to $475). There were three hollowbody electrics: the Corvette at $137.50 in sunburst and $147.50 in natural; Streamliner at $225 sunburst, $235 Jaguar Tan (dark gold), $245 natural; and Country Club $375 sunburst, $385 Cadillac Green, $395 natural. There were also three semi-solid electrics: the black Duo Jet at $230 (with four-string baritone ukulele and tenor-guitar options listed at the same price); the new Silver Jet at $230; and the orange Round Up at $300.

Meanwhile, over in Michigan, Gibson was enjoying much success with that gold Les Paul Model solidbody, selling well over 2,000 in 1953 alone. This alerted other manufacturers, including Gretsch, to the value of a signature model endorsed by a famous player. Today, the practice is wearyingly familiar, but back in the 50s it was a new and potentially profitable kind of instrument marketing. A signature guitar named for a musician was a step beyond Gretsch's regular advertising, which simply highlighted the use of this or that model from the company's line by particular players.

Mitchell Morrison, Gretsch's New York City-based ad agency, devised a series of Gretsch Spotlight ads that appeared in musicians publications and trade magazines in the early 50s. They featured mainly jazz and studio guitarists such as Al Caiola (with an Electro II), Mary Osborne and Billy Mure (with Country Clubs), and Hank Garland (with a Duo Jet). Phil Grant liaised between Gretsch and Mitchell Morrison. "Every musician liked a little publicity," Grant recalled. "They figured it would help them with their career: your name and your picture in the papers. But, to be honest, Al Caiola had a limited following – he would only be known to studio musicians – and Mary Osborne was pretty much the same, though of course she had the glamour angle. Really, those ads didn't have much impact. They were just a name and a picture."[22]

Gretsch needed its own Les Paul – in other words, a well-known player whose name it could put on an instrument and exploit to attract fresh, untapped interest in its guitars. Around 1954, Jimmie Webster came up with the answer: Chet Atkins. It was a solution that in time, directly and indirectly, would turn Gretsch's fortunes around.

Chester Burton Atkins was 18 years old in 1942 when he became staff guitarist at WNOX in Knoxville, Tennessee, and he spent much of the rest of the decade working for other radio stations around the country. During the late 40s and into the early 50s, he was regularly playing electric guitar, at first a Gibson L-10 with an added DeArmond pickup (he got the L-10 from Les Paul through his half-brother, Jim Atkins, who played bass with Paul), then a Gibson L-7 acoustic, to which he added P-90 pickups, and later a D'Angelico Excel Cutaway with a Bigsby pickup (he later also added a P-90). Atkins had John D'Angelico put smaller f-holes in the top of that guitar and sound posts inside the body, because he felt this would help reduce feedback, increase sustain, and thus allow him to play at louder volumes.

Atkins recognised the practical value of an electric guitar almost from the start, and in the late 30s he'd bought a small amp from Allied Radio (which became Radio Shack). Perhaps he was an electric-guitar pioneer? "I ordered an Amperite pickup," Atkins recalled. "It had a clamp and you could attach it to the bridge of a flat-top guitar. So I was electrified back in those days, and I would take it down to the church where my dad directed the choir in Columbus, Georgia, on a Saturday – we didn't have electricity at home, so I had to take it down there, play all day, and then I'd bring it back. So I suppose you could say I was pioneering … but I didn't feel like it. I was just trying to sound like George Barnes and Les Paul, you know?"

Meanwhile, Atkins found there was growing demand for his playing skills. In 1947, he landed a recording contract with RCA while still in his early twenties, and he began to work hard on both sides of the studio glass. Around this time he began touring as the accompanying guitarist with The Carter Sisters, the country group led by Maybelle Carter with her three daughters. In Nashville, RCA put him in charge of its new studio, where he helped to create the so-called Nashville Sound, a sort of modernised vocal-centric version of country music. He played rhythm guitar on some of the records cut there, including hits for the likes of Elvis Presley and The Everly Brothers. But it was the run of instrumental gems he made under his own name – from 'Main Street Breakdown' to 'Yakety Axe' – that had guitarists staring slack-jawed at their record-players as they tried to emulate his impressive multi-line picking style. He was among a small group of trail-blazing guitarists who made records that defined the new potential of the electric guitar by mixing playing skills, effects units, and studio tricks to open up an exciting world of possibilities.

Atkins was well aware of his growing stature in the 50s when he was offered the chance of a signature guitar. "I was already doing well at the time Gretsch made their approach," he said in 1995. "I was on the Opry, I was playing on network radio shows, and I think I was already on national television. I was pretty popular nationally when I went with Gretsch." He remembered meeting Jimmie Webster in Nashville, at a time when he was still using his D'Angelico. "I had seen people playing Gretsch guitars – a couple of my friends played them," he said. One of those Gretsch-toting friends was Louis Innis, who recorded in the 50s on Mercury and King. "Jimmie Webster would come to town to demonstrate Gretsch guitars, and he wanted me to play them. They had some design, but I didn't like it. But he kept after me. I remember once he took me over to a music store to try some things. He really wanted me to play one of their guitars. So finally he said, well, why don't you design one that you would like? He invited me out to the factory in New York."

Atkins was interested in the offer, and he made some preliminary enquiries. "Les Paul had his endorsement with Gibson and so I called him – he and my brother Jimmy had worked together in a trio. I said to Les, how much royalties should I get? He hummed and hawed around, finally gave me a number, don't know if it was right or not. Then

1955 COUNTRY CLUB 6196

THE GRETSCH ELECTRIC GUITAR BOOK

JOIN THE COLOURFUL CLUB

1956 *COUNTRY CLUB 6196*

1956 *STREAMLINER 6189*

■ The Electro II morphed into the Country Club model in 1953, and the "new" model was promoted in Gretsch ads by American studio guitarists including Mary Osborne (opposite) and Billy Mure (above). Gretsch's accent on colour options continued, with a Cadillac Green finish popular on the Club (top) or less common two-tone grey (left), as well as the regular sunburst and natural varieties. This Streamliner (right) is in a pleasant combo of Bamboo Yellow front and Copper Mist (brown) back. It has the hump-top markers added at this time to many models.

THE GRETSCH ELECTRIC GUITAR BOOK

someone else said to me, why don't you get a lawyer to go with you? But I didn't do that, I was afraid a lawyer would queer the deal by asking too much or something. When you're young like that, money doesn't matter."[23]

When Webster first talked to Fred Gretsch Jr about hiring Chet Atkins to endorse a guitar, the boss was dismissive, asking why on earth Gretsch should pay some "hillbilly guitar player" to use his name on its guitars.[24] Webster must have persuaded Fred of the advantages. Soon after Webster's offer, Atkins flew up from Nashville to New York City. "I went over to Brooklyn to the factory," Atkins recalled, "and visited with Mr Gretsch, Emerson Strong, Jimmie Webster, and Phil Grant. They were very nice, and we came up with the design for the orange Gretsch Chet Atkins. I think if Jimmie Webster were alive today, he would tell you the most important thing he ever did was to sign me, because they started selling the hell out of guitars."

Gretsch put together a prototype to show to Atkins, probably early in 1954. In a similar way to Les Paul and Gibson, Atkins had little input to the original design of his signature model. The label inside identified the sample guitar as a Streamliner Special, although it was more like a Country Club: it had a Melita bridge, a second DeArmond single-coil at the bridge, and Gretsch's two-pickup control layout (four knobs plus one selector). "That's the first one I received," Atkins explained when he showed it to me in the 90s. "They sent it over and said: how about this? But I wanted a Bigsby vibrato on it, and I especially didn't like the f-holes, and later on we changed those. They also put all this junk on it, the cattle and the cactus, which didn't appeal to me at all."[25]

Gretsch had reckoned that with Atkins's country associations there was an opportunity to re-use the Western decoration from the earlier Round Up guitar. Duke Kramer: "Instead of giving a pair of cowboy boots with every guitar, we put this Western stuff on it."[26] Atkins had strong reservations about the cowboy paraphernalia – a belt buckle on the tailpiece, a steer's head on the headstock, steers and cacti engraved on the block inlays, and a G-brand on the body. But he gave in to Gretsch. "I was so anxious to get my name on a guitar, so I said oh … that's fine. I was thrilled to have my name on a guitar, like Les Paul had his name on the Gibson. At the time I was full of ambition. I wanted to be known all over the world as a great guitarist, and that was one brick in the edifice that would help that happen."

Gretsch would gradually remove the Western "junk" from the original Chet Atkins models over the following years. (As for the f-holes, Atkins had to wait until the Country Gentleman for a change there.) Gretsch did give a little ground right away by adding a Bigsby vibrato to the production model, in line with Atkins's request – Atkins had added Kauffman vibrolas to most of his earlier guitars. He recalled that it was Fred Jr who gave the nod to the vibrant orange colour of the new guitar. "They brought him some colour samples, and he said let's do that, that's a great idea! And it turned out it was," Atkins remembered. "It was different."[27] The two new guitars were announced, with a hazy idea of model names, at the end of 1954 in *The Music Trades* under the heading "Gretsch To

NEW YORK CLASSICS

Have New Guitars, Chet Atkins Country Style". The news item below read as follows: "Chet Atkins, top favorite of the Grand Ole Opry and one of the nation's best guitarists, plays and endorses the new Gretsch 'Chet Atkins Country' model guitar. Chet Atkins Country Style Electromatic guitars are available in the conventional hollow body or the solid body. Both have Gretsch DeArmond built-in pickups, slim, fast playing Miracle Neck, and built-in vibrola. Both models will be available for delivery after January 1, 1955, and are priced at $360 list (case extra)."[28] That price would be the equivalent of about $3,200 in today's money.

The "solid body" model mentioned in that report was the Chet Atkins Solid Body 6121, issued alongside the "conventional" Hollow Body 6120 and essentially a Round Up with a Bigsby vibrato replacing the belt-buckle tailpiece (and, despite the name, the Solid Body still had Gretsch's customary semi-solid construction, just like the existing Jet models). Atkins had little to do with the 6121, and one Gretsch insider went so far as to describe it as a mistake. The guitar was quietly dropped during the early 60s.

The Hollow Body, however, was for a short while Atkins's exclusive instrument for his increasingly popular work. "I was very honest about it," he said. "I played the Gretsch guitar, the orange one, even though I didn't like it. I was trying to get a better sound out of that Gretsch guitar – that's the reason for the zero nut and the metal bridge and those things that we did."[29] It went on to become one of the most revered of Gretsch's original models, and it has become known simply by its Gretsch model number, 6120, which is what we'll call it throughout this book.

Upon its official release in the early months of 1955, the 6120 looked unlike any other guitar around. The body – 15½ inches wide and 2¾ inches deep – had a maple-plywood back and sides and Gretsch's customary pressed maple-plywood top. Fred Gretsch Jr was evidently proud of the company's way with plywood, supplied to Gretsch for many years by Jasper Wood Products of Indiana. "One of my father's ideas, which has changed the industry, was the introduction of the three-ply rim," he told an interviewer way back in the 20s. "Instead of trying to make a drum or tambourine by taking one piece of wood and bend it under steam pressure, he put in operation the plan of making each rim from three separate rims glued together."[30]

The finish of the 6120's body was what Gretsch called "Western style in amber-red", a semi-transparent deep orange colour that allowed any figuring in the top laminate to show through. There was a G-for-Gretsch logo branded into the front of the body and two large bound f-holes. Gretsch stamped a serial number on to a paper label, pasted inside the body and visible through the lower f-hole.

The mahogany neck was glued to the body and the bound rosewood fingerboard was glued in place over a strengthening truss-rod in a slot in the neck. The 22-fret board had eight block-shape position markers with engraved Western motifs: steer's head (at frets 1, 7, 12); cactus (3, 5, 9); and fence-post (15, 17), although early examples with 21 frets are missing the 17th block. White plastic binding was glued and secured to the edges of

1954 PROTOTYPE STREAMLINER / CHET ATKINS HOLLOW BODY 6120

30 THE GRETSCH ELECTRIC GUITAR BOOK

STRINGIN' ALONG WITH CHET ATKINS

Chet Atkins was well known for his easy-on-the-ear style and a relaxed delivery, which disguised an exceptional talent. Jimmie Webster at Gretsch persuaded Atkins to put his name to the company's first signature electric models, the Hollow Body 6120 and Solid Body 6121, launched in 1955 in the wake of Gibson's successful Les Paul models. The 6120 and 6121 are featured in Gretsch's catalogue of 1955 (opposite). A prototype sent to Atkins (left; back, below) was based on the earlier Streamliner and had a belt-buckle tailpiece. A second prototype (bottom) added the Bigsby vibrato that Atkins demanded (and both guitars were later modified by Atkins). He is pictured with the first prototype (below) in a poster for an exhibition about him at the Country Music Hall of Fame in Nashville in 2012.

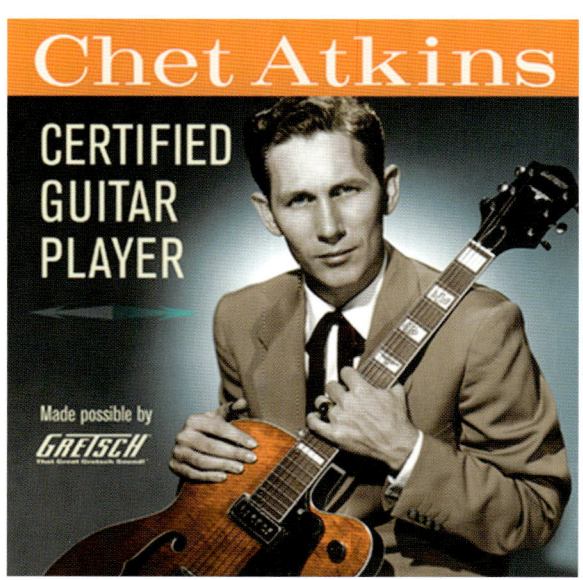

1954 PROTOTYPE CHET ATKINS HOLLOW BODY 6120

THE GRETSCH ELECTRIC GUITAR BOOK

the body and fingerboard, and there was a brass nut at the top of the neck, stopping and spacing the strings there.

The hardware included two of Gretsch's locking strap buttons and a plastic pickguard painted gold underneath, with a Gretsch T-roof logo and a facsimile Chet Atkins signature on a Western signpost. The guard was fitted to the body with a screw at the neck and a metal bracket screwed to the side of the body. There was an output jack on the side of the body. On the body were four knobs and a selector switch, Gretsch's regular control layout at the time for a two-pickup guitar: a volume knob per pickup and master tone knob down beyond the bridge, a master volume on the cutaway bout, and a pickup selector switch (bridge/both/neck) on the upper bout. The metal knobs had knurled sides and an arrow indicator on top, and the Bigsby vibrato tailpiece was partnered with Bigsby's compensated (notched) aluminium bridge.

Six Waverly tuners were fitted to the headstock, each with an open back and an oval-shape metal button on a thin metal shaft. A black plastic bullet-shape cover on the headstock hid the truss-rod adjustment channel, and there were two logos on the headstock: a Gretsch T-roof logo and a steer's head that matched the fingerboard inlay. There were two DeArmond DynaSonic single-coil pickups, each with six polepieces in a distinctive black-topped chrome case and a row of screws that allowed adjustment of each polepiece individually for height.

Gradually over the next few years, Gretsch modified and improved the 6120. The Western "junk" that Atkins detested so much began to disappear: a horseshoe replaced the steer's head on the headstock around '56, while a year or so later the block markers lost their engraved designs and the G-brand went. The Bigsby B6 tailpieces went through a few changes, too, moving from the original anodised gold to a silver colour with black infill, and from the original fixed "spoon"-shape arm to a shortlived breakaway arm and then a better swivel arm, all during '56. As we've seen, Atkins wasn't happy with some aspects of the instrument. "I played that orange Gretsch 6120 guitar, but I hated the sound of the pickups at first," he said, referring to the single-coil DeArmond DynaSonics fitted to all early 6120s. "The magnets pulled so strong on the strings that there was no sustain there, especially on the bass."[31] It wasn't until 1958 that Gretsch would swap the single-coils for new humbuckers and modify the body's internal bracing – of which more later.

In his book *Gretsch 6120*, Edward Ball estimates that fewer than 250 6120s were made in the model's first year of production, 1955, at a time when the Brooklyn factory was producing around 2,000 guitars a year. He goes on to estimate the total number of single-cut 6120s made between 1955 and 1961 at about 3,800. Gibson's bestselling ES model at this time was the ES-175, the two-pickup version of which listed at $290, a good deal cheaper than the $360 6120 – the nearest Gibson in price was the $410 ES-350T, new for 1955. Gibson sold around 3,000 ES-175Ds and fewer than 1,000 ES-350Ts between 1955 and 1961. In its field, the 6120 was clearly a sales success.

Meanwhile, Gretsch was happy to see the effect of the new endorsement deal. Atkins had his first solo hit single in 1955, 'Mister Sandman', which made number 13 on the US country chart, and this coincidental success did the new guitar no harm at all. Gretsch's '55 catalogue trumpeted: "Every Chet Atkins appearance, whether in person or on TV, and every new album he cuts for RCA Victor, wins new admirers to swell the vast army of Chet Atkins fans." Phil Grant, Gretsch vice president at the time, said later: "I think the following that Chet had in country music surpassed even Les Paul's general following. You can't undervalue Chet's importance – he was the greatest thing that ever happened to us. The Gretsch Chet Atkins models put us on the map."[32]

Not content with the coup of attracting Chet Atkins to the company, Jimmie Webster worked during 1954 on ideas for a guitar that would become Gretsch's top-of-the-line model. "I have a feeling the White Falcon was his dream guitar," Webster's daughter Jennifer remembers. "When he was developing it, there was talk that this was going to be something real special."[33]

Special it certainly was. Gretsch first marketed the White Falcon in 1955, and it was an overwhelmingly impressive instrument. The 17-inch-wide single-cutaway hollow body was finished in a gleaming white paint finish, and so too was the new "winged" headstock. Both had gold sparkle decorations, yet again borrowed from the Gretsch drum department. All the guitar's metalwork was gold-plated, including the fancy Grover "stair-step" Imperial tuners and the stylish new tailpiece, since nicknamed the Cadillac because of its bold V similar to the car company's logo. The new hump-top fingerboard markers had suitably ornithoid engravings, and the gold plastic pickguard featured a flying falcon about to land on the nearby Gretsch logo.

Webster's daughter remembers him drawing the logos for different guitars. "I think he may have drawn that falcon symbol," Cohen says. "He used to sit and draw a lot of that stuff, different symbols for the different guitars – I can recall seeing him sketching them. There's one on a Chet Atkins that looks like a piece of wood with jagged edges, for example. I can remember him experimenting with different Gretsch logos and things like that, too."[34]

The White Falcon was, quite simply, a stunner. "Cost was never considered in the planning of this guitar," Gretsch boasted in a '55 catalogue, and it's hard to disagree. "We were planning an instrument for the artist-player whose caliber justifies and demands the utmost in striking beauty, luxurious styling, and peak tonal performance, and who is willing to pay the price." To be precise, the new Falcon's retail price was $600 (equivalent to about $5,300 in today's buying power). The next highest in the Gretsch line was a $400 Country Club. Gibson's most expensive hollowbody electric in 1955 was the $690 Super 400CESN – and while a fine instrument, it was by comparison a sedate, natural-finish product of the relatively conservative Kalamazoo-based company. Meanwhile, over in New York, Gretsch proclaimed the idiosyncratic White Falcon as "the finest guitar we know how to make – and what a beauty!" For Jimmie Webster, a white guitar was not such

■ The semi-solid companion to the Chet Atkins Hollow Body 6120 was the Solid Body 6121 (below), but it was never as popular. It was in the style of Gretsch's Jet models, and it sat awkwardly alongside the existing and similar Round Up. Atkins himself hardly played it, and it disappeared from pricelists by the early 60s.

1955 CHET ATKINS SOLID BODY 6121

1956 EXPERIMENTAL GUITAR

34 THE GRETSCH ELECTRIC GUITAR BOOK

COWBOY STYLE OR WESTERN JUNK?

1955 *CHET ATKINS HOLLOW BODY 6120*

1956 *CHET ATKINS HOLLOW BODY 6120*

■ The Chet Atkins Hollow Body 6120 would become one of the most revered Gretsch electrics. Upon its launch in 1955 (top of page) it had a G-brand, DeArmond pickups, gold-plated metalwork, an anodised Bigsby vibrato, engraved block markers, and that famous orangey-red finish. The Bigsby was changed, including a "breakaway" arm (on the 1956 example, above), and by the '59 catalogue (above right) the 6120 had lost most of the decoration Atkins called "Western junk", but it retained the "carved saddle leather" strap (above). This experimental black sealed-top 6120 (left) was sent to Atkins, who plays it here on a 50s TV show (top). It had prototype humbuckers but was later modified by Atkins, who had Ray Butts set polepieces into the top of the fingerboard, apparently for octave effects.

THE GRETSCH ELECTRIC GUITAR BOOK

a new idea. Jennifer Cohen kept a picture of her father playing in Iceland in his Army Air Corps band during World War II, in which he was clearly using a Harmony guitar with a white finish. Even more intriguing among her collection of memorabilia was a newspaper cutting from 1943 that Webster sent home from Iceland during the war. Cohen says: "He's mentioned in the article, and there's a little arrow pointing to 'me'. Then if you flip it over, you can see that this forces newspaper is called *The White Falcon*. I really think that's where the name for the guitar came from."[35]

Another influence on the style of the White Falcon may have come from the banjos that Gretsch marketed – for example, Gretsch had acquired the Bacon & Day banjo company in the late 30s. Some of the more ostentatious models had gold trim, fancy fingerboard markers, and rhinestone inlays. It's fair to deduce that some features of the White Falcon – including its distinctive jewelled knobs and feathery fingerboard inlays – were inspired by these banjos. There's no reason to suppose that borrowings would be limited to the drum department, and Jimmie Webster was probably fond of wandering around the entire factory in his search for new ideas.

"We were always looking for something new to bring out at the NAMM conventions," Gretsch's Duke Kramer said of the White Falcon. The purpose of demonstrating proposed new models at these important regular gatherings of the National Association of Music Merchants was to line up customers – the dealers who visited from across the country – in advance of production. An early White Falcon prototype was displayed at one of Gretsch's local promotional events in March 1954, but the guitar's first big showing was at the major NAMM show in Chicago four months later. Gretsch enticed store-owners by billing the still experimental Falcon as one of the "Guitars Of The Future" alongside the green Country Club and the dark-gold Streamliner.

"We followed the automobile industry," Kramer explained. "General Motors had what they called the Autorama or Motorama show where they would display a dreamlike futuristic car model. We felt we could do that on a guitar. So we made the White Falcon for the show. It created quite a stir. We had it on a turntable with spotlights on it and it looked very special. Because of the response at that show, Fred was forced to go into production on the Falcon – which he didn't want to do, because it's a miserable guitar to have to make!"[36]

Gretsch's Phil Grant remembered the Falcon's reception among music store owners and that the flagship model became a help to Gretsch's general marketing efforts. "Our sales force always had a struggle getting our guitars accepted, because Gibson was number one," Grant said. "So if Gibson had one dealer in a city, we had to look to find a dealer that wasn't quite as hip and quite as knowledgeable to put our guitars in. And of course the best dealers in town would obviously have Gibson. It became easier when Jimmie Webster got the thing going and we had the White Falcon and guitars like that. The dealers were getting calls for the Falcon, and when that happens they're a little more agreeable to putting in stock."[37]

Gretsch began to supply dealers with the first Falcons in 1955, and news of the impact of this spectacular new model reached other guitar manufacturers. Don Randall, head of Fender Sales at the time, recalled later that Gretsch's coloured guitars influenced Fender's decision to officially offer in 1956 its "player's choice" colour options, known from the following year as Custom Colors. "I was out in the field and sales oriented," Randall explained, "so I saw that Gretsch had their green Country Club and the White Falcon. We offered our colours to diversify and get another product on the market."[38] Despite earlier Gretsch and Gibson models featuring gold-plated hardware, it was the White Falcon that finally convinced Fender of the visual bonus that sparkling golden metal could provide. Randall didn't want Fender to be outdone, and from around 1957 Fender began officially to offer some of its models with the option of gold-plated hardware.

In the same way that Gretsch had issued a companion model to the Chet Atkins 6120, it produced a partner to the White Falcon in semi-solid style. This was the White Penguin. It had most of the Falcon features and was first released in 1956. "The name came about because a penguin has a white front," Duke Kramer insisted,[39] although it's hard to imagine how Gretsch expected anyone to buy a guitar with such an unappealing and comical name. It even had a little penguin waddling across the pickguard. Sure enough, very few people bought a White Penguin. The model didn't appear in any of the company's catalogues, and it only made fleeting appearances on a couple of pricelists and was briefly name-checked in a single brochure. From the small number that surface today, it's obvious that very few Penguins were made, and the model has since become regarded as one of the most collectable of all Gretsch guitars.

When it came time to compile the 1955 catalogue, Gretsch decided to pull out all the stops and create a document that showed off its new models and bright finishes to best effect. The company produced a striking brochure with a full-colour cover, a rarity among guitar companies at the time. Eight vivid models were displayed over the outside front and back covers, including Convertible and Streamliner in two-tone finishes, a green Country Club, a dark-gold Corvette, and, of course, a White Falcon. Gretsch also took the opportunity to parade in colour the two orange Chet Atkins models, on the inside front page, plus the black Duo Jet, orange Round Up, and the recently added red Jet Fire Bird on the inside back. "One look at these new Gretsch guitars will tell you why musicians all over the country are raving about them," Jimmie Webster said inside as he gazed out at the reader from behind his Country Club. "Whether you play hillbilly, jazz, progressive or just plain strum an' sing, there's a Gretsch guitar for you," he continued, modestly hinting that Gretsch now had lines that catered for virtually all the guitar-playing tastes of the era.

In October 1956, prices for Gretsch's line of 11 electric guitar models were detailed in a catalogue bound into the latest issue of *Country & Western Jamboree*. There were six hollowbodys: the Clipper at $175 in sunburst or $185 in two-tone Desert Beige/Shadow Metallic Gray; Streamliner $250 sunburst, $260 two-tone Bamboo Yellow/Copper Mist,

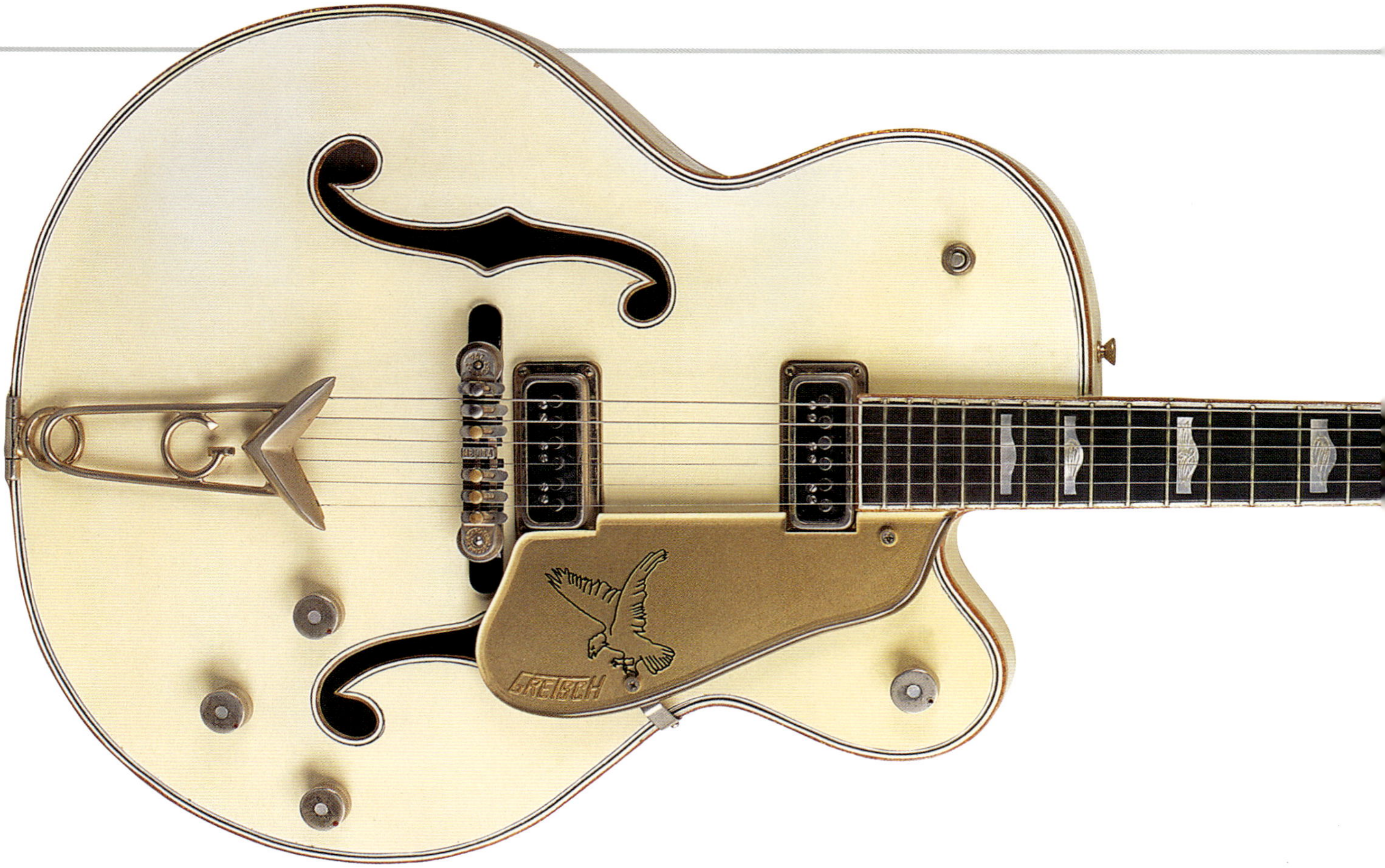
GRETSCH

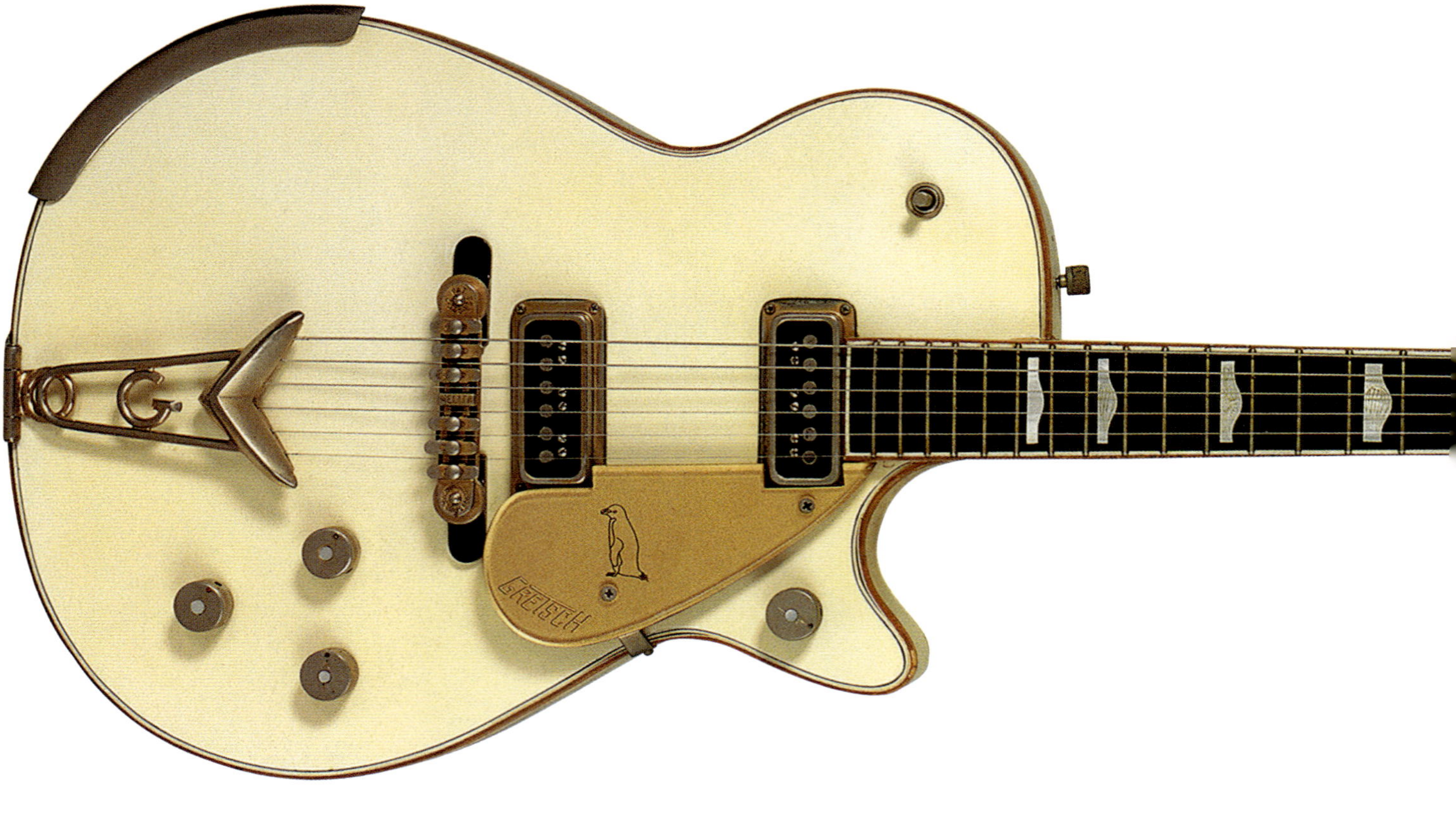
GRETSCH

THE FALCON HAS LANDED

1956 WHITE FALCON 6136

1956 WHITE PENGUIN 6134

■ It was, said Gretsch, "the utmost in striking beauty, luxurious styling, and peak tonal performance". Players had to agree that the $600 White Falcon was a stunner, as this early example (top) testifies. The Falcon's mutant offspring was another of Gretsch's semi-solid companions, the peculiar White Penguin (left), which is now considered to be one of the rarest and most collectable Gretsch guitars ever made. Jimmie Webster (with Phil Grant and prototype Falcon, early 1954, above left) was largely responsible for the Falcon's design and ostentatious looks, and he may have got the idea for the name when he was posted to Iceland during World War II and regularly sent home the forces newspaper, The White Falcon (top). The cover of Gretsch's 1955 catalogue (above) was a glorious affair that celebrated the company's increasingly colourful models, including the new White Falcon.

THE GRETSCH ELECTRIC GUITAR BOOK

$260 natural; Convertible $320; Chet Atkins Hollow Body 6120 $400; Country Club $400 sunburst, $420 Cadillac Green, $420 natural; and White Falcon $650. Five semi-solids completed the picture: the Duo Jet at $290; Jet Fire Bird $300; Silver Jet $310; Round Up $350; and Chet Atkins Solid Body $400.

Gretsch was busily widening its line of electric guitar models and improving the visibility of its guitars with glossy new brochures and popular endorsers, and the company decided it was time to employ a quality-control person to increase the chances that the instruments coming out of the factory were equal to all this fresh attention. The new man who joined the guitar team at the Brooklyn factory was 24-year-old Dan Duffy. Duffy had been studying guitar with New York jazzman Sal Salvador, best known for his time as a sideman with Stan Kenton, and he played a Gretsch Convertible.

The 17-inch-body Convertible, introduced in 1955, was named because, like many early electrics, it was in effect an acoustic that was offered in a "converted" style that made it suitable for electric playing. The pickup and controls "floated" on the pickguard, avoiding interference with the resonance of the hollow body and, as Gretsch put it, "preventing the combination of electric and acoustic properties". Salvador became so closely linked with the Convertible that, toward the end of the 50s, Gretsch renamed it the Sal Salvador model.

Constantly in touch with Gretsch, Salvador knew that the company wanted a keen young player to work as a quality controller … a keen young player just like his pupil Dan Duffy, in fact. Duffy started work at Gretsch in 1957. "I was in the small assembly department," he says, "which is where they put the pickups and tailpieces on, strung the guitars up, and tuned and adjusted them. It was up on the ninth floor of the ten-storey Gretsch building. Guitars were made on two of the floors at that time; the rest was let to other people. Next door to us was the machine shop where they made bridges, tailpieces, and so on, and next to that was the plating department."

Duffy remembers that the seventh floor housed the wood shop and the finishing room, where the guitars were painted. "Beyond that area at the time was the shipping department," he says, "which dealt with Fred Gretsch's wholesale business: accordions, banjos, band instruments, that type of thing. The other part of the seventh floor was taken up with the drum department. As the years went by, the drums were moved out, the finishing department became immense, and guitars were made throughout the whole area. But that's how it was in the 50s and into the first part of the 60s."

In his two books on Gretsch, author Edward Ball has established that from about 1950 until the mid 60s the company produced specific models in batches, usually of 50 or 100 at a time and serial-numbered as a group. Dan Duffy says Gretsch's foremen did an important job throughout the factory to ensure that production ran relatively smoothly, and he emphasises that the instruments which defined the firm's success would not have existed without the skills of those foremen and the workers on the shop floor. "Probably Fred Gretsch's success was due to surrounding himself with good players and good foremen," Duffy says. "When I got there, some of those guys had already been there 25 years. They were super-mechanics, experienced tool-and-die makers. They were devoted to him and to that company."

Duffy remembers the names of some of the foremen who made Gretsch guitars happen: Vincent DiDomenico and Jerry Perito in the wood shop; Jimmy Capozzi in plating; Sid Laiken in the machine shop; Johnny DiRosa in finishing; Felix Provet in assembly; and Carmine Coppola in repairs. "We all got along so great," Duffy says. "If we had problems with rejected guitars, finishes, whatever, everyone would help out everyone else. It was like one big family."

When Jimmie Webster interviewed Dan Duffy at Gretsch for the quality-control job, he explained a new system of green cards they would use to keep a running check on every guitar's progress through the factory. They were called O.K. Cards, and each had checkboxes for Finish, Workmanship, Construction, Nut, Bridge, Action, Intonation, Electrical Equip[ment], and Playing Test, plus an "O.K.'d by" space for the quality controller's signature at the bottom. Each guitar would be shipped to the dealer accompanied by its green O.K. Card. There was also a red card for rejected instruments, Duffy recalls, which obviously stayed in the factory. "You'd just fill out the red card with what was wrong with it," he says. "Throughout the years, we had a quality-control meeting once a week where each foreman would discuss any problems. There were always finishing problems: scratches, nicks, dents, and dust in the finish that had to be buffed out. Then in the wood shop the hand-sanding had to be perfect: the better the wood is sanded, the better the finish lays on. There were periods where we had neck-pitch problems, wood shrinkage problems, and binding problems, especially on the White Falcon guitars. But we tackled that whole thing together. There was a lot of talent in that company, and that's what made it work."

Some of Duffy's "problems" from back then are what today make each vintage Gretsch guitar a potential surprise. Anyone who has played more than a few old Gretsches will be aware of this – and some might put it less charitably. It's the frustration of never being sure what to expect, of knowing that you are just as likely to find yourself struggling with a poor instrument as rejoicing at how well this particular guitar plays. That's old Gretsches for you. Duffy concludes: "You go into a guitar store, and you buy a name. But if only you realised what went into that guitar, all the lives, and all the years that guys took to make those guitars the way they were. And it wasn't Fred Gretsch Jr, as much as we loved him. It was the guys who got there every morning at six o'clock. They did it. You remember that."[40]

When Jimmie Webster rounded up the contemporary guitar styles in Gretsch's '55 catalogue, there was one new musical category absent: rock'n'roll. Hit records continued through 1956 and '57 for Chuck Berry, Bill Haley & His Comets, Buddy Holly, Jerry Lee Lewis, Carl Perkins, Elvis Presley, and others, spreading the popularity of the fresh new sound. We know now that this would eventually sweep the old guard from the map as

■ Gentle two-tone finishes graced many a Gretsch in the 50s, like the guitars shown on these pages. The Convertible (above) came with Lotus Ivory (cream) front and Copper Mist (brown) back and similar pickguard, while the Clipper (right) came with another Lotus Ivory top but Shadow Gray back and pickguard. The Constellation (below) is an example of a Gretsch f-hole acoustic model adapted here for electric playing by adding a floating pickup – and this one is in custom two-tone grey.

1957 CLIPPER 6187

1957 CONSTELLATION 6030

THE GRETSCH ELECTRIC GUITAR BOOK

TRY A TWO-TONE CONVERSION

1957 CONVERTIBLE 6199

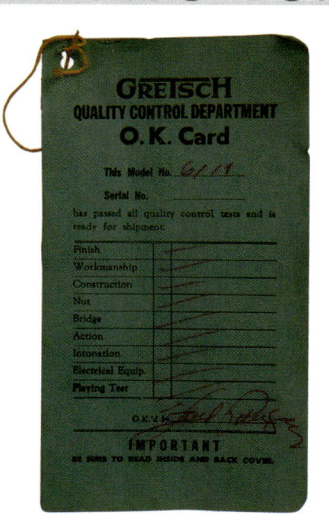

1957 RAMBLER 6115

■ The Convertible (main guitar, above) had a pickup and controls fixed to the pickguard, offering a production-model take on the way some players would add a floating pickup to an acoustic (see Constellation, opposite). The Convertible's name hinted at the "conversion" of acoustic to electric, although it was later renamed for its best-known player, Sal Salvador, who is pictured with one (below) fronting his band in the 50s. Later in that decade, Gretsch started to use a new system to track production and provide a quality-check assurance for dealer and customer. The visible evidence of this was the O.K. Card (above), with checkboxes and signature, that left the factory with every guitar. Another two-tone model from this period was the budget Rambler (right) with small body and 20 frets on a short 23-inch scale.

THE GRETSCH ELECTRIC GUITAR BOOK

43

groundbreaking musicians headed toward modern pop music. Back then, at the birth of the music, none of the guitar companies chased rock'n'roll guitarists to get them to play this or that guitar. Like many at the time, they probably thought it was a passing fad. Instead, Gretsch, Gibson, Guild, and the rest mostly publicised established jazz, country, and studio pickers. But Gretsch gained enormous benefit from some unsolicited associations with successful artists in the early years of rock'n'roll, and two of the most important used 6120s to power their sound.

Eddie Cochran was a talented, accomplished guitarist. He started out as a session player, but at 18 years old his moody good looks landed him a cameo spot in the Jayne Mansfield movie *The Girl Can't Help It* (1956) where he performed 'Twenty-Flight Rock'. Cochran is best known now for some basic, blasting rock'n'roll singles, including the classic 'Summertime Blues', a US number 8 in 1958, but his talents were wide-ranging. His music was a churning mix of rockabilly, country, and blues, which he played on acoustic as well as electric guitars, and at its heart was his '55 Gretsch 6120, which he bought at Bell Gardens Music Center in the suburb of Los Angeles where he lived. The guitar was effectively secondhand – it had been on loan for a few months to a guitarist waiting for his new Country Club to arrive. Cochran continued to play sessions as well as make his own records, and in the studio he became fascinated by the developing technology, using overdubbing and other techniques before they became widespread.

Darrel Higham plays good rockabilly guitar with Imelda May, and he's almost always played Gretsch. We'll meet him again a bit later in the book, but for now we're interested in his collaboration with Julie Mundy on a book about Cochran, *Don't Forget Me*. Higham worked in the USA for six months in the 90s with Cochran's last road band, The Kelly Four, he met Cochran's family, he played the ex-Cochran 6120 at length, and he even had a stint appearing as Cochran in a UK theatre tour, so he was uniquely qualified to appreciate and evaluate Cochran's achievements.

Cochran was a proper, credible musician, Higham explains, despite the subsequent concentration on his hit singles. He was coming up with tough rock'n'roll at a time when the music was being ironed out and smoothed over, and so his records came to fit more comfortably into the early 60s than they had into the late 50s. Many of the guitarists who emerged in the 60s admired and recognised Cochran's exploits, including Jeff Beck, Hendrix, Pete Townshend, and others.

"Eddie understood rock'n'roll," Higham says, "that it wasn't all about blazing guitar solos. It was a beat, and it was lyrics that were memorable, a catchy hook. It irritates me when they do these hundred greatest guitarists or whatever: Eddie's usually in there, somewhere towards the back, and they'll pick 'Summertime Blues' as an example of his work. And you think oh, for god's sake: dig a bit deeper! It's not that hard, you know? The session work he did for other players – that's when he really went to town."

Higham picks some highlights from those sessions: Ray Stanley's 'My Loving Baby', and a Skeets McDonald date where Cochran played on 'You Ought To See Grandma

NEW YORK CLASSICS

Rock' and 'Heart Breaking Mama', which Higham nominates as two of the greatest examples of rockabilly guitar playing ever. Then there was a Bo Davis session where Cochran added lead guitar to 'Let's Coast Awhile' and 'Drowning All My Sorrows' – again, according to Higham, one of the best double-sided rockabilly 45s ever released. And there's plenty more where those came from. There are also some notable Cochran blues cuts, including 'Eddie's Blues' and 'Milk Cow Blues', mostly from a single solo session in 1959. Higham remembers hearing B.B. King interviewed on the radio and asked to name the best white blues player he'd worked with. King, to the evident surprise of the interviewer, said Eddie Cochran.

Cochran might have seemed light-years away from Chet Atkins's musical stylings, yet he was certainly influenced by Chet's fingerstyle picking – and to some extent he seemed to agree with Chet about the quality of DeArmond pickups, replacing the neck pickup on his 6120 with a meatier-sounding Gibson P-90. Cochran also admired Merle Travis, another P-90 player, and he usually played with both pickups on to get a very fat sound.

Higham says that Cochran was a big jazz fan and a fine jazz player, and he probably found the neck DeArmond not quite mellow enough when he wanted that kind of tone. Perhaps he thought adding a P-90 at the neck gave him the best of both worlds: a tough, brittle rock'n'roll sound from the bridge DeArmond and a smooth, mellow jazz tone from the neck P-90. "In fact," Higham says, "Eddie could do all that western swing stuff, all the pretty country stuff, jazz as well – he understood chords, and he was obsessed with Johnny Smith, the jazz player from the early 50s."[41] Gretsch would issue a signature Cochran model in all but name in 2001 and a detailed repro of the original guitar in 2010.

There's a clip of Cochran early in 1959 on a TV show, *Town Hall Party*, that includes a short interview by a remarkably boring host called Johnny Bond. "How long do you predict that rock'n'roll music will stay?" Bond asked, clearly unimpressed by the racket he'd had to put up with on his show. "I think, actually, rock'n'roll will be here for quite some time, but I don't think it's going to be rock'n'roll as we know it today," Cochran replied, perceptively. "I think it'll be around for a long time … but changing."[42] It's a pity Cochran never got a chance to be a part of those changes – his career was cut terribly short when he was killed, just 21 years old, in a car crash while on tour in Britain in 1960 – because it seems that he and his 6120 could have been right at the centre of it all.

Meanwhile, back in the rock'n'roll 50s, Duane Eddy turned out a string of hit records based on his deceptively simple instrumental style, forever known by the word attached to so many of his albums: Twang. That twangy tone came as Eddy concentrated on playing melodies on the bass strings of his 6120. He made full use of the pitchbending potential of the guitar's Bigsby vibrato, his amplifier's tremolo, and the studio's echo facilities, resulting in gloriously haunting hits such as 'Rebel Rouser', a US number six in 1958.

Eddy's first decent electric guitar, at age 15, was a Gibson Les Paul Goldtop. He grew up in Phoenix, Arizona, playing in high-school bands. "Electric guitar was the mainstay of country music and had been for many years at that time," he recalls. "I don't ever remember not hearing electric guitar. It was around in the 40s, though of course it wasn't featured much in pop music or big-band music, but it became featured in country music very early on, and I suppose in blues as well – but I wasn't into blues then, we didn't hear much of it out there in the desert. I was focused on country, because we'd turn on the radio and that's what we'd hear. It was very natural to play an electric guitar then, and we'd heard of Chet Atkins, Merle Travis, and Les Paul, who was having hits."

He regularly checked out the local music store, Ziggie's Accordion & Guitar Studios. One day early in 1957, the 19-year-old made what turned out to be a very important discovery. "I just went into Ziggie's with a friend of mine to look around," Eddy says. "My Les Paul didn't have a vibrato on it, and I wanted that bar: Chet Atkins had it, Merle Travis had it. I could play the fingerpicking thing a little, but I wanted to do the vibrato part." Eddy went into the store, and he couldn't help but notice a Gretsch White Falcon hanging on the wall. "It was beautiful, but it was a lot of money, nearly $700," he recalls. "I asked Ziggie what he had that's nice but not so expensive. He pulled out two or three guitars, and the first case I opened had the 6120. It was the first time I saw the red Gretsch, with a Bigsby on it, and I settled on that. Took one last look at the White Falcon, but the neck wasn't as nice on it as the red Gretsch – and I didn't care for the gold trim, which looked a little chintzy."

The $420 6120 suited him straight away. "First time I picked it up it just took to me, settled right in there, the neck was just perfect. There's nothing more exciting than finding a new guitar, but that was such an experience that I've not bought many new ones since then. Felt no need for it."[43] Eddy found that the 6120's DeArmond pickups suited his style well. When I asked Chet Atkins about this, he told me, laughing: "I think Duane Eddy was the only one who liked the DeArmond pickups! He got a big bass sound out of those things."[44] Eddy enjoyed some studio flirtations with a Danelectro six-string bass in the late 50s and a Guild signature hollowbody for live work in the early 60s, but otherwise he's been served well by that original 6120, right through his long and successful career. Gretsch issued a signature model in 1997, then Eddy switched allegiance to Gibson in 2005, but he was back home to Gretsch for a further signature guitar in 2012.

Eddy says it was his producer, Lee Hazlewood, who described the sound he made with the 6120 as twangy. "It became a running joke, and then we decided to name the first album *Have Twangy Guitar Will Travel*. They decided to call it twangy guitar, and it stuck, just became a trademark kind of thing. It's rather a silly word, and not entirely descriptive, but it was something for the average person in the street to identify with." How would Eddy describe it? "Oh well, it's a rock'n'roll sound. I guess twangy is as good as anything. I don't know how you'd do it in one word. There's times it does get twangy, other times it gets smooth and dragging and menacing. Then I can turn around and do a pretty song, a ballad or something, with a gentle warmth."

Looking back, Eddy is also proud that by having hits with instrumental guitar tunes, he gave guitarists something to show off with. "It gave all the guys who'd been doing what

I'd been doing not too long before – performing in clubs for $10 a night – something to play. The guys that didn't want to sing and that played guitar in a group, they had a song that was a hit that people would recognise that they could play. They could play 'Rebel Rouser' and 'Ramrod' and 'Cannonball' and get up there and actually be a star for a little while at their local club." And he promoted a certain Gretsch electric guitar at the same time. "I probably sold more Gretsch guitars than anybody other than Chet Atkins," Eddy says with a chuckle.[45]

Gene Vincent and his Blue Caps hit in summer 1956 with 'Be Bop A Lula', a 45 full of guitarist Cliff Gallup's beautifully concise jazz-rockabilly stylings. His unmistakable fills and solos were there again later that year on Vincent's second single, 'Race With The Devil', and across the first LP, *Blue Jean Bop*, on tracks such as 'Jump Back, Honey, Jump Back'. Gallup once named his main influences as Les Paul and Chet Atkins. "Like most musicians, you listen to a lot of people," Gallup said in a 1983 interview. "Pick up a lick here, a lick there. Pretty soon you originate some kind of style." Were his solos on the Vincent records spontaneous? "Just as they come to mind," Gallup replied in his amiably laidback manner.[46] He used a Duo Jet and nicknamed it Pancake because of the flat top. It was probably a '55 or maybe a '56 model, complete with original DeArmond pickups and a Bigsby, and Gallup got a great sound from it.

Gallup in turn influenced many players since, not least Jeff Beck. Beck bought a '56 Duo Jet in the 90s because, he says, he'd come to realise that getting the exact model was key to getting the Cliff Gallup sound, something he'd been chasing since first hearing the brilliant playing on Vincent records. "He got a characteristic bell-like sound," Beck explains. "Cliff was doing stuff in the mid 50s, at breakneck speed, and we'd never heard anything like that. What's this diddly-diddly stuff! Then he was playing runs, climbing octaves, which totally blew me away. I had to slow the record down to try to figure that out. It was so spot on, and it was as though he'd never even thought about the solo – and all the people who follow rockabilly since have been standing aghast at how he played these things and how he reckons that he didn't spend all his life perfecting solos. You can tell if you listen carefully that they're just random brilliance. That's how things were: you were only allowed to be signed to a record company if you had something really special to offer."[47]

Gallup didn't stay long in Vincent's band, mostly because he was averse to long bouts of touring, and he was gone by the end of '56, replaced by a few short-stay guitarists and then Johnny Meeks. Gallup died in 1988 at the age of just 58, but he will always be remembered by those who appreciate the art of fine rock'n'roll guitar playing.

One more early rock'n'roll guitar hero closely associated with Gretsch is Bo Diddley, notably for a series of peculiarly shaped guitars. Like many things with Mr McDaniel, it's not entirely clear how all this came about, but it seems that at one stage he may have taken the neck and pickups from a Gretsch and added them to a rectangular guitar body that he'd made himself. Realising the shortcomings of his own handiwork, he then asked the Gretsch factory to make him a custom rectangular guitar from scratch. A short item in *Billboard* magazine early in 1958 said that Gretsch "has made a special custom-built square guitar for Bo Diddley … This is a strong artist who would probably sound great even with glockenspiel accompaniment."[48]

Years later, Bo recalled that Gretsch made him four of the distinctive rectangular guitars: that first one in 1958, another in '60, and then two more in '62. "It didn't record real well," he said, "so I used other guitars mostly on the records, but it was great for stage."[49] One of the guitars he probably used on his early recordings was a Jet Fire Bird that he bought from a store in Chicago, as pictured on the jacket of his 1959 album *Go Bo Diddley*. Clearly impressed by Gretsch's work, he had them make further oddities with a spectacular winged-rocketship shape. The modern Gretsch company would reissue the rectangular guitar in 2000 and the rocketship in 2005 as the "Billy-Bo" Jupiter Thunderbird, named for Bo Diddley and Billy Gibbons.

Chet Atkins wasn't oblivious to rock'n'roll: after all, he played rhythm guitar on Elvis's 'Heartbreak Hotel' in 1956, and he could be heard more obviously – also on rhythm – on many of the Everly Brothers hits. But you wouldn't call him a rock'n'roller. And whatever his musical role, he was still unhappy with those Gretsch single-coil pickups. Fortunately, he met Ray Butts, an electronics expert who owned a music-store in Cairo, Illinois. It was an auspicious meeting. Chet's difficulties with those darned DeArmonds were about to dissolve.

Ray Butts went to Nashville in 1954 hoping to meet the city's guitarists and interest them in his combo amplifier, which offered echo from a built-in tape loop, an unusual facility at the time. Players were becoming used to echo effects in the studio, and Butts reckoned they would jump at the opportunity to make similar sounds relatively easily on stage. Chet Atkins became a customer for Butts's EchoSonic amp, and he recalled using it first in 1954 on his debut 12-inch album for RCA, *A Session With Chet Atkins*, on tracks such as 'Caravan' and 'Red Wing'. Elvis Presley's guitarist Scotty Moore got an EchoSonic from Butts, too, and so did Carl Perkins. (A few years later, Gretsch discussed marketing Butts's EchoSonic amp. "Mr Gretsch and I had a long session with Chet Atkins about your EchoSonic amp," Jimmie Webster wrote to Butts in July 1958, suggesting that it might become a Gretsch Chet Atkins amp. "It must be remembered, we must all make a buck on it, and at the same time keep it at a retail level that the average consumer can afford."[50] Sadly, nothing came of the idea.)

Meanwhile, Atkins got talking with Butts about other topics of common interest. Butts helped him choose recording equipment for a garage studio, and then the subject turned naturally to Atkins's quest for an improved guitar pickup. "Chet didn't like the DeArmond pickups that Gretsch were using at the time," Butts remembered. "It just didn't fit his style of playing then: he said they didn't sound right. Primarily what he wanted was a proper balance between the bass and the treble and the midrange, for that thumb effect he used, and he really didn't get it with those pickups. For one thing, the magnets were too strong. They kept sucking the strings and stopping the sustain. I saw some where he'd broken the bass-string magnets in two in a vice with a hammer. So he said to me, why don't you make me a pickup? I had done some experimenting with pickups before, so I said OK. My idea from the beginning was to build a humbucking pickup. I knew about the concept from working with transformers, and Ampex used the humbucking principle in the pickups of their tape-recorder heads. It wasn't a new idea, and it's a very simple principle."[51]

The main idea with a humbucking pickup is to reduce the hum and electrical interference that can cause trouble for regular single-coil pickups. That's why they're called humbucking: they can buck, or cut, hum. The design, as Butts said, is reasonably simple. A humbucking pickup has two coils with opposite magnetic polarity, wired together so that they are electrically out-of-phase. The result is a pickup less prone to picking up noise, and in the process it provides a pleasingly clear balanced tone.

Butts made a prototype and took it to Atkins, who was immediately impressed. "I got in touch with Gretsch," Atkins said. "I told them that this guy has an improved pickup I like, that it gets the sound I want."[52] The timing was dead right: a change of pickup suited Gretsch, too. Duke Kramer: "We wanted to drop DeArmond, because all of a sudden they were building pickups for anybody and everybody. It had become no great asset to have a DeArmond pickup on a Gretsch guitar, because other makers were putting them on cheap guitars as well as on expensive guitars. So we were very anxious to make this deal when it came up, because we needed another pickup."[53]

Butts went to New York City to meet with Fred Gretsch Jr and Jimmie Webster at the company's offices in Brooklyn, probably some time in 1956. "They wanted to make the pickup themselves, because they wanted to be sure of having supply. I wasn't experienced at manufacturing," Butts recalled, "so I agreed to that. We came to an agreement on a royalty basis. I furnished all the information and everything to make the pickups, and they went and got tooling. I worked real closely with Jimmie, and I designed new control assemblies and switching to go with the new pickups."[x]

Gretsch debuted its new pickup publicly at the summer '57 NAMM trade show in Chicago. The company was not alone in displaying a humbucking pickup: Gibson, too, had developed one and also probably showed it off to the instrument trade for the first time that summer in Chicago. Seth Lover from Gibson's electronics department was inspired to apply the humbucking principle to a pickup after he saw a Gibson amplifier with a choke coil designed to eliminate the hum produced by its power transformer. Butts and Lover came up with their ideas for a humbucking pickup independently and at around the same time, although Lover managed to file his patent application much earlier than Butts. "I feel I was first with it," Butts insisted. "It's the conception that counts, and I feel I had better documentation on that. I had earlier pictures of Chet playing a guitar with my pickups on it, for example. But Gibson complained, and Mr Gretsch discussed it with Mr McCarty at Gibson. They decided to let each go his own

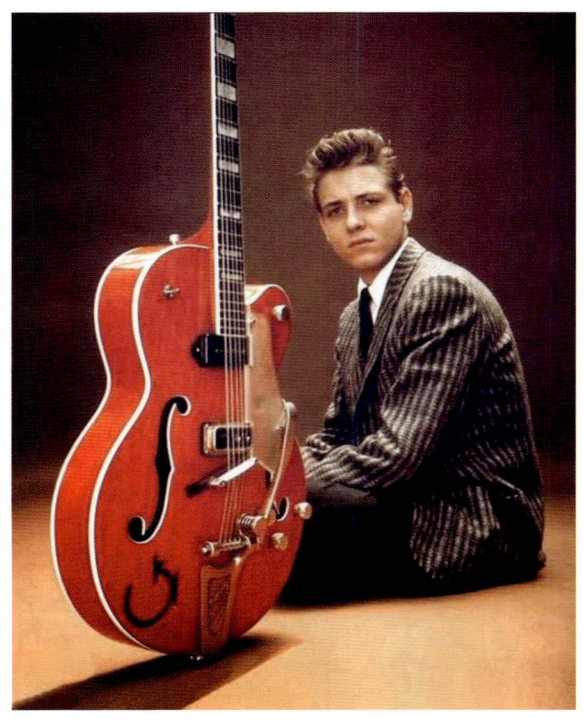

EDDIE COCHRAN'S 1955 *CHET ATKINS HOLLOW BODY 6120*

50 THE GRETSCH ELECTRIC GUITAR BOOK

C'MON EVERYBODY

■ Eddie Cochran (portrait, opposite) is best remembered for his pop hits, but he was a talented musician and underrated guitarist. He used a 1955 6120 exclusively, and today the instrument (left) is on display at the Rock & Roll Hall of Fame in Cleveland, complete with its personalised strap and Cochran's other mods, including a Gibson P-90 pickup at the neck and a see-through pickguard.

JEFF BECK'S 1956 *DUO JET 6128*

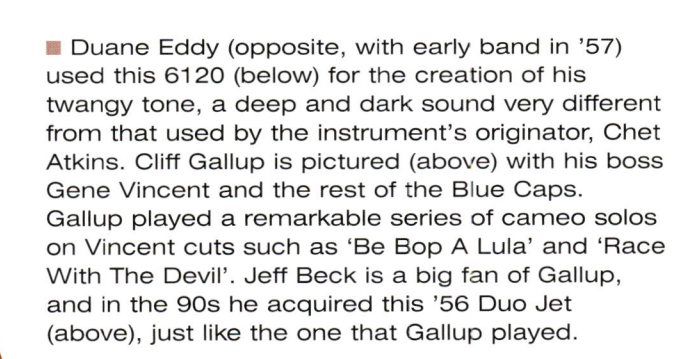

■ Duane Eddy (opposite, with early band in '57) used this 6120 (below) for the creation of his twangy tone, a deep and dark sound very different from that used by the instrument's originator, Chet Atkins. Cliff Gallup is pictured (above) with his boss Gene Vincent and the rest of the Blue Caps. Gallup played a remarkable series of cameo solos on Vincent cuts such as 'Be Bop A Lula' and 'Race With The Devil'. Jeff Beck is a big fan of Gallup, and in the 90s he acquired this '56 Duo Jet (above), just like the one that Gallup played.

DUANE EDDY'S 1957 *CHET ATKINS HOLLOW BODY 6120*

THE GRETSCH ELECTRIC GUITAR BOOK

way without the one challenging the other."[54] In typically grand style, Gretsch called its new humbucker the Filter'Tron Electronic Guitar Head. The bombast continued in the company's explanatory leaflet: "Good electronic reproducing units such as Hi-Fidelity, Stereophonic and such, have created a demand for perfect sound and performance. ... It is with this knowledge in mind that we present the new Filter'Tron heads for guitar. The finest engineers in the country were engaged in the development of the Filter'Tron and their main object was to produce the greatest sound with as many color combinations as possible."

Years later, that patter amused Ray Butts. "The finest engineers in the country! That was me," he said with a laugh. "But they never associated me with anything, in the literature, advertising, anything else. Of course, they had their interest. But there's people to this day don't know I had anything to do with those pickups."[55]

By 1958, Gretsch was advertising Filter'Trons as standard on all models except the thinline-body Clipper, which for a short while continued with the DynaSonic single-coil and during '59 was given an early version of Gretsch's own single-coil pickup, the HiLo'Tron. (Dan Duffy wrote later that Jerry Perito in Gretsch's wood shop designed the HiLo'Tron.[56]) Gretsch proudly claimed that the Filter'Trons "eliminate absolutely all electronic hum – you get pure guitar sound".

Butts revised the control layout to complement the new Filter'Trons. A two-pickup Gretsch now had two volume knobs, one for each pickup, in the regular position on the lower part of the body, plus a master volume knob on the cutaway bout. (Gretsch had around 1957 upgraded most models to include its stylish G-indent knobs, with an arrow through a G-for-Gretsch set into the top, replacing the earlier arrow-only versions introduced around 1955.) On the top bout there were now two three-way selector switches: the one furthest from the player was a regular bridge/both/neck pickup selector; the other replaced the old tone knob and was for what Gretsch called "tone color". It selected between bass-emphasis, neutral, or treble-emphasis settings. Some Gretsch fans know this now as the mud switch, because they consider it offers less than useful sounds, and most keep it permanently and safely stuck in the neutral middle position.

The internal geometry of the guitar changed, too. Gretsch was worried about problems with feedback. Guitarists were playing live music, especially rock'n'roll, at louder volumes, and when they played hollowbodys, often they were plagued by howling feedback when they turned up the amp. Feedback happens when pickups pick up their own sound from the amp's speakers and feed that back into the system, creating an unpleasant howl-round effect. The increasingly amplified soundwaves move into and around the body of the guitar, agitating the strings and top and setting up vibrations that in turn promote more feedback. During the mid 60s, guitarists would begin to discover feedback's musical possibilities, but for now players considered it a technical nuisance to be avoided.

"I figured out what was causing the feedback and made a suggestion," Butts remembered. "Gretsch started out primarily with what was an acoustic-type guitar, and I said in an electric guitar you don't really need the same things that you need in an acoustic guitar: it's a different situation. I said the way to stop the feedback – and probably get better sustain and better performance all around – is to fasten the top to the neck, to do away with all that vibrating. The feedback was coming from that top vibrating with the pickups on it, mounted to the top. When you fasten the top to the back, it's locked in and it can't vibrate. So that solved that problem."[57]

What Gretsch did was to install what it called truss bracing, which has since become known as trestle bracing. The company regularly glued to the underneath of hollowbody tops a parallel pair of wooden rails, to which the pickups were screwed, but now it added a wide upside-down-U-shape wooden section to each of the rails – the "trestle". The two "legs" of each trestle connected to the back, providing four curved solid vertical posts that joined the top to the back: a pair each side under the bridge, and a pair near the neck block. The result was a guitar where the top and back vibrated more sympathetically with one another, providing into the bargain more sustain and less feedback.

Gretsch started to use trestle bracing around 1958 on many of the hollowbody models, including the 6120, Country Club, Tennessean, and White Falcon, until about 1962. (Coincidentally or not, 1958 was also the year that Gibson introduced its ES-335 and 355 models, which had a completely solid neck extension within the body, done for similar reasons.) Gretsch's factory manager Harold Woods wrote to Butts in summer 1958: "We have been, for some time, building a solid truss-type bridge into [hollowbody] guitars, running under the bass bars and anchored, solidly, to the backs and tops. We have not had any feedback since using this type construction."[58] For Gretsch, the new bracing further blurred the lines between solidbody and hollowbody guitars.

Two new Chet Atkins electrics that Gretsch released during 1958 were the Country Gentleman (Atkins had released a single with that name four years earlier) and the Tennessean. Gretsch's idea was to play on Atkins's growing fame to sell a higher-end model, with the Gent, and to reach a wider audience, with the Tennessean.

"Gretsch were selling so many of the orange guitar, they wanted to put out one that was a little more expensive," Atkins explained. "So the Country Gentleman had good tuning pegs, better wood selection, and the body was generally a little larger and thinner. I started to use the Country Gentleman on my records continually. I would use the 6120 once in a while – I know I've seen pictures of me with it in the studio – but I didn't use it as much as I used the Country Gentleman." Despite the "improved" versions of the Gent that came later and that Gretsch would send regularly to Atkins as they appeared, he continued to play his single-cutaway original – simply because he felt it was a better instrument and that most of the changes Gretsch made were for the sake of change.

One of the key design features that went into the Gent was its sealed body with "fake" f-holes, an idea that came from an experimental 6120 that Gretsch had made for Atkins around 1956 and that appeared on his *Finger-Style Guitar* album of that year. It had a thick solid top with painted-on f-holes and prototype Butts humbuckers feeding two

■ The new Country Gent (above) was a high-end addition to the Chet Atkins line in 1958, complete with new Filter'Tron humbuckers and sealed body. Ray Butts devised the Filter'Trons (patent, opposite). A new single-coil appeared, too, the HiLo'Tron (pamphlet, right). Atkins is pictured (opposite) with the Gent in the studio and also with Jimmie Webster at its launch at a '58 trade show. Atkins had an experimental sealed-top 6120 before the Gent, seen on a '56 LP (top). Meanwhile, the 6120 continued with the new Filter'Trons – and this example (below) has an especially figured top. Some Duo Jets (opposite) were offered in the Cadillac Green finish usually seen on the Country Club.

Introducing – THE NEW Gretsch HILO'TRON Electronic GUITAR Heads

- FULL HI-FIDELITY
- BRILLIANT HIGHS
- MELLOW LOWS
- EXTRA LIVELY RESPONSE

1960 *CHET ATKINS HOLLOW BODY 6120*

54 THE GRETSCH ELECTRIC GUITAR BOOK

A TRUE GENTLEMAN

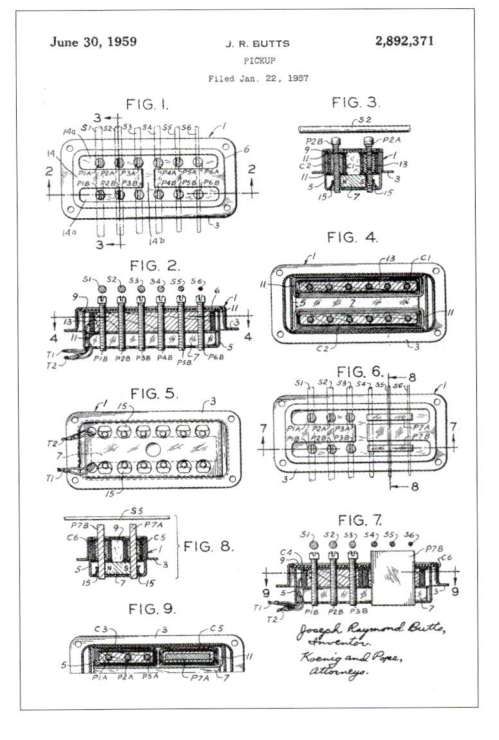

1959 *CHET ATKINS COUNTRY GENTLEMAN 6122*

1958 *DUO JET 6128*

THE GRETSCH ELECTRIC GUITAR BOOK

55

output jacks. "This was the so-called red guitar pictured on the original cover of that album," Atkins remembered. "It was a special model with closed f-holes which Gretsch made for me."[59]

Ray Butts recalled that he and Atkins fooled around with the way to give a visual impression of f-holes on a sealed body. "Chet came up with a design for a guitar that was basically semi-solid, one of the first he made that had the artificial f-holes. I was out at his house when he was working on that. I know we went and got some superglue when he was putting those f-holes on there," Butts said, chuckling at the memory, "and we glued those f-holes on top of the guitar."[60] Gretsch would reproduce this instrument, calling it the Chet Atkins Stereo Guitar 6120-CGP, in 2008.

The sealed body and fake f-holes appeared on the Country Gentleman 6122 when it first went on sale in 1958, following Atkins's mission to cut feedback and increase sustain. The new Country Gent was also the first Atkins model with the new FilterTron pickups, and the first Gretsch hollowbody with a thinline body – about two inches deep, as opposed to most similar models that were generally around an inch deeper: the 6120 was 2⅜inches deep at the time, for example. Gibson had popularised the thinline idea with its Byrdland and ES-350T models, both introduced in 1955. The Gent was also the first Atkins model offered with a slightly wider 17-inch body, like the White Falcon, Country Club, and Convertible; the 6120 was 15½ inches wide, as was the new Tennessean.

Gretsch was content to add the new trestle bracing inside the Country Gentleman's body. Atkins, however, was still less than content. "I continually tried to get them to make the guitar more solid from the neck down to the end," he remembered. "I wanted more of a sturdy guitar that gave more sustain. Originally, the Country Gent did have two braces that went from the end of the guitar to the neck, but they didn't join it, so it still killed off the sustain. They finally made it semi-solid back to the bridge, and had a piece of wood going out to the back, which helped, but it didn't go all the way to the end of the guitar. They never could do that for me."[61]

Gretsch announced to its dealer network that "guitar star Chet Atkins will be in the Gretsch Guitar room to greet you personally" at the summer 1957 NAMM show in Chicago, where the dark brown Gent was previewed to the music trade. The retail price of $525 put the new instrument second only to the White Falcon in the company's hollowbody electric line.

The other new Chet Atkins model was the red Tennessean 6119, effectively a less fancy one-humbucker version of the 6120, launched in 1958 at $295 (about $100 less than a 6120). Gretsch now had three Chet Atkins models: relatively low (the $295 Tennessean); midrange (the $400 6120); and upper-mid (the $525 Country Gentleman). It sat well with the company's general intention to offer clearly different models at a range of price-points.

General Motors was a big influence on American manufacturers with its methods to expand consumerism and create a segmented market with a range of models, providing what the car firm called the "organised creation of dissatisfaction" with new models every year. Fred Gretsch Jr wrote in the late 50s in a magazine ad aimed at music dealers: "You can capitalize on [your customers'] range of taste and spending much more easily than the auto industry – and do it with Gretsch instrument lines, too. Gretsch can supply you with 'Cadillac' or 'Volkswagen' models, whatever the instrument."[62] Naturally, Gretsch hoped its trio of Chet models would secure a bigger share of a market that Gibson continued to dominate.

A number of new features began to appear on the guitars. Most noticeable was the latest bridge, the Space Control. No doubt the company reasoned that if it could now make pickups in-house, then it could certainly make its own bridges – enabling it to dispense with Mr Melita's services, as well as those of Mr DeArmond, and thereby gain more control over the production and supply of key components. The Space Control bridge was a Jimmie Webster design, and it was, unsurprisingly, a lot simpler than Melita's Synchro-Sonic unit. It had six wheel-like grooved saddles, each of which could be positioned at any point along a threaded bar. Intonation adjustment was not possible, but Gretsch must have considered the benefits outweighed such drawbacks, and the Space Control began to replace the Melita around 1958.

Also new was the Neo-Classic fingerboard, which Gretsch eulogised in a handy leaflet. "Centuries ago, when string instruments were first built, the early craftsmen discovered that pure ebony offered the best playing performance, and that discovery stands to this very day. As time passed, man decided to decorate these fine playing boards with fancy pearl inlays which were beautiful but in no way helped the playing performance of the board; it only destroyed the wonderful feel only pure satin ebony could give. It is with these proven facts in mind that we introduce the new Gretsch Neo Classic fingerboard – the finest in playing performance and sheer beauty. The beautifully inlaid mother-of-pearl half moons on the bass side of the board are perfect position markers and do not in any way detract from the classic feel which is so essential to perfect performance. Neo Classic construction preserves the full strength of the fingerboard." It was hard to refuse. The Neo-Classic markers, better known now as thumbnails or half-moons, first appeared along the side of many Gretsch fingerboards during 1957 and 1958, and many of the boards were switched from rosewood to ebony. Around the same time, Gretsch decided to screw a metal plate to the headstock of some models and put on it the name of the model (and, sometimes, the serial number).

In 1958, Gretsch marked the 75th anniversary of its formation and, having already tried the idea with 70th anniversary accordions in 1953, issued special Anniversary model guitars. They were launched with all the new appointments – one (Anniversary) or two (Double Anniversary) Filter'Tron pickups, trestle bracing, G-indent knobs, Space Control bridge, Neo-Classic fingerboard – and the guitar's 15½-inch-wide body was offered in an attractive two-tone green as well as sunburst. As instruments related to the importance of a solitary year in the company's history, they lasted remarkably

■ Another new Chet Atkins model debuted in 1958, the less expensive Tennessean (bottom). For now, it had a single humbucker, as seen also in this late-50s ad (left). "You get the same fine sound, easy playin', and good looks as the Gretsch people put into their most expensive guitars," Chet insisted in the ad. The Tennessean, as we'll see, would be changed in the coming years, most dramatically in the early 60s when the humbucker was swapped for two single-coils.

BIRTHDAY ON A BUDGET

HAPPY ANNIVERSARY FROM GRETSCH!

1959 ANNIVERSARY 6125

In 1958, Gretsch marked its 75th birthday (ad, top) with two Anniversary models, with one (left) or two pickups (right). The two-pickup model was known as the Double Anniversary. These were budget guitars, and the only hint of luxury that you might expect for an anniversary came with the attractive two-tone green finish, officially called Smoke Green. A few changes came in the 60s when the ebony board was replaced with rosewood and the Filter'Tron humbuckers were swapped for HiLo'Tron single-coils (see the Double here). The Anniversaries had Gretsch's new Neo-Classic fingerboard markers (50s pamphlet, above), better known as thumbnail markers.

1960 CHET ATKINS TENNESSEAN 6119

1962 DOUBLE ANNIVERSARY 6118

THE GRETSCH ELECTRIC GUITAR BOOK

well, continuing in the line until 1977 (and revived in 1993). The relatively low-end Anniversarys were stripped-down 6120s and something of a cheap celebration. "Priced for promotional selling" was the euphemism employed by Gretsch's admen. At least the party was a long one.

Stereo and stereophonic were magic words in the late 50s, reflecting all that was new and exciting in hi-fi, with the first stereo LPs appearing from the major record labels. Jimmie Webster was immersed in the potential of electronics and sound, and he wasted no time putting his fertile brain to work on the possibilities of a stereo guitar. Webster was almost certainly involved in that experimental 6120 which Chet Atkins received around 1956 with two jacks to feed the bass strings to the amp's echo channel and the treble strings to the regular channel.

Webster asked Ray Butts to design a stereo pickup, which Butts achieved simply by splitting the windings of a Filter'Tron so that the signal from the three bass strings could be directed to one amp and the signal from the three treble strings to another. That, in a nutshell, was Gretsch's Project-o-Sonic stereo system, the subject of a Jimmie Webster patent filed in December 1956. The system was launched during 1958 as an option available on the Country Club and the White Falcon. Gretsch continued to call these models Project-o-Sonic (Country Club) and Super Project-o-Sonic (Falcon), only naming them Stereo in pricelists and catalogues from about 1967.

The stereo Country Club and White Falcon had the bridge pickup located much closer to the neck pickup than usual. The control layout and functions were similar to a regular guitar with two Filter'Trons, but the master volume knob on the cutaway bout was replaced with a three-way switch that selected various combinations of pickups and amps, while the two switches on the upper bout offered independent control of tonal emphasis for each pickup. A special Dual Guitar Cord connected the guitar to a Dual Jack Box, which provided two more jacks to connect to the two amplifiers necessary for stereo reproduction. Gretsch offered its own pair of amps to make a complete stereo outfit.

Webster recorded an album for RCA Records in December 1958, *Unabridged*, produced by Chet Atkins, where Webster made full use of his stereo White Falcon. Gretsch must have been delighted, because the May 1959 release amounted to a high-profile demo of its new stereo system. The stereophonic version of *Unabridged* was one of the first stereo albums to feature electric guitar.

The launch of the stereo guitar gave Gretsch an advantage over Gibson, for once. Gibson had to follow Gretsch's lead, issuing its own interpretation of a stereo guitar in 1959: first with the ES-345, and then the ES-355. Gibson's more straightforward process directed the output of each of the guitar's two individual pickups to a separate amp.

Gretsch soon modified its system, and a more complex version began to appear during 1959, previewed on an experimental White Falcon at the company's Guitarama show in Boston in April. Visitors to the Boston demo saw a Falcon with conventional looking Filter'Trons but a more complex control layout. Webster and Butts once again split the twelve poles of each pickup into two, but added two more three-way selector switches on the upper bout for a total of four there, giving the guitar a grand and somewhat overwhelming total of three control knobs and five selectors. The new pair of switches provided nine combinations of the split pickup sections, and Gretsch calculated that this, in combination with the six tonal options provided by the other two selectors, offered what it called "54 colors and shadings in stereo sound". Presumably the Boston audience would have needed a little time to take all that in.

On the cover of Gretsch's 1959 catalogue, the company pictured two White Falcons: one with the revised stereo system built in, the other a regular mono example (although surprisingly neither was featured in detail within). This second-type White Falcon Super Project-o-Sonic was made available for sale during 1959, and the revised version of the stereo Country Club appeared the following year. Gretsch also issued an Anniversary Stereo in 1961, reverting the control layout to the original style but using split HiLo'Tron single-coil pickups.

Gretsch had underestimated the conservative nature of many guitar players. Despite Webster's rich imagination and Butts's technical prowess, the stereo models did not sell well (although stereo Falcons, with gradual revisions to the way the controls were laid out, continued to appear on pricelists until around 1980). Duke Kramer from the company's management team recalled that both types of Gretsch's stereo guitar were just too complicated. "A few players could use the system, but on the Falcon stereo there were 54 different tone variations," he said, "and that got to be a little too much for anybody to handle. And in fact there wasn't that much difference between some of the colourings. It never really became too popular."[63]

During 1959, Gretsch began to fit to many models a zero fret, an extra fret directly in front of the nut. The aim with a zero fret is to please players by making the tone of open strings more like that of fretted notes – and to please the factory by reducing the amount of setting-up time. Chet Atkins said that he persuaded Gretsch of its advantages, because he'd seen a picture of Django Reinhardt playing a Selmer guitar with a zero fret and figured it must help to achieve correct string height. By providing the start of the string's speaking length, the zero fret creates the string height at this end of the fingerboard, meaning the only job for the nut is to keep the strings spaced apart. In Gretsch's customarily fanciful marketing hype, the zero fret was an Action-flow Fret Nut. It remained a feature of many Gretsch models until the early 80s, and then appeared later on relevant reissues.

The December 1959 pricelist showed a contemporary line-up of 15 electric models. There were 11 hollowbodys: Clipper at $175; Single Anniversary $225, Double Anniversary $310; Chet Atkins Tennessean $325; Sal Salvador $375; Country Club $450 sunburst, $475 natural or Cadillac Green; Chet Atkins Hollow Body 6120 $475; Country Club Project-o-Sonic $500 sunburst, $525 natural or Cadillac Green; Chet Atkins Country Gentleman $575; White Falcon $750; and White Falcon Super Project-o-Sonic

c.1957 *SILVER JET TESTBED*

■ Gretsch supplied Ray Butts with this unfinished Silver Jet (above) in the late 50s so he could test ideas for pickups and circuits. He fitted the large board to the front so he could change components around easily. Butts used the testbed Jet to develop Gretsch's stereo system with Jimmie Webster.

62 THE GRETSCH ELECTRIC GUITAR BOOK

3 + 3 = STEREOPHONIC

1958 WHITE FALCON SUPER PROJECT-O-SONIC 6137

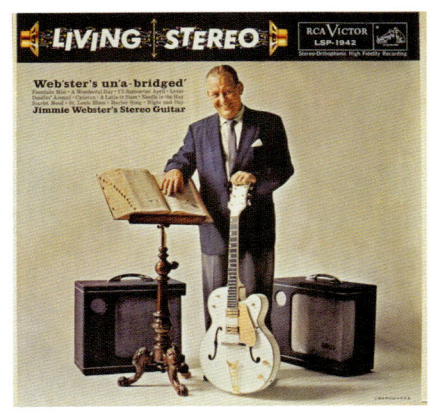

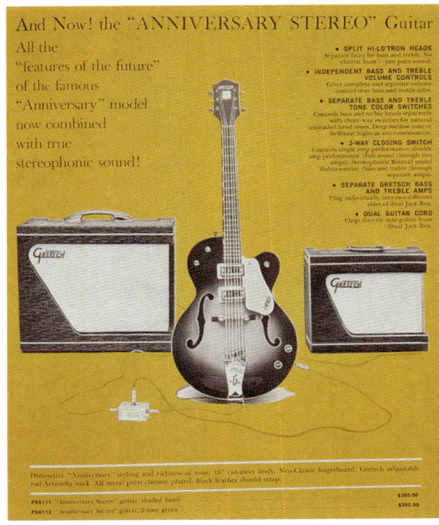

1959 COUNTRY CLUB PROJECT-O-SONIC 6103

■ Gretsch's new Project-o-Sonic models, launched in 1958, were the first stereo guitars. The idea, developed by Jimmie Webster and Ray Butts, was to split the pickups so that the sound of one set of three strings went to one amp and the other three to a second amp.

Webster (pictured, above, with a later stereo Falcon in the early 60s) released an LP in 1958 called Unabridged (centre) to promote the notion of the stereo guitar. The stereo White Falcon (above) was the Super Project-o-Sonic and the stereo Country Club (left) the Project-o-Sonic. There was also a stereo Anniversary model, seen on a page of the 1961 catalogue (above). Despite a beautiful cover for the '61 catalogue (top left), with mono and stereo Falcons, stereo was too complex for most players, and the idea quietly faded away.

THE GRETSCH ELECTRIC GUITAR BOOK

$900. There were four semi-solids: the Duo Jet at $310; Jet Fire Bird $325; Silver Jet $330; and Chet Atkins Solid Body $475.

During the first few years of the 60s, Gretsch made some significant changes to the shape and construction of the hollow electrics. The first move, from around 1960, was to make some of them thinner. Gretsch had found with the thinline Country Gent that many players preferred the easier feel of a slimmer guitar. So the team whittled down the White Falcon from two and three-quarters to two and a half inches deep and took a good inch off the two-and-three-quarter-inch deep Country Club. The single-cut 6120 was trimmed twice in the first years of the 60s, a quarter of an inch at a time, and the Tennessean was thinned down, too, in 1960. A year later, in 1961, the Tennessean gained the sealed body of the Gent and accompanying fake f-holes, while its single Filter'Tron humbucker was swapped for a couple of single-coil HiLo'Trons – a transformation that would ensure a new popularity for the good-value $350 Tenne during the 60s.

The White Falcon was the first to go double-cutaway, in 1960, but the model (mono or stereo) retained its open-f-holes body. Gibson was, as ever, the primary inspiration for this shapely decision: since 1958, the Kalamazoo bods had been using double-cuts to successful effect. Players could more easily reach the higher frets of the fingerboard with this kind of body design and make fuller use of the upper register when soloing.

The Country Gent and 6120 each moved to a double-cut body a year later, in 1961, but the 6120 also gained the sealed unit of the Gent, as usual with fake f-holes painted on for a reasonably traditional look. Of course, Gretsch couldn't resist giving its new sealed double-cutaway body a grand name: Electrotone.

Jimmie Webster wasn't content with these sweeping changes to many of the company's models. He continued during the early 60s to come up with ideas for add-on gadgets, too, which he felt could give the brand's guitars the edge over the competition, and a subsequent outcrop of weird devices would provide Gretsch instruments with an increasingly complex look as the decade progressed.

He came up with a mechanical damper: Gretsch called it a muffler; most people call it a mute, and so shall we. Webster's patent for the mute was filed in February 1962, although it began to appear on guitars a couple of years earlier. Depending on the model and the period, the mute consists of a single or double felt pad close to the bridge and under the strings. The pad(s) can be brought into contact with the strings by turning one or two "dial up" control knobs (also known as "screw down" knobs), situated either side of the tailpiece; these were changed around '63 to "flip up" lever-action switches, which look like smaller angled knobs. Most players preferred the edge-of-the-hand method when they wanted to damp the strings and simply ignored Gretsch's shortlived mutes.

Next came the padded back. "For added comfort and playing," ran the catalogue hype, "a springy pad of foam rubber on the guitar back cushions pressure and eliminates fatigue." Gretsch omitted to mention that the pad also conveniently hid an ugly plate on the back of the body, the one over the hole for access to the guitar's mute system.

NEW YORK CLASSICS

Webster's daughter Jennifer remembered going with her father to obtain the padded material from a Long Island supplier of convertible tops and seating covers for cars.

A standby switch was added to the control layout of some models from around 1961, and it simply turned the guitar's output on or off, saving you the trouble of leaning over and turning down the amp. The Tone Twister was a Webster idea, too. His patent was filed in June 1962 for a small device that clipped on to the dead string area between bridge and tailpiece. Manipulating the small attached arm allowed a brave guitarist to induce vibrato effects. It also allowed startling string-breaking effects, which rather limited its popularity.

Webster next came up with the idea of slanted frets, and he grandly called it T-Zone Tempered Treble. He was down at the patent office again in February 1962 for this one. Gretsch slanted the guitar's frets by one degree from the 12th fret and above, which sharpened the treble strings slightly. The White Falcon and Viking models that bore this questionable addition from 1964 had offset dot markers in the slanted zone. "You will never notice the slight degree in your fingering but you will notice a beautiful change in your treble range," Gretsch said, hopefully.

Next, around 1966, was the Floating Sound Unit (patent filed August 1965), another idea Webster pulled from his piano-tuning bag. Strings were threaded through a three-bar frame that sat between bridge and mute. Fixed to the underside of the frame was a tuning fork that passed downward through a hole in the top of the body and made contact with the guitar's back. The theory was that this would improve sustain, but mostly the unit just rattled around and ruined any attempts to intonate the guitar accurately. Many of the Floating Sound Units were subsequently removed by exasperated guitarists.

Chet Atkins said: "Jimmie's tuning-fork idea was supposed to make the guitar sustain, but the bass strings didn't have any balls. I had them make me a tuning fork that just was on the first four strings, but I never did utilise it." He said that marketing was behind Webster's 60s gizmos. "Jimmie said to me that you've got to give guitarists something different all the time. It's like a car: you've got to come up with something new, they want new features. And I guess he was right. He was a hell of a salesman. But I never liked them all."[64]

And the Gretsch view? Duke Kramer said: "Some of Jimmie's ideas were good; some were bad. The padded back was OK, the Tempered Treble was a little far fetched, and the Floating Sound Unit was an absolute pain in the neck."[65] Dan Duffy said: "I didn't always agree with Jimmie, but you had to train yourself to be commercially minded. You couldn't go into the factory every day and be a jazz guitar player. You had to go in there and be a businessman. Those guitars had to play right and get the hell out the door so the money came in. That's what it was all about."[66]

Like the hollowbodys, the semi-solid line went double-cutaway, starting in 1961, although very few Chet Atkins Solid Body models were made in this style, and a twin-winged White Penguin would turn out to be an even rarer sight than the single-cut

■ As the 50s became the 60s, Gretsch changed the shapes and depths of some bodies. For now, the 6120 was single-cut (the '60 opposite is in rare walnut finish). But the Falcon, meanwhile, moved from the single-cut body ('59 mono example, below) to Gretsch's new double-cut shape ('60 stereo example, above). The changes continued through the line, and a 1963 UK catalogue (opposite) showed a double-cut Gent, the resolutely single-cut Tennessean, and a double-cut 6120. Jimmie Webster introduced a series of add-on gadgets to Gretsch guitars during the late 50s and into the 60s. They included the padded back (right), which hid access to a switch-activated mute system (see patent, opposite, top). The T-Zone Tempered Treble (tag, opposite) was a series of slanted frets meant to improve intonation.

1959 *WHITE FALCON 6136*

66 THE GRETSCH ELECTRIC GUITAR BOOK

BODY IMAGE

1960 WHITE FALCON SUPER PROJECT-O-SONIC 6137

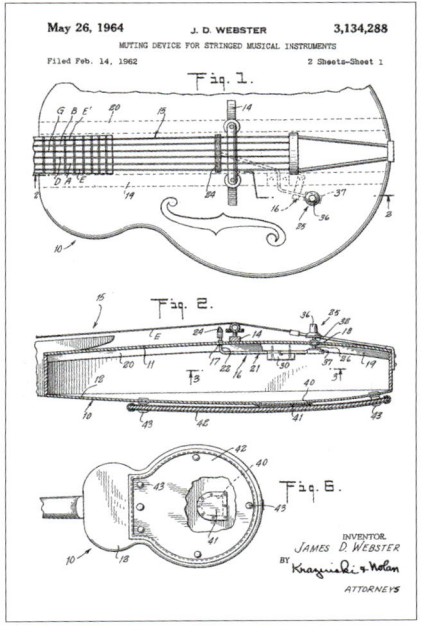

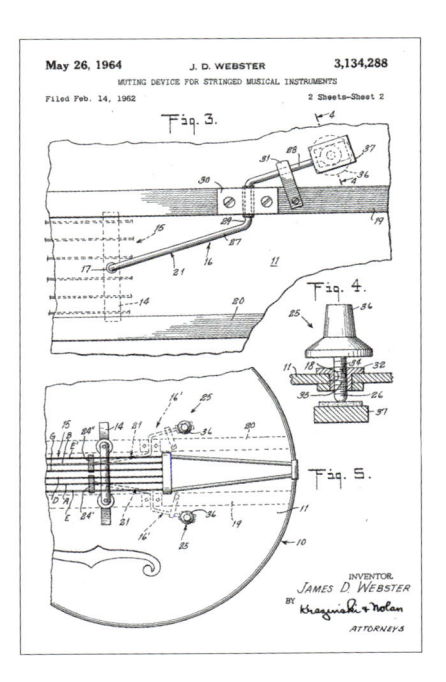

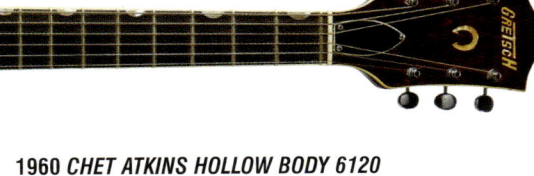

1960 CHET ATKINS HOLLOW BODY 6120

THE GRETSCH ELECTRIC GUITAR BOOK

67

version. Soon after Gretsch changed the solids to the double-cut style, it replaced the Bigsby vibrato tailpieces with units designed by Burns in the UK, probably because of supply irregularities from Bigsby. Quite why Gretsch chose the product of a small maker from Britain is a mystery – although it's fun to speculate that if Jimmie Webster and Jim Burns had met at a trade show, these two eccentric and gifted designers would surely have had a great time discussing bizarre guitar gadgetry. Whatever the reason, Gretsch carried on using the Burns vibratos on its solid lines into the mid 60s.

During the early part of the 60s, Gretsch toyed with a number of oddball solidbody designs. Local guitarist Charles Savona brought the idea for the Bikini model to the company, explaining that he had in mind a hinged folding body into which you could slide interchangeable guitar and bass necks. The body was to be made in single or double-neck styles, and the result was intended to be a versatile, portable guitar. Or so Savona argued. However, Dan Duffy remembers something of a struggle to produce the Bikini. "People at the factory worked diligently to design the butterfly backs so that the slide-in track would work right. It was a great idea, but in my estimation it wasn't really engineered correctly."[67]

A Bikini neck and body listed at $175; a bass neck and body, $195; and a double body with guitar and bass necks was $355. Single bodies could be bought separately for $25; double bodies for $35. Bill Hagner, who replaced Harold Woods as factory manager at Gretsch in 1961, also recalls that the Bikini caused suffering at the workbenches. "You talk about a hard guitar to make," he says with a weary smile. "Forget about it. Headache! To get that thing on correctly and sliding up and down – it was awful. We didn't make that many of the Bikini, thank god."[68]

Gretsch needed a cheaper solidbody to compete with Gibson's $155 Les Paul Junior, and in 1961 it came up with the $139.50 Corvette, the company's cheapest solid. It was Gretsch's first true solidbody guitar, without the routed-out areas of earlier designs. It came with a HiLo'Tron single-coil pickup, and it started life with a simple slab-style body similar to the old Junior's, but subsequently it gained bevelled-edge contours, influenced by Gibson's new SG design.

An interesting variation on that later contoured Corvette was the colourful Princess model of 1962. "For the first time in guitar manufacturing history an instrument has been selectively constructed only for girls," Gretsch's hype ran. "This is the unique adaptable Gretsch Princess Guitar, engineered with identical Gretsch precision to meet the needs and standards of young women all over the world." Gretsch had simply finished the Corvette in special pastel colour combinations designed to appeal to the delicate female sensibility. The boys at Gretsch offered White body with Grape pickguard, Blue body with White pickguard, Pink body with White pickguard, or White body with Gold pickguard. The girls failed to respond to such charms, however, and the Princess retired from public view. Another opportunist variant of the 1962 Corvette was Gretsch's Twist model. Chubby Checker's single 'The Twist' topped the US chart for the second

NEW YORK CLASSICS

time in January and set off the twist dance fad. "You follow a trend," Duke Kramer explained. "The twist dance was an absolute craze. Everyone was doing the twist. What better than to bring out a Twist guitar?"[69] This coloured Corvette had a pickguard bearing a twisting red and white "peppermint" design. Of course, it did not last long.

Gretsch's pricelist of September 1962 summed up a line of 19 electrics. There were 12 hollowbodys: the Clipper at $189; Anniversary $225, Double Anniversary $295; Chet Atkins Tennessean $350; Sal Salvador $375; Anniversary Stereo $375; Chet Atkins Hollow Body 6120 $495; Country Club $495; Country Club Project-o-Sonic $550; Chet Atkins Country Gentleman $595; White Falcon $800; and White Falcon Super Project-o-Sonic $1,000. There were seven solids and semi-solids: the Corvette (one-pickup) at $148, or with vibrato $185; Twist at $149, or with vibrato $189; Princess $169; Duo Jet $350; Jet Fire Bird $350; Silver Jet $350; and Chet Atkins Solid Body $425.

The last of Gretsch's new early-60s solidbodys was the $295 Astro-Jet, which appeared around 1963. "Hand-carved edges highlight its unusual body design," the catalogue said. When Gretsch, no stranger itself in the land of weird, said something was unusual, you knew it would be truly outlandish. The Astro-Jet was indeed a very strange looking guitar, almost as if it had been left out too long on a hot Brooklyn summer day and melted into several disfigured lumps. Salvador Dali might have painted an electric guitar that looked like this. It was big, too, with a body measuring sixteen inches across, some three inches wider than most Gretsch solids.

The Astro-Jet featured Gretsch's new Super'Tron humbucking pickup, visually characterised by the absence of polepieces; instead it had two long bar-shaped laminated poles on the top. The intention was a hotter humbucker than the regular Filter'Tron, but the Super was never as popular. As for the peculiar Astro-Jet, Duke Kramer recalled it as an effort to bring out something that would compete with Fender but not look like Fender. "It was a heavy guitar," he said, "and an awkward shape. It didn't play too bad, but it just didn't catch the imagination of the players. I don't know who was responsible for the design, but I suppose I can push it on to Jimmie Webster."[70]

In 1964, along came the Viking, Gretsch's first new hollowbody-style electric model for some years. At $650, the 17-inch-body Viking was second only to the $850 White Falcon in list-price, and decked out with all the paraphernalia of the period – mutes, T-Zone frets, padded back, telescopic vibrato arm, and all – it could almost be considered as a mono Falcon for those who didn't fancy a white guitar with a winged headstock. The Cadillac Green-finish Viking was, like the sunburst variety, priced at $650, while a natural no-paint-at-all job would, perversely as ever, cost the 60s guitarist an extra $25.

In August 1960, a group called The Beatles had set out to start a run of 48 nights at the Indra club in Hamburg, Germany. It was the first time they'd travelled abroad, and 17-year-old George Harrison took with him his Futurama, a cheap Czech-made solidbody electric that looked a bit like a Stratocaster. Harrison had already decided he needed something better. After all, his co-guitarist in the group, John Lennon, had

c.1969 DUO (SILVER) JET 6128/6129

1962 CORVETTE 6132

■ Meanwhile in solidbody world, Gretsch gave some of its semi-solid models the new double-cut style, such as this late-60s Silver Jet (top). In fact, the sparkle colours were sold officially as finish options of the Duo Jet from about 1963. A catalogue from 1961 (opposite) shows double-cut takes on the Duo Jet and Jet Fire Bird. The Corvette was Gretsch's first true solidbody, launched in 1961. This example (above) has another of Jimmie Webster's gadgets, the Tone Twister, which was a sort of clip-on vibrato. The Princess (in '61 catalogue, above) was a pastel-finish Corvette that, Gretsch said, was "selectively constructed only for girls". It's not clear who the Astro Jet (opposite, top) was aimed at, but this weird solidbody, with Burns vibrato, lasted only a few years. Meanwhile, the Viking (flyer, opposite) was a new hollowbody model, and the 6120 (right) went double-cut in '62.

70 THE GRETSCH ELECTRIC GUITAR BOOK

ASTRO JET MISFIRES

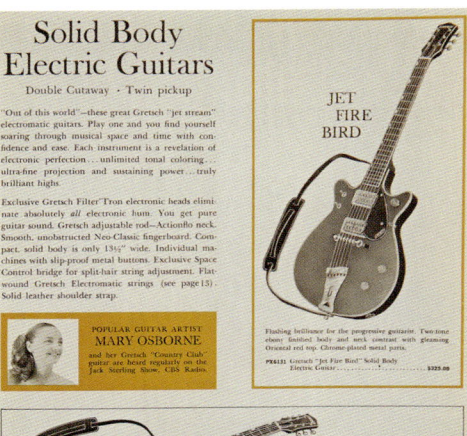

1967 *ASTRO JET 6126*

1962 *CHET ATKINS HOLLOW BODY 6120*

THE GRETSCH ELECTRIC GUITAR BOOK

recently bought a new Rickenbacker 325, which was exactly what most British guitarists wanted but few possessed: a real American guitar. "I might manage a red Fender Stratocaster with gold plating … but the one I want is the Gretsch," he wrote to a friend in October.[71] The following summer he got lucky.

Harrison heard about a Duo Jet up for sale by a merchant seaman, Ivan Hayward, and hurried over to Wavertree in Liverpool to see this rare object for himself. A ban on importing some US goods had been lifted only a year or so earlier, and an American guitar was still quite hard to come by in Britain. Hayward bought the Jet new during his travels, in New York in summer 1957, adding a Bigsby a year later. Now he was getting married and needed to sell the guitar, for £90. Harrison had 70 with him and signed an IOU for the remaining money (which, in fact, he never paid). Now he had what he wanted. "It was my first real American guitar," he remembered, "and I'll tell you, it was secondhand, but I polished that thing. I was so proud to own that."[72]

Over the next few years, The Beatles began their dramatic rise to fame, and Harrison continued to use his beloved '57 Duo Jet – with its DeArmond pickups, hump-block markers, and G-indent knobs – right through the group's early gigs and recordings. Buoyed up by his group's great success in Britain, Harrison next bought a new Gretsch Country Gentleman, around April 1963, at the Sound City store in central London. He paid £264 for the guitar – the equivalent at the time of about $740, which would amount to around $5,700 in today's money.

Harrison, a Chet Atkins fan, was pleased to own a guitar named for his hero. Asked to provide a sleevenote for Atkins's 1966 album of Lennon & McCartney covers, *Picks On The Beatles*, he wrote: "I have appreciated Chet Atkins as a musician since long before the tracks on this album were written; in fact, since I was the ripe young age of 17. Since then I have lost count of the number of Chet's albums I have acquired, but I have not been disappointed with any of them. For me, the great thing about Mr Atkins is not the fact that he is capable of playing almost every type of music, but the conviction in the way he does it. … 'I'll Cry Instead', 'She's A Woman' and 'Can't Buy Me Love', having a country feeling about them, lend themselves perfectly to Chet's own style of picking, which has inspired so many guitarists throughout the world (myself included, but I didn't have enough fingers at the time). All the other tracks have Chet adding harmonies and harmonics in the least expected places, bringing out that crystal-clear sound of the guitar to his audience's benefit."

A few weeks after buying his new double-cut Gent, Harrison used it to record 'She Loves You', but in October he acquired a replacement after that first one became damaged. The new Gent can be spotted in photos because it has angled mute switches either side of the tailpiece – the earlier one had knobs there – and it quickly became his prime instrument. (Like most Gretsch players, Harrison completely avoided the mutes, of course.) That second Gent was one of the guitars most associated with Harrison, who used it regularly until it was destroyed in an accident – it fell off the back of the group's car – at the end of 1965. Crucially for American fans, it was the guitar Harrison was seen with in February 1964 when the group played their first concerts in America and made appearances on the *Ed Sullivan* TV show. By that time, he'd indulged his passion for Gretsch still further, acquiring over the 1963/64 new year a two-pickup single-cut Tennessean, which he used in the studio and for live shows in '64 and, especially, in '65.

Following their domination of Britain, The Beatles had a devastating effect on American youth. Hundreds of bands were formed across the country in the wake of the Sullivan shows, and many of them sought the guitars played by the Liverpudlian invaders. One such was David Crosby of the fledgling Byrds, who bought a Tennessean. Asked much later what inspired the choice, Crosby said it was simple. "That's what George Harrison had. And he had that Rickenbacker, which is what Roger McGuinn got. We went straight for their shit! We said OK, that's how you do it. And once you play a Gretsch, you find out there are tricks to it. Take a Gretsch and roll the volume all the way up on the guitar and then control it from the amp. Then you get that crunch that Gretsch guitars have got."[73] McGuinn also used the Tennessean: he said later that while most people referred to it as Crosby's Gretsch, it actually belonged to the band, and that he used it, for example, to play lead on 'Have You Seen Her Face' and elsewhere on The Byrds' first album, *Mr Tambourine Man*.

Many more 60s pickers tried Gretsch guitars in the wake of the success of The Beatles and George Harrison's shining example. Brian Jones of the Stones bought a green Gretsch Anniversary, also at Sound City, using it on stage from mid '63 and well into the following year. Steve Marriott of The Small Faces was one of the few who opted for a Chet Solid Body, which he later painted white. Chris Britton's Country Gent graced many a Troggs track, including the stirring opening of 'Wild Thing', and Hilton Valentine of The Animals said later that he used his Tennessean for the distinctive arpeggios on 'The House Of The Rising Sun'.

Gerry Marsden strummed a Tennessean for many a Pacemakers show, and Eric Clapton briefly tried a double-cut 6120 while in The Yardbirds but gave up after finding it "too complicated". Neil Young played a single-cut 6120 to great effect in his first notable group, Buffalo Springfield, and he would go on to give Gretsch a new prominence in the following decade. Mike Nesmith was seen in a Monkees TV episode with a 12-string, and in 1966 Gretsch issued a Monkees model six-string. Lou Reed almost managed to get a Country Gent in tune on the early Velvet Underground records.

George Harrison was well aware of the impact that he and his group had on instrument sales. "I read somewhere that after The Beatles appeared on [the Sullivan shows] Gretsch sold 20,000 guitars a week, or something like that," he said later. "I mean, we would have had shares in Fender, Vox, Gretsch and everything, but we didn't know."[74] Gretsch naturally tried to make the most of the fact that the lead guitarist in the most famous group in the world was actively and visibly playing its instruments. An ad aimed at its dealers showed an illustration of the top of a Beatle mop-topped head over the

1964 *CHET ATKINS TENNESSEAN 6119*

P.S. I LOVE GRETSCH

GEORGE HARRISON'S *1957 DUO JET 6128*

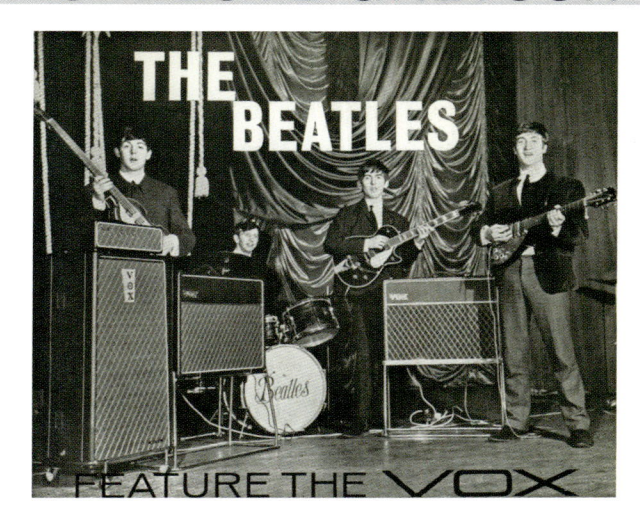

In 1961, George Harrison bought this Duo Jet (left) from a sailor in Liverpool who'd acquired the guitar in New York four years earlier (and soon added a Bigsby vibrato). Harrison is seen in an early Vox ad (top right) proudly playing his prized American guitar, and at some point he had the back of the body and neck (left, centre) sprayed black. He used his Duo Jet on many early Beatles gigs and recordings, until he got a Country Gentleman in early '63 (see next colour spread). Indulging his passion for Gretsch still further, during the 1963/'64 new year he acquired a Tennessean, similar to the one shown here (below). This shot of him with the Tennessean (right) was taken during rehearsals for an American TV show in summer 1965.

THE GRETSCH ELECTRIC GUITAR BOOK

image of a Country Gent. "This shape … and this Gretsch shape … mean success!" ran the copy. "One is the famous Gretsch Country Gentleman guitar. The other is a member of the top rock'n'roll Liverpool group that plays it. And together … they mean success."[75]

Of course, The Beatles were caught in a whirlwind of success, and offers for marketing opportunities surfaced from every entrepreneur with a Beatles wig or a plastic guitar to flog. Gretsch's Jimmie Webster did make a promotional visit to Britain in April 1964 and apparently intended to meet with Harrison while he was there. Webster's daughter Jennifer recalls that there was supposed to be a meeting but it didn't happen. "I don't think my father really cared that much personally," she says, laughing, "but he was willing to explore the idea of developing a guitar with him. And business had picked up when George used a Gretsch. My father was raving about that. Keep doing it, keep doing it, he'd say, that's what we need!"[76]

It seems likely that if Webster had met Harrison, they would have talked about a Harrison signature model, because Gretsch was keen to produce one. Later, in October, the company custom-built a 12-string guitar and delivered it to Harrison during a British tour. The one-off guitar was something like a black single-cut Tennessean, but with real f-holes, Super'Tron pickups, no Bigsby, and, of course, 12 strings. It also had a somewhat presumptuous plate on the headstock reading "George Harrison Model". But Harrison didn't care for the guitar – after all, he had a fine Rickenbacker 12-string – and before long he gave it away to a musician friend. Presumably Gretsch, too, soon forgot about the idea.

The Beatles and the groups who came in their wake triggered a boom in guitar popularity during the middle 60s, and the US industry hit a peak in 1965 with sales of around a million and a half instruments. A strong link to the biggest group of the time – even without any official partnership – certainly did Gretsch little harm. Thanks to Harrison and his highly visible Gent and Tennessean, business was good and the orders came flying in. "The guitar is truly the sound of the day," a jubilant Jimmie Webster told a trade gathering at the time.[77]

Gretsch was not entirely taken by surprise at the way a pop fad could affect its business. More than 30 years earlier, way back in 1932, Gretsch's Emerson Strong had explained how a craze for Cuban music followed 'The Peanut Vendor', a hit for Don Azpiazu. "Overnight a new market sprang into existence," Strong told a Brooklyn reporter, "a market for queer West Indian instruments, which found the business totally unprepared." Gretsch and other instrument houses were faced with a sudden demand for such queer things as guiros, claves, bongos, and maracas. Strong finished the 30s interview with a line that could just as easily have come from the 60s. "One sensational song like that," he said, "introduced over the radio by a nationally known band, can change the whole trend of the country's musical taste in a single night."[78]

The trend for electric guitars sparked by The Beatles in the 60s meant some organisational changes were necessary at the Gretsch building in New York City to deal with this exceptional shift in the balance of its trade. One insider estimated that Gretsch had around 5,000 orders for electrics stacking up at the time, and a customer wanting one of the most popular models might have to wait over a year. One of those hanging on for Gretsch to supply his guitar received a letter from Duke Kramer in August 1965. "Your order has been entered and we hope to make shipment before the end of this year," Kramer apologised to the guitarist in Missouri, who had been waiting for his Country Gentleman since May. "Projected production figures are not too reliable, however, but we can only promise to do the very best we can." Something had to change. In October that year, Gretsch announced it would move the drum department out of the Brooklyn factory to another location a few blocks away, on South 5th Street, and would stop many of its wholesaling operations or move them to the Chicago office. Gretsch did all this to allow the whole of the seventh floor to be turned over to guitar production.

Quality controller Dan Duffy, who by now had taken on extra people such as Fred Rodriguez to cope with the increased demands on him, remembers well how the changes affected his working day. "The transformation was amazing, totally mind boggling," he says. "The changes in that factory during the ten years or so since I started in 1957 were amazing. You have to picture a company back in the 50s trying to make twelve guitars a day, and possibly only getting out eight. In '66, we'd be aiming for seventy-five, and some days we'd make a hundred and more. We had racks made to hold twenty guitars. You'd see Country Gents, Anniversary models, White Falcons – they were all lined up, twenty to a rack, being moved throughout the factory. It was the most spectacular experience in my life."[79] Meanwhile, in the company's boardroom, far-reaching plans were being drawn up that would drastically change the future of Gretsch.

■

Shockwaves echoed through the guitar industry in 1965 when Fender was sold to the CBS corporation for $13 million. It was by far the biggest sum ever paid for an instrument business, and other large predatory companies began to look at the potential of guitar firms as part of what Fender's purchaser called "the expanding leisure-time market".[80]

D.H. Baldwin was an Ohio-based musical instrument company specialising in the manufacture of pianos and organs. It wanted to buy a guitar-making operation, and in 1965 it had bid unsuccessfully for Fender. Baldwin then bought the Burns guitar company of Britain for £250,000 (about $700,000 at the time) and applied the Baldwin brandname to many existing Burns models. The company's annual report for 1966 described a rosy picture: for the first time in Baldwin's long history, overall sales exceeded $40 million, and for the fifth year running sales and profits were up. Keyboard instrument sales had declined, but "since guitars and amplifiers were introduced in the latter part of 1965, there were substantial increases over the figures of the previous year". Baldwin decided it could benefit further with a guitar brandname that had an existing high profile in the USA, and the bosses turned their attention to Gretsch. Every year,

78   **THE GRETSCH ELECTRIC GUITAR BOOK**

GEORGE'S GENTS

1964 CHET ATKINS COUNTRY GENTLEMAN 6122

■ George Harrison got his first Country Gentleman around April 1963, in time to record his group's next hit, 'She Loves You'. Harrison was a big Chet Atkins fan (Atkins is pictured, opposite, with a double-cut Gent in a '62 ad), and the Beatle jumped at the chance to get a guitar named for his hero. That first Gent was like the '62 example here (below), with large mute knobs each side of the vibrato. Later in '63 that first Gent was damaged and he acquired a replacement – Harrison is pictured with both in a dressing room (right). The new Gent is on the left, and like the example pictured (top) it has smaller "flip-up" angled mute knobs. He continued to use the second Gent until it was broken in an accident when it fell from a car roof in late '65. Meanwhile, Gretsch was delighted with all this hugely valuable free publicity, and an artful 1964 trade ad (right) carefully skirts around the lack of any official endorsement.

1962 CHET ATKINS COUNTRY GENTLEMAN 6122

This shape... and this Gretsch shape... mean success!

One is the famous Gretsch Chet Atkins Country Gentleman Guitar. The other is a member of the top rock 'n' roll Liverpool group that plays it. And together... they mean success. There has been a big upsurge of Gretsch guitar sales reflecting the growing interest in today's popular music. As more young, talented guitarists join the trend, they look for quality when they buy. That's why it pays to display and promote Gretsch guitars. You too can profit from Gretsch!

THE FRED. GRETSCH MANUFACTURING CO.
60 Broadway, Brooklyn, N.Y. 11211

THE GRETSCH ELECTRIC GUITAR BOOK

Duke Kramer and Phil Grant, Gretsch's vice-presidents based in Chicago and New York respectively, would go to dinner with Fred Gretsch Jr on their return from the trade fair in Frankfurt, Germany. Early in 1967, the regular dinner date came around with their 62-year-old boss. Kramer: "We were back from a very successful fair, and Fred drops this bomb on us that he was selling the company to Baldwin. It was a real shake-up."[81] Grant: "He mixed us a stiff drink each and said I have some news for you – I'm selling the company to Baldwin. Well, we didn't know how to take it. And there was nothing much you could do about it."[82]

Dick Harrison was Baldwin's treasurer at the time of the acquisition (he went on to be vice-president and then chief executive officer) and he dealt with the negotiation and completion of the transaction, reporting to Baldwin's top man Morley Thompson, who spearheaded the deal. Harrison recalled the reasons why Fred Gretsch decided to sell. "I don't believe he had any offspring who were interested in pursuing the company. He had a young daughter, I believe, and that was all. I'm sure that he knew he had a company in an industry that was growing, and if he was ever going to diversify, it would be a smart time to do that. I'm sure that's why he did it, and that's what he told me. Of course, we were dealing with a man who's giving up everything he owns in the way of a company, and naturally he wants to be careful how he does it. But they were good negotiations with no major problems."[83]

The sale was completed on July 31 1967, and *The Music Trades* reported the price as "10,000 shares of Baldwin common stock and an undisclosed sum of cash," which has since been estimated at $4 million. The report continued: "A new Baldwin subsidiary, organized to acquire these assets, will have Fred Gretsch as president. No change in the management of Gretsch is contemplated. … Gretsch's sales in 1966 were in excess of $6 million. The acquisition of Gretsch will expand Baldwin's business in the guitar field and will put Baldwin in the drum and band instrument business."[84]

Just before the sale, Gretsch's pricelist of November 1966 detailed 15 electrics in the line. There were 11 hollowbodys: the Clipper at $200; Anniversary $245, Double Anniversary $300; Chet Atkins Tennessean $400; Country Club $475 sunburst, $500 natural; Chet Atkins Hollow Body 6120 $500; 12-String $500; Chet Atkins Country Gentleman $650; Viking $675 sunburst or Cadillac Green, $700 natural; White Falcon $900; and White Falcon Super Project-o-Sonic $1,000. There were four solids: the Corvette (two-pickup) $265; Astro-Jet $350; Duo Jet $375 (including colour sparkle options); and Jet Fire Bird $375.

The first catalogue issued after Baldwin took over in 1967 highlighted the return of Bigsby vibratos to the solidbody models, after the dalliance with Burns, and introduced the first new Gretsch model of the Baldwin era, the $395 Rally. It was a double-cut thinline hollowbody with 16-inch-wide body and was unusual in that it featured a built-in active treble-boost circuit, which was also added to the Corvette. The circuit may have been derived from Baldwin's Burns connection, as the British company had pioneered active circuitry in the early 60s. Quite why Gretsch wanted to boost the treble of a guitar already equipped with toppy HiLo'Tron single-coil pickups is unclear.

Gretsch made a number of limited-run instruments at this time for retailers, players, teachers, and so on. Not that Gretsch had ever been shy of custom work, most famously exemplified by that handful of odd-shaped solids it built for Bo Diddley. Duke Kramer explained: "Gretsch was always small enough to be flexible, and always tried to fill small niches in the business. That's why nobody can nail down what Gretsch did on a particular model, because maybe ten percent of our business was custom guitars. If someone wanted a pink guitar with blue stripes, we made it. If somebody wanted a guitar with a narrow neck at the nut, we made it. It cost the customer extra money, but we were small enough to be able to do that."[85]

There were small-order batches in the 60s of specially modified models for Gretsch dealers such as Sam Ash (an Anniversary-style "Cat's-Eye Custom" guitar with cat's-eye soundholes), Sam Goody (a double-cut hollowbody with G-shape soundholes), and Sherman Clay (a gold or silver-finish Corvette, later nicknamed the Gold Duke and Silver Duke). Kramer continued: "Dealers liked the idea of an exclusive instrument, because they could point to it and say no one else has this, and they could charge a certain amount of dollars and know that nobody could quote a cheaper price."

Gretsch also made special small-run personalised guitars, including a small number for Ronny Lee, a player, teacher, and store-owner in New York City, a Sal Febbraio model for another New York teacher (effectively a Rally with cat's-eye soundholes), and six and seven-string models named for guitarist George Van Eps, the seven-string version of which remained in the catalogue for ten years.

Gretsch meanwhile continued to keep an eye on the major makers and habitually monitored the moves of its longtime rival, Gibson. In the late 60s, some guitarists were rediscovering old Les Pauls, and finally in 1968 Gibson reintroduced the early-style single-cut model that almost everyone seemed to be looking for. Gretsch responded by bringing back its own discontinued single-cut solidbody design, last seen around 1961 in the form of various Jet models and the Chet Solid. The $350 Roc Jet appeared in 1969, and shortly afterward Gretsch dropped the remaining double-cut Jet models.

Long-standing Gretsch man Bill Hagner saw changes as the takeover took hold. "The Baldwin company were the greatest manufacturing company of organs and pianos," he says, "but they tried to put their men into the guitar and drum business, and it wasn't the right thing to do. They had their own so-called engineers and so-called chemists and so-called this and that, and they wanted to incorporate their methods that they used in making pianos and organs. They said now we're going to do it this way – and I would say wait a minute, we made that mistake 20 years ago!"[86]

Phil Grant said he couldn't blame Fred Gretsch Jr for selling. "But the usual thing happened: a company was bought up and the president promises nothing's going to change, your jobs are all secure, don't worry. And your cheque's in the mail," Grant

JIMMIE WEBSTER'S 1966 *WHITE FALCON*
SUPER PROJECT-O-SONIC 6137

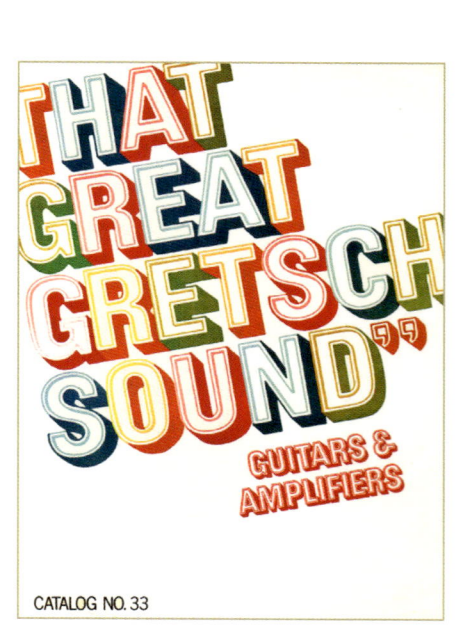

1968 *RALLY 6104*

82   THE GRETSCH ELECTRIC GUITAR BOOK

INTO THE BALDWIN ERA

■ This mid-60s Falcon (main guitar) was owned by Jimmie Webster and typifies Gretsch style of the time, with double mute switches and pads, telescopic vibrato arm, multiple stereo controls, Space Control bridge, T-Zone slanted frets, thumbnail markers, two Filter'Trons, and, of course, That Great Gretsch Sound (1968 catalogue cover, opposite, bottom). Gretsch trumpeted the "ultimate" Falcon's $1,000 price-tag in this contemporary ad (below).

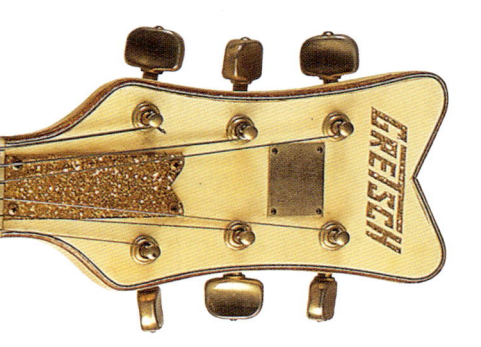

1966 *CORVETTE 6135 "GOLD DUKE"*

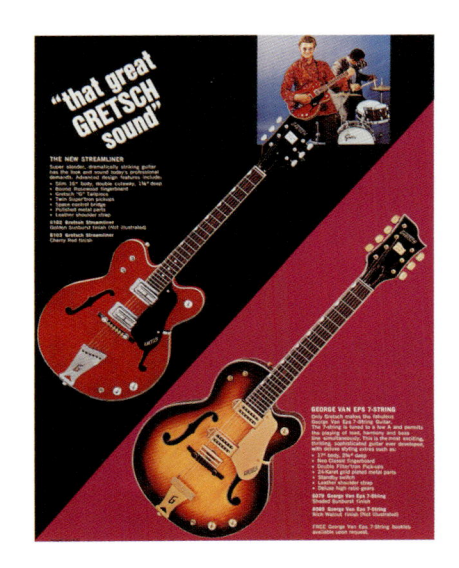

■ Two rare sparkle-colour options of the Corvette were later nicknamed the Gold Duke (right) and Silver Duke. The Baldwin piano and organ firm bought Gretsch in 1967, and the first new model after the takeover was the Rally (left), a colourful contender that lacked real inspiration. This late-60s ad (above left) adds another, the cheaper thinline Streamliner, alongside the seven-string Van Eps.

THE GRETSCH ELECTRIC GUITAR BOOK

83

added with a smile. "Anyway, I went along with it, and after a while you could see that things weren't going to be the way that you hoped they would be. Baldwin would press a button, say let's do it this way, and anybody's personal feelings never entered into their decisions at all."[87]

It didn't take too long for Baldwin to become disappointed with the business results of the merger. "When you put two companies together, you like to believe that one plus one equals three," Dick Harrison explained. "If you have a sales force out there that would be capable of selling Gretsch guitars in addition to Baldwin pianos, that would have represented some synergy. In other words, you would come out better by having done it. But the products were so different, and we felt that it would have been a great mistake to put the Gretsch guitar in the hands of our Baldwin sales people, so we never did that. Another example of synergy would have been if our factories that make pianos, primarily woodworking operations, could make guitars. Again, they're so different that that didn't come about."

Harrison said that from Baldwin's perspective, Gretsch did well for a while, but then the industry in general hit a dip. "That hurt us," he remembered. "I would say that it really wasn't a financial success for us. And that certainly wasn't the fault of anybody from Gretsch. That was as much the industry's fault and our fault as anything else."[88] Baldwin had begun to move away from its original core business in music and into financial services, including banking and insurance. The company's annual report for 1969 noted a 12 percent drop in Gretsch sales, conveniently attributing over half the fall to a three-month strike that began in October 1969.

By 1970, Baldwin decided to move the Gretsch factory out of the 54-year-old site in Brooklyn to Booneville, Arkansas. This was well over a thousand miles away. Baldwin already operated a number of factories there and enjoyed the fruits of a cheaper and more amenable workforce. Of course, the idea of a move did not please the already disgruntled workers, and virtually none made the long journey south-west in September 1970. The Brooklyn sales office had already moved to Chicago, in August 1969, and in May 1972 it would shift again, to a dusty old six-storey warehouse across the street from Baldwin's HQ in Cincinnati, Ohio.

All this meant that by the early 70s, Gretsch had severed the last connection with its longstanding HQ at 60 Broadway, Brooklyn. (Years later, in 2003, the Gretsch Building would be converted to 120 luxury condominiums; one of the largest, a six-bedroom penthouse, was for sale at six and a half million dollars in 2014, perhaps the ultimate Gretsch collectable. "I'm sure the tenants are haunted by the faint sound of the Gretsch guitars playing 'The Fred Gretsch Blues'," Dan Duffy wrote later, referring to the title he gave the scales and licks he'd play when testing guitars at the old factory.[89])

Bill Hagner was one of the few New York people who relocated to the new Booneville site. He had started at Gretsch back in 1941, working his way up from office boy to become production manager in the 50s and then factory manager in 1961, overseeing drum manufacturing as well as guitars. He moved everything down to Booneville in July 1970 with an engineer, Jim Fulvery, and set it up. "And I taught the new people what to do and how to do it," Hagner says. "That lasted several years. The factory was a big converted barn up on top of the mountain, about five miles out of a small town of 3,000 people. You had to take people off the farms and try to teach them how to work. When you're used to New York, well … you move down there and they'd be polishing a guitar for four hours instead of a half hour."[90]

Charlie Carrington became plant manager and Hagner was moved to Baldwin's Ohio offices to work with the sales force – although, as we'll see, he would soon return to Booneville. Some of the old names remained: Fred Gretsch Jr had become a Baldwin board member in December 1967. Duke Kramer went to Ohio in 1972, as Gretsch's general sales manager. Dan Duffy left in 1970, at first going back to full-time playing and teaching, and then on to positions in various instrument companies. Phil Grant left in 1972 to set up a grocery business in Vermont; he died in July 2002.

Jimmie Webster made some Guitarama-type appearances for Gretsch after the sale to Baldwin, but gradually he drifted away from the guitar company he had done so much to establish. Webster died in 1978 at the age of 69. Chet Atkins would switch to a deal with the Gibson company around 1980.

At the time of the sale, Baldwin knew it wasn't just the brandname and products of its new acquisition that could be valuable, and it recognised that Chet Atkins was the most important name still associated with Gretsch guitars. "I was important to the sale," Atkins recalled. "Mr Gretsch came to me, said he was gonna sell to Baldwin, and asked me if I would sign a contract for so many years. I said why don't I get some stock? And he wouldn't do it. I was real busy at the time, and I didn't have an attorney or anything, so I went ahead and signed it."[91]

During 1966, the 6120 had switched identities, when Gretch changed the official model name from Chet Atkins Hollow Body to the more friendly Chet Atkins Nashville. The guitar itself stayed much the same – double-cut sealed body, thumbnail markers, string-mute, standby control layout – with the addition of a Nashville nameplate on the head and the new name on the pickguard.

In 1972, a new Gretsch Chet Atkins design hit the market in the form of two broadly similar guitars, the Deluxe Chet and the Super Chet. They were big single-cut hollowbody models – the bodies were 17 inches wide and 2½ inches deep – and they resulted from a collaboration between Chet Atkins, Dean Porter, and Clyde Edwards. Atkins had been concerned about the changes with the move to Booneville. "They just couldn't build Gretsch guitars there," he said later. "I complained, and they hired a man called Dean Porter. He moved to Arkansas and got the guitars so they would play. But the quality never was like it was in Brooklyn."[92] Gretsch called Edwards its "master string-instrument designer". A company newsletter of the time explained what happened. "The surest way of getting this super guitar was to turn these three men loose and tell them to

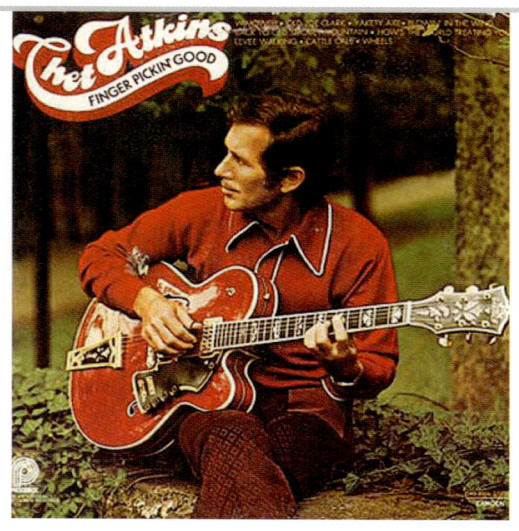

■ In 1970, Baldwin moved Gretsch production from the site in New York, where it had been since the 1910s, to a factory in Booneville, Arkansas. Among the new models developed there was the Super Chet (opposite, top), with controls unusually situated on the edge of the pickguard. Atkins played the Super (ad, above left, and early-70s LP sleeve, centre), which was partnered by a simpler version, the Deluxe Chet (pictured in a 1972 catalogue, opposite). Both were devised by Atkins in collaboration with Dean Porter, Gretsch's new guitar technician, and Clyde Edwards, the company's new guitar designer. The Deluxe soon left the line, but the Super Chet remained available until 1980.

THE GRETSCH ELECTRIC GUITAR BOOK

NEW CHETS, NEW JETS

1972 SUPER CHET 7690

c.1973 ROC JET 7610

1967 CHET ATKINS NASHVILLE 6120

Deluxe Chet
7680
Hollow Body
Electric Cutaway

■ The Chet Atkins Hollow Body had a name change, to the Chet Atkins Nashville (main guitar), around '66, although most people call it simply the 6120. Meanwhile, the White Falcon was no less than "a rainbow of breathtaking sound" according to a late-60s ad (opposite, top right). Booneville's new Roc Jet (above) was a sort-of updated Jet reissue, with some of the style of the single-cut Duo Jet, last seen in the early 60s, but with newer features such as Super'Tron humbuckers.

THE GRETSCH ELECTRIC GUITAR BOOK

design the best guitar they could, no holds barred. ... More fussing went into this guitar than you can imagine."[93]

A lot of the fussing must have been spent on the profuse decorative work on the Super Chet. The guitar had flowery inlays sprouting on the fingerboard, the headstock, and the tailpiece. It also sported an unusual row of control wheels built into the edge of the pickguard, and the sides of the body were decorated with an attractive inlaid centre stripe. Atkins was responsible for this. "I had a little acoustic guitar from the 1800s that a lady had given me. It had a lot of inlay on it, and inlay in the centre of the sides, so I had them do that. We were trying to make a really beautiful guitar. Clyde just tried to build the prettiest guitar ever."[94] The Deluxe Chet was a plainer version, with conventional controls and none of the foliage, and it did not last long. The Super Chet stayed in the line for about seven years – Atkins used one for many of his shows and sessions in the 70s – and it would be reissued as the Super Gretsch in 1998.

The August 1972 pricelist showed 14 electric models in the Booneville-made Gretsch line, of which 13 were hollowbodys: the Clipper at $250; Double Anniversary at $345; Streamliner $395 (a lower-price double-cut launched in 1967); Chet Atkins Tennessean $495; Country Club $500 sunburst, $525 natural; Chet Atkins Nashville 6120 $595; Van Eps seven-string $675; Chet Atkins Country Gentleman $695; Viking $700 sunburst, $725 natural; Deluxe Chet $750; Super Chet $850; White Falcon $975; and White Falcon Stereo $1,100. The solitary solid was the single-cut Roc Jet at $395 in red, orange, or black and $425 in brown. It was around this time that a gear-box system for truss-rod adjustment was adopted, borrowed from Baldwin's Burns-originated guitars and accessed through the back of the body at the neck heel. Hollowbody models once again allowed air inside with the revival of real, open f-holes from around 1972.

Although sales picked up a little in the early 70s – Gretsch's Don Manchester insisted that in the first half of 1972 "sales records were broken every month"[95] – still Baldwin was not seeing a profit from the business, despite cutting costs wherever it could. In January 1973, there was a bad fire at the factory, adding to the general gloom.

Baldwin decided to contract out manufacture of Gretsch products to Bill Hagner, whom Baldwin had reinstated as factory manager in late '72. He formed the Hagner Musical Instrument Corp for the purpose, still operating from the Booneville site. Hagner and Gene Haugh were instrumental in getting the new operation up and running. "Baldwin didn't want to be bothered with it any more," Hagner remembers, "and assuming that I knew what I was doing, they decided to take a chance and do it that way."[96] Another fire, in December of '73, completely destroyed the factory, and a larger replacement building was put up nearby.

The odd new Roc II and Streamliner II appeared in 1973. The Roc II was a single-cut solid with an elliptical control plate and circuitry intended to produce copious quantities of treble and distortion. "High degree of treble booster for 'screaming' rock sounds," said the press release. Most guitarists seemed unimpressed. The Streamliner II was a stripped-down version of the Streamliner, in red, with the same active circuitry and elliptical control plate but missing a pickguard.

Following on from the Roc Jet, first seen in 1969, which was prompted partly by a growing sense of nostalgia among players for older-style instruments, Gretsch added the Country Roc to the line in 1973. It was a Western-appointed solid that evoked but hardly matched the Round Up model of the 50s. In the same year, Gretsch reintroduced a single-cutaway deep-body mono White Falcon. The Falcon had last been made with this kind of body style some 12 years earlier, and it now partnered the contemporary double-cut thinline mono and stereo versions. It was significant because it was the first reissue of a 50s-style Gretsch hollowbody, and it underlined the growing fashion for old guitars.

It's not clear exactly when old guitars began to be called vintage guitars, but it was probably some time in the early 70s. Guitarists were talking openly in interviews about the mysterious and apparently contagious idea that the older the guitar, the better it played. Charlie Daniels, for example, said: "If a guitar sounds good and plays good, I don't care if it's a '58 or a '75. It just happens that most guitars that sound good and play good are old ones."[97] A trend was settling in. Somehow, went the vibe, only vintage guitars are worthy of attention by "real" players. Vintage dealers appeared, too, and they were more than happy to charge increasingly large premiums for the most desirable of the classic axes from the 50s and 60s.

The trend caught hold of Pete Townshend. Joe Walsh gave him a '59 or '60 Chet 6120, which he used for some pleasant noise on a good deal of *Who's Next* (1971) and *Quadrophenia* (1973). Despite the fact that Townshend largely avoided the guitar on stage because it "won't stay in tune", he soon discovered that here was a good studio companion. When it first arrived from Walsh, he thought the bright orange colour rather horrible. But Walsh usually knew his stuff, so he persevered. "I went home and went into my studio and plugged it in – and it totally wrecked me out. It's the best guitar I've got now," Townshend said in 1972. "It's the loudest guitar I've ever owned. It is so loud, man, it whips any pickup that I've ever come across. It's maybe six or seven times louder than anything I've come across. If I plugged it in my amp tonight, normally I'd be working on volume 6 or 7, but I would work this guitar on 1."[98] In 1973, Townshend demolished his 6120 during a performance of '5:15' on the British TV show *Top Of The Pops*, but it was rescued and he continued occasionally to use the remodelled guitar.

Also during the early 70s, in Crosby Stills Nash & Young, Stephen Stills and Neil Young added to the growing interest in old Gretsch guitars. Young's Falcon-fuelled intro to 'Ohio', a Top 20 hit for CSNY in summer '70, was more than enough to intrigue many guitarists. "Neil Young and I are going to go to Gretsch in the next couple of weeks," Stills told an interviewer that year. "I think they were really amazed at the pure White Falcons we had, because they're kind of old, both of them. So they offered to let us design one for them. And you know what the design is? There is no new design! Just build the old one, man."[99] Stills said more recently that he recalled Chet Atkins giving him a demo

c.1975 COUNTRY ROC 7620

■ Starting around the late 60s and early 70s, some players were looking for older instruments, soon to be called vintage guitars. The trend was based on the idea that old guitars were somehow inherently better, while current guitar-making skills had dimmed. Some of Gretsch's new models reflected this, such as the Country Roc (above), which evoked the 50s Round Up model, complete with G-brand. Others were newer, such as the Streamliner II (below), with active circuit and unusual control plate.

1975 WHITE FALCON 7593

THE GRETSCH ELECTRIC GUITAR BOOK

OLD GUITARS ... NEW GUITARS

■ Gradually during the 70s Gretsch began to notice the vintage trend, as new and not-so-new musicians began to play the company's old guitars. One very visible example was Pete Townshend (above) who was much taken with a circa-1960 Atkins 6120, given to him by Joe Walsh and all over The Who's work in the early 70s. Also at this time, Gretsch reintroduced the original-style single-cut White Falcon (opposite, and on the cover of the 1975 catalogue, right), its first reissue of a 50s hollowbody.

1973 STREAMLINER II 7667

THE GRETSCH ELECTRIC GUITAR BOOK

of a single-cut Country Gent. "Chet did finger-picking, like I wanted to," he remembers. "When I first saw [Gretsch guitars], I liked the woody ones, the orange ones. That's the Buffalo Springfield sound, because the Gretsch on the records was an orange one, but they got swiped at the Whisky." He still has a '58 Falcon, which might just be the one he used when CSNY played Woodstock. "Well, it's old, and it's spent 30 years on the road with me," Stills continues. "The flash of this guitar – actually Neil talked me into it. As much as finding two good ones, it was the look of two White Falcons on either end of the stage."[100] Gretsch would issue a Stills signature Falcon in 2000.

Other musicians ensuring high visibility for Gretsch included Randy Bachman, with his late-50s 6120 in Bachman-Turner Overdrive (and a notable Gretsch collector), and Malcolm Young of AC/DC. Young powered his band's growing fame through the mid and late 70s with a '63 double-cut Jet Fire Bird, given to him by his elder brother George, who'd been in The Easybeats. He bashed it around to suit his driving rhythm-guitar stylings for AC/DC, stripping the red paint to reveal the natural wood and leaving just the bridge pickup in place. Gretsch would issue a couple of Young reissue Jets in 1996.

Meanwhile, Bill Hagner's Booneville-based Gretsch operation released two budget-price Broadkaster models in 1974, a solid and a semi-hollow, in an attempt to attract rock players to Gretsch with new designs. As usual, Gretsch was to some extent following Gibson's lead – and on this occasion the path was an unpopular one. Gibson had launched the Marauder, its first solidbody guitar with a Fender-style bolt-on neck, in 1974. The Broadkaster solid was the first Gretsch with a bolt-on neck, and it had strong influences of Stratocaster styling. Neither the solid nor the semi raised much interest.

At the very start of 1976, Hagner opened a new factory in Booneville. It was reported at the time as "ultra-modern" and "a spanking new plant affirming Gretsch plans to grow".[101] The new building – appropriately located at 84 Baldwin Road – was 42,000 square feet, far bigger than the 1,500-square-feet building destroyed in the December '73 fire or the 2,500-square-feet plant that replaced it.

Baldwin had issued a Japanese-made Strat-like solid electric with the Dorado brandname in 1970 to add to its already wide distribution of other instruments under the Dorado umbrella. This was separate from Gretsch but significant because it was the company's first brush with guitar manufacturing in Asia. The connection led in 1976 to Gretsch's selection of a Japanese supplier to provide new pickups for several models.

Ray Butts's patent for the Filter'Tron pickup reached the end of its official 17-year run in '76. The previous year, he got a letter from Duke Kramer at Gretsch saying royalty payments would end.[102] "I had made a handshake agreement on my humbucking pickup with Mr Gretsch," Butts recalled. "He told me they'd done business that way with K Zildjian in Turkey, the cymbal makers, for over 50 years, and also with Cuesnon band instruments of France. So we had no written agreement, which was fine at the time."[103]

After Gretsch was sold, it seemed to Butts that Baldwin more or less forgot about the arrangement. With the letter he got in '75 came a little money and a note saying that

BALDWIN & BOONEVILLE

Baldwin felt the agreement no longer applied – and, by the way, would Butts like to come up with a new pickup for the Roc Jet, the Broadkaster, and "the new Chet Atkins Hi-Roller model guitar"? When Butts understandably declined, Gretsch turned to the Japanese supplier for pickups for the existing Roc Jet and Broadkaster models. In fact, Butts did no more business with Gretsch, the company for whom he had created so much. He died in April 2003.

As for the Atkins Hi-Roller, this was the original name given to a design that quickly became the Super Axe and Atkins Axe of 1977. Gretsch was still hazy about a name late in 1976: an ad published at that time mentioned an upcoming instrument to be called the Atkins Yakety Axe. The big new guitars had a distinctive look, with a sweeping, pointed cutaway and 16-inch solid bodies, all the subject of a patent for ornamental design issued to Gretsch designer Clyde Edwards. Chet Atkins and Gretsch's general manager Duke Kramer were also involved in the project.

"Chet wanted to call it the Hi-Roller guitar," Kramer recalled, "and he wanted to put on dice as position markers. We made a few with the dice – we even had it down as the Hi-Roller on a pricelist – but the Baldwin people thought the name and the dice gave the guitar a bad connotation of gambling, and they didn't want that. So we left the markers plain, and we called it the Super Axe. Chet wanted more sustain, so he put on a compressor, and he wanted a phaser on it, which the Baldwin engineers came up with."[104]

When the two models were officially launched, the effects-laden version was called the Super Axe and the less expensive gadget-less one the Atkins Axe – despite the fact that it was Chet's idea to have the built-in effects. He appeared in Gretsch's ads at the time pushing the Super Axe, which was clearly the version he liked. Further confusion arose because Gretsch tried to get an endorsement deal with Roy Clark, the country guitarist. Kramer said the company at first decided not to put Chet Atkins's name on the new guitars. "We were going to pay Chet a royalty because he helped design them, but we weren't going to have his name on them. I took one out to Roy Clark, and he fell in love with it. He wanted to play it, and I said OK, we might make it the Roy Clark model. He said that'd be great. I got back and told Chet, and he didn't like that at all, so we never did it – although Roy did use and play the guitar, and we did some advertising with him."[105] The Atkins Axe would be reissued as the Axe in 1995 – and this time it had the dice-style markers along the fingerboard.

Mike Jones has become the historian for the Booneville period of Gretsch's story, channelling much of his research into his website *Gretsch's Lost Weekend*.[106] This is Jones's ironic title for Gretsch's Baldwin period, because he believes the guitars made in that period are undervalued by many guitarists, especially by some snobbish vintage collectors who care only for Gretsch's 50s and 60s classics and think of the Booneville models as poor relations.

"The Booneville era became interesting to me because I couldn't find any real flaws in the models I owned or had examined," Jones explains. "Sure, there were styling

CHET ATKINS'S 1977 *SUPER AXE* 7680

■ More new Chet Atkins models appeared in 1977, with the effects-laden Super Axe (above) and the simpler Atkins Axe (1978 catalogue, below right). In an ad (below) for the Super, which he preferred, Atkins called it "the ultimate guitar for the rock musician", but unfortunately few agreed with him. The Corvette II (right) appeared in 1976 as a revised take on the existing Corvette solidbody, keeping the two-and-four tuner layout on the distinctive headstock, and providing simpler electrics than the previous Corvette's active circuit and distortion effects.

1976 *CORVETTE II* 7630

94 THE GRETSCH ELECTRIC GUITAR BOOK

SUPER AXES FOR THE SEVENTIES

1976 ROC I 7635

■ Several new models appeared from Booneville, such as the Roc I (above), a straightforward guitar aimed squarely at rockers, and the Broadkaster semi-hollow (pictured in the 1975 catalogue, below). More players were finding that old Gretsch guitars made useful tools, including Malcolm Young (above) of AC/DC, with a modified Jet Fire Bird, and Stephen Stills and Neil Young (below), here with vintage Gent and Falcon.

Broadkaster #7607 Hollow Body Electric

Also available in shaded sunburst finish. Model #7608

Broadkaster #7604 Hollow Body Electric

Also available in natural finish. Model #7603

THE GRETSCH ELECTRIC GUITAR BOOK

differences and there were models they introduced that were meant to attract the rock crowd, but for the most part they were still very well made instruments. The Booneville era gets a bad rap, in my opinion, and that's why I started to dig. The more I dug, the more interesting it became – and the more interesting it became, the more passionate I became." Over the years, he's bought many of the so-called apocryphal guitars, he's interviewed Gretsch people from the time, he's catalogued the models, and gradually he's pulled the story together.

Looking closely at the solidbody guitars from this period, Jones concludes that the new mid-70s models – Corvette II, Deluxe Corvette, Roc I, Super Roc, and Broadkaster – were Gretsch's attempts at making guitars for rock players. The firm needed sure-fire sellers that could be produced in large enough quantities so that Bill Hagner could fulfil his demanding contract with Baldwin. "Part of the deal was that he not only had to pay Baldwin a million dollars for the operation," Jones says, "but he had to increase output 100 percent per year – which he did. It wasn't until after his second year at the new factory that he realised that meant 100 percent every year … in perpetuity. What they asked Bill to do was just ridiculous – and impossible. He really got things moving, increased production, balanced costs, and so forth – and he got screwed. By late 1976, Booneville had increased production almost 300 percent. It looks to me like Baldwin just wanted the fruits of Bill's labour."

The Broadkasters were cheap and easy to make and supposed to be the answer, in 1974, but they didn't sell well. "They were aimed at the rock crowd but they were probably seen by guitarists as just another Stratocaster knock-off with humbuckers," Jones says. "Similarly, the Roc I was probably viewed as too much in the shadow of the Telecaster. And the Deluxe Corvette and the Super Roc didn't do well: they were too time-consuming and too expensive to make. The Corvette II was considered because Gretsch had a thousand leftover Corvette bodies from the 60s that travelled to Booneville from New York."

This all led to Gretsch's next move in its doomed quest to find a rock guitar for the masses. In early 1977, production manager Tom Kimble came to Gene Haugh and asked him to design a guitar that they could turn out like popcorn … and design it by tomorrow. It had to look different and be inexpensive to make. Jones recalls Haugh's story of how the "popcorn model" came to get its official name. "The next morning," Jones says, "Gene called Tom over to his bench and said well, here it is. He said he figured they could probably make about 300 a month of this guitar. Tom looked pleased and a bit excited, and he asked what Gene was going to call it. Gene said he was thinking it could be the TK – for Tom Kimble – 300. Looking a bit surprised, Tom asked why not the GH – for Gene Haugh – 300? Gene smiled and said well, I wouldn't have designed it if you hadn't asked me to – and, more importantly, if this thing bombs, I don't really want my name on it! They both laughed. According to Gene, Kimble said: 'It won't bomb … and I like it. OK then, TK 300 it is.'"[107]

BALDWIN & BOONEVILLE

The TK 300 was added to the line in 1977, alongside another easy-to-make solidbody electric, the Committee. The TK 300 had a bolt-on neck and a strange asymmetric body that has led some to consider it the ugliest guitar ever produced. The Committee followed a trend of the time for solidbody through-neck construction, where the neck runs the length of the guitar with added body-wings to complete the shape. Both were uninspiring guitars that lacked the character once at the heart of Gretsch design, two more victims of the drive to produce an all-purpose rock guitar.

A pricelist from April 1977 summed up a Gretsch line of 18 electrics. There were 11 hollow or semi-hollow models: the Broadkaster at $495 in sunburst or natural ($550 with vibrato), $525 red; Double Anniversary $625; Chet Atkins Tennessean $695; Country Club $725 Antique Maple, $750 natural; Chet Atkins Nashville 6120 $795; Van Eps seven-string $795; Chet Atkins Country Gentleman $895; White Falcon single-cut $1,050; Super Chet $1,150 hardtail, $1,200 vibrato; White Falcon double-cut $1,175; and White Falcon Stereo double-cut $1,295. There were seven solids: the TK 300 at $295; Broadkaster $450; Committee $475; Roc Jet $595 black or red, $600 Walnut; Country Roc $695; Atkins Axe $750; and Super Axe $895.

The manufacturing deal with Hagner ceased at the end of 1978, and control passed back fully to Baldwin. Hagner recalls the way that Baldwin pressed him continually to increase production, knowing the targets were impossible. "I told them, wait a minute, I don't even have the room to do everything that you want. And the question came down to well, you either produce what we want, or you're avoiding your contract, and so bang, bang, bang ... goodbye."[108] Baldwin then appointed one Ben Johnson as plant manager.

In early 1979, Baldwin bought the Kustom amplifier company, and by the end of the year it had merged Gretsch with Kustom, moving the sales and administration office for the new combined operation to Chanute, Kansas, under the direction of Charlie Roy. In 1979 and '80, Baldwin's last new Gretsch guitars appeared. The Beast solids came in different styles, some with a single-cut body something like a scaled-down Super Axe, as well as a couple of double-cut versions. Gretsch seemed to want to be all things to all guitarists with the Beasts, absorbing design elements from Gibson and Fender as well as contemporary Japanese makers. "All the sound you can ask for," a promotional leaflet boasted. "New pickups, new electronics, completely new designs make it all happen."

The Beasts ranged in price from $299.50 for a mahogany bolt-on-neck model (BST-1000) to $695 for a walnut-and-maple through-neck guitar (BST-5000). They seemed functional rather than inspirational, and although few people realised it at the time – "this is only the beginning of what you can expect from the Beast family" was the way the optimistic leaflet put it – they would be the last gasp from Gretsch until the brand's revitalisation at the close of the 80s. As such, they marked the end of a difficult period with a depressingly low note.

Baldwin's bosses finally decided they'd had enough and would stop production of Gretsch guitars, probably some time during 1980, and it seems that very little was manufactured beyond the start of 1981 (just short of Gretsch's 100th anniversary, due in 1983). Baldwin continued to build Gretsch drums at Booneville until '81, when it transferred the business to a Baldwin factory in De Queen, Arkansas, about 80 miles south of Booneville, and later to Texarkana, Arkansas, still further south. Gretsch also made Sho-Bud steel guitars at the De Queen premises. In early 1982, Charlie Roy bought the business from Baldwin and moved his offices to Gallatin, Tennessee, just outside Nashville. One report in summer 1982 had Roy claiming he would build a new Gretsch factory in Gallatin, to "replace the present facility in Chanute, Kansas", but that idea soon faded.[109]

By now, Chet Atkins's endorsement deal had ceased, and he soon transferred allegiance to Gibson, which issued its first Chet Atkins model, a solidbody classical, in 1981 – not long after the death in 1980 of Fred Gretsch Jr, with whom Atkins had made his original Gretsch deal. Gibson issued a Chet Atkins Country Gentleman model in 1986 and a Chet Atkins Tennessean four years later. Atkins said Gibson was able to use the Country Gentleman name as he owned it, because of the song by that name that he'd written (with Boudleaux Bryant) and recorded in the 50s. "The Gibson Country Gentleman was built sturdier than the Gretsch," he said in 2001, "and had the advantages of newer technology, so I think it's a better guitar overall."[110] As we'll discover, Gretsch would eventually regain the right to use the Chet Atkins name.

Charlie Roy continued to sell his existing Gretsch guitar stock probably as late as 1983. The last known Kustom–Gretsch pricelist is dated January '83 and shows only Committee and Beast models, presumably unsold leftovers from the '79–'81 production runs. Baldwin regained control of the Gretsch company soon after this, when the deal with Roy ceased. Jerry Perito, another of the few longtime Gretsch workers who moved from Brooklyn to Booneville, came up with an idea to rename Country Gents with a label that declared them as Southern Belle models (and dated them to around the middle months of 1983). A few years earlier, the Gent was briefly renamed the Country Squire, presumably related to Gibson's adoption of the Chet-related name. Perito then led a last-ditch plan to revive Gretsch guitar production at a Baldwin piano-action factory in Ciudad Juarez, just across the border in Mexico, but when a trial batch of five Southern Belle husks were sent to Gene Haugh, he rejected them all for poor quality, and the idea was dropped.

Dick Harrison had been promoted to chief executive officer at Baldwin in 1972, and he recalled dramatic changes to his company during the 70s, which by about 1978 was known officially as Baldwin United. "By the early 80s, it had become predominantly a financial services company," Harrison said, "and the music division, while always doing well, was a very small part of the total." Baldwin's musical strength was in its piano and organ business and, despite much effort, it never did well with Gretsch guitars, amplifiers, or drums. "Baldwin United went bankrupt in September 1983," Harrison continued. "Out of that, the music company was purchased by myself and another gentleman. We completed the deal by June of 1984."[111] The new Baldwin Piano & Organ Co sold Kustom and then took a hard look at Gretsch.

This is the point at which yet another Fred Gretsch came into the picture. It wasn't Fred Gretsch Jr – he had died in 1980 at the age of 75. As far as the fate of brand new Gretsch guitars was concerned, if it hadn't been for our "new" Fred, then the book you hold might well have finished right here. And it's worth remembering that in the 80s, there was relatively little interest in Gretsch guitars in America much beyond collectors on a quest to complete their sets of Beatle-related axes. Dealers would sell the occasional old White Falcon or early 6120 for over $1,000; other Gretsch models went for a great deal less. There was Poison Ivy in The Cramps with her 50s 6120, and Brian Setzer of The Stray Cats headed up a rockabilly revival with a vintage 6120 – more about him shortly.

In Britain, there was a fad for relatively affordable old guitars that looked the part and played OK. It seemed almost compulsory for Scottish bands to include a Gretsch – for instance Edwyn Collins, of Orange Juice, who played an unusual Black Hawk, a shortlived late-60s double-cut model. A little further south, John Squire of The Stone Roses used a 60s Gent (with Super'Tron neck pickup) at the time of the band's acclaimed first album, Johnny Marr wrestled a Super Axe in the early months of The Smiths, and Robert Smith of The Cure played a red 60s Tennessean on stage. Even Martin Gore of the synth-laden Depeche Mode bravely strummed an Anniversary, and Edge chose a Falcon when U2 rehearsed 'Desire' in the band's *Rattle And Hum* movie.

The 80s are still lazily characterised as a decade full of superstrats for shredders and metal-inclined rockers. No wonder Gretsches had trouble finding their place among all that. But in reality, there were yet more voices to be heard. Billy Duffy found fame with The Cult during the 80s, and he explored some lush territory with his White Falcon. "I was around at the time when all those Jacksons and Charvels were about," he says, "and they just … I don't know, they took all the soul out of it. It became a bit nerdy, for me. People were approaching it like a violin. If I'd wanted to be the guy that stayed at home and did that, I would have joined the orchestra at school and never had a girlfriend."

Duffy grew up in Manchester, England, and he remembers a growing admiration for White Falcons that began in his earliest days of playing guitar. "Half the guys in my high-school band were into Neil Young, and then when punk came around there was Sylvain Sylvain using a Falcon on their famous *Old Grey Whistle Test* appearance. Later, I saw Bow Wow Wow debut at Hammersmith – I was working in a shop, a semi-pro aspirational guitar player – and Matthew Ashman had a Falcon. I really went to see them because of that guitar! But I never could really afford one, so I just kind of hustled with what guitars I could get by on. And it almost became this mythical thing to me, the White Falcon, almost like the great white buffalo: a mythical quest that led me to own one."

He went through a (white) Les Paul Custom and a Junior – and then in 1982 he joined Kirk Brandon's Theatre Of Hate. In lieu of an audition, Brandon visited Duffy at his London flat, where he spotted two pin-ups stuck to the wall. One was of a dog that

Duffy liked, an English Bull Terrier; the other was a Gretsch guitar. Brandon said his dad had those Terriers when he was growing up.

"I hadn't played a note of music," Duffy remembers, "and then he said why do you like Gretsches? I said I've always had a bit of a fascination for a White Falcon, I've just never been able to afford one, but if I got in a decent band that was a living … and he said what guitar would you get? I said I'd get a White Falcon. He said: 'That's interesting, because I play a Gretsch.' I had no idea he played a Single Anniversary, that green thing with just the one pickup at the neck. So that was it, lo and behold: I showed up for Theatre Of Hate with a Gibson Les Paul Junior, got the gig, and got a White Falcon. I basically sold everything I owned to get a White Falcon, all my savings from working in the clothes shop, I invested all my money. It was the best 800 quid I ever spent."

That first Falcon, a mid-70s stereo double-cut, turned out to be "kind of a terrible model", but it had the nice neck and the long-arm Bigsby that Duffy came to love. "I liked the feel of the 70s Falcon more. I know it seems like heresy to Gretsch guys, but I like the way they felt from that period, and I still do." That first double-cut Falcon didn't last too long, and then Duffy got his now-famous '75 mono single-cut Falcon. He also got his own band, first known as Death Cult and then The Cult. "I call it the Sanctuary guitar," Duffy says, "because that's the one I played on 'She Sells Sanctuary'. It's the guitar I did all the *Dream Time* album on and all the early Death Cult stuff, and I did the whole of the *Love* album on that. I was off and running with the Gretsch, and it became a sonics thing: we were looking for a guitar that had a different voice. The punk thing was great and we were all fans of punk, but we wanted to find our own sounds."

Gretsch would issue a signature Falcon for him in 2013, but Duffy explains that he considers himself as something of a blue-collar guitarist. "To me, guitars are just work tools that I enjoy," he says. "I'm more of a Land Rover bloke than I am a sports-car guy, and the same thing with guitars – although the Gretsch is very fancy! But I still look at it as a work tool. That first Falcon, I just beat it to death. It still works, you know? To be honest, I had it out on the road again a couple of times but I've sort of retired it now. And the new ones sound fantastic – they've got a lot of life, and they're good."[112]

■

The Fred Gretsch who owns Gretsch today is a nephew of Fred Gretsch Jr, and his father was Bill Gretsch, who ran the company from 1942 until his premature death six years later. Fred himself worked at Gretsch for six years from 1965, starting in product engineering and working on the factory expansion in '66. "I'd been going to the Brooklyn factory since about 1951 when Fred Sr, my grandfather, took me there as quite a young fellow," Fred recalls. "I probably started going there at five years old. I credit him with activating in me quite a good interest in the business." When his uncle, Fred Jr, sold out to Baldwin in '67, he was disappointed, because it was his long-term ambition to own

FRED & FENDER

it himself one day. "But that was going to take another 17 years to achieve." When he left Gretsch in 1971, Fred started his own business, importing and wholesaling instruments, and in 1980 he bought the Synsonics brand from Mattel, using it for acoustic and electronic percussion and electric guitars. He stayed in touch with Dick Harrison of Baldwin and kept an eye on the bankruptcy of the Baldwin parent company.

Baldwin brought in Duke Kramer to sell off the two instrument parts of the business, and at first Kramer set up the sale of the piano operation. Then he turned to the guitar firm, and first he called Bill Schultz at Fender, but Schultz was busy with a plan to buy Fender from CBS. So Kramer spoke to Fred about buying the guitar and drum business. "Negotiations began and were ultimately successful in November of 1984, and I bought the business in January of '85," Fred says. "The plan was to continue drum making in Arkansas for a year, then to move it to our location in South Carolina, and subsequently to get the guitar business going again."[113]

Kramer worked with Fred on plans to introduce a set of revived guitars, and the two began to draw up the various specifications. The next move was to find someone to make them. Kramer met with several American makers, including Heritage (ex-Gibson workers located in the old Gibson factory in Kalamazoo, Michigan), Guild, and Gibson itself, but he was unable to make a deal.

"Our only option was to go offshore," Kramer explained, using the US term for anything made outside the country. "I went to Japan and selected Terada. They were used to making hollowbody guitars, whereas the rest were used to making mainly solidbody guitars."[114] The Terada Musical Instrument Co Ltd was established in 1916 and has a factory located in Kanie, a suburb of Nagoya, Japan. Terada continues to manufacture the majority of Gretsch guitars to this day.

Back in 1989, Gretsch offered an unusual forerunner to the forthcoming new line with a series of Korean-made electrics intended to capitalise on the popularity of the Traveling Wilburys, the fictional family supergroup with George Harrison (Nelson Wilbury), Jeff Lynne (Otis), Bob Dylan (Lucky), Tom Petty (Charlie T Jr) and Roy Orbison (Lefty). These cheap and rather primitive guitars were loosely based on some old Danelectro instruments the group had. Various shortlived models were issued, all boldly finished in what Gretsch called "original graphics" with an appropriate travel theme.

Fred Gretsch Enterprises Ltd delivered its first proper Gretsch guitars to dealers by the second half of 1989. The company was unable to use the names of Chet Atkins and the associated models, following the guitarist's earlier defection to Gibson, so some of the model names had to be modified, while others kept the familiar originals.

A pricelist from September 1989 showed nine electric models. There were five hollowbodys: the Tennessee Rose (post-Chet name for a Tennessean) at $1,495; the Nashville (a plain 6120) at $1,750; Nashville Western (6120 with G-brand etc) at $1,875; Country Classic I (a post-Chet Country Gent single-cut) at $1,975; and Country Classic II (Gent double-cut) at $1,975. There were four solids: the Duo Jet at $1,300; Silver Jet

THE GRETSCH ELECTRIC GUITAR BOOK

1979 *BEAST BST-1000 8210*

1989 *TRAVELING WILBURYS TW-300*

1978 *TK 300 7625*

OLD GRETSCH ... NEW GRETSCH

Baldwin's Booneville-based Gretsch operation was running out of steam, and their last new models were the Committee (catalogue, above left), the TK 300 (opposite, bottom) and the Beast series (opposite, top). They were part of Gretsch's continuing search for a successful rock solidbody, but they failed to make a mark with enough players. In the early 80s, Baldwin finally called it a day, and later in that decade Fred Gretsch, nephew of Fred Gretsch Jr, bought the company. An interim project was the Traveling Wilburys series of models (opposite, centre), after which the first Gretsch guitars appeared from the new operation, made in Japan and featured in catalogues in '89 (above centre) and '90 (right). Meanwhile, players still sought old Gretsch guitars, including Billy Duffy of The Cult, in this recent portrait (below) with his original 70s Falcon (right) and playing Gretsch's 2013 signature version.

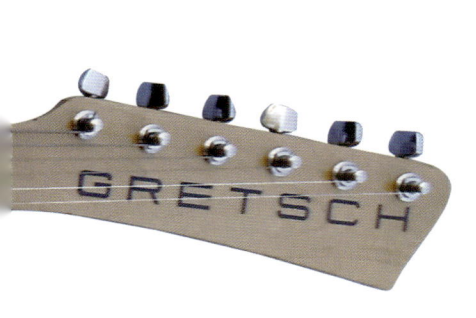

THE GRETSCH ELECTRIC GUITAR BOOK

at $1,400; Jet Firebird at $1,400; and Round Up at $1,550. An '89 catalogue added a few White Falcons to the list, at nearly $3,000 each.

This was just the start, and more reissues would come along, including Anniversary models, Country Clubs, and a White Penguin, and signature models for Bo Diddley, Elliot Easton, Duane Eddy, Keith Scott, Brian Setzer, Stephen Stills, and Malcolm Young. There were new twists, too, such as Falcons finished in black or with silver-coloured metalwork, scaled-down versions of various models, a number of coloured sparkle-finish Jets, a 12-string or two, a double-neck Jet, and some new Spectra Sonic models (six-string, baritone, and bass) designed with pickup specialist TV Jones, who created several pickups and consulted for Gretsch on various matters for a few years from 1998.

The path toward accurate re-creations of old designs started in 1992 with the new firm's attempt at a vintage-style 6120, the Nashville 6120-1960. It was a commendable first try, with thumbnail markers, zero fret, three knobs and two selectors, and a two-and-a-half-inch deep body, but other details like the Bigsby and the bridge seemed adrift. Further bids for vintage veracity came with oldie-style takes on the Country Classic (Gent), Country Club, Duo Jet, Falcon, Nashville (6120), Silver Jet, and Tennessee Rose (Tennessean), and even the Atkins Axe and Super Chet. But it would be a while before the vintage-intended guitars were shuffled much closer to the originals.

Brian Setzer and The Stray Cats personified the rockabilly revival of the early 80s. Back when it was born in the 50s, rockabilly came about when country guitarists tried to play rock'n'roll (rock'n'roll plus hillbilly makes … rockabilly). Now, in the 80s, some said that the new popularity was simply a thirst for music that shared the raw power of punk and that it remained a 50s throwback. Setzer, however, was always more than a mere re-enactor. True, he often displayed the trappings of a rockabilly: the hair, the clothes, the 6120, the Bassman amps. But more than all of that, Setzer is a fine, versatile guitarist. And his instrument of choice has been a Gretsch 6120, ever since he got his first one back in the late 70s.

He remembers it as if it were yesterday. He'd been hunting a 6120 because he wanted to look like Eddie Cochran. "Nobody knew who Eddie was in the States, especially back then," Setzer says. "I saw the ad in my local want-ads paper, the *Buy-Lines*. It said: 'Gretsch guitar, orange, $100.' I called the ad, and I said is it like Eddie Cochran's? And the the guy said: who? He said I don't know who Eddie Cochran is, but it's orange, and I've got the pickups and all the electrics in a shoebox. He said I've got the guitar standing alone and I'm gonna refinish it, so if you want to buy it you'd better come over."

Setzer was there in a flash. It certainly looked like the Eddie Cochran guitar, even if he didn't realise at the time that Cochran's had a DynaSonic and this had Filter'Trons. The owner had sanded down a small section in preparation for the ill-advised refinishing work. "I said OK, I'll take it: here's a hundred bucks. I ran out of his house with the guitar in one hand and the shoebox with the bits and pieces in the other." He took a bus to the local Sam Ash store. "And I go hey – you have to remember, I'm 15, 16 maybe – do you have a case for this guitar? They kind of rolled their eyes at me: oh god, just what we need, some pain-in-the-ass kid looking for a case. So they had a conveyor belt. The guy shouts down: 'Sal, send up a Gretsch case!' And up comes a white cowboy case. I didn't know that was the right one for the guitar – he just happened to have it in the basement. So I gave him ten bucks, whatever it was, threw the guitar in the case, and back home I went on the bus. It was crazy. What's the word when everything lines up? Providence, yes."

He'd found a wonderful 6120, which he subsequently referred to as his '59 Stray Cat guitar (although Edward Ball's recent research places it as a 1960 guitar). It was one fine Gretsch axe that would serve Setzer well as he and The Stray Cats began their successful run of albums and gigs and rockabilly rioting. "I rate guitars Monday through Friday," Setzer says with a grin. "And I got a Friday, you know? On Monday the guy is standing there trying to nurse his hangover, he's got to sand this guitar or he's got to paint it, but he doesn't want to be bothered. By Friday he's on ten and he's having a lot of fun doing it. You've got to find a Friday!"

From the start, the revived Gretsch company had its eye on Setzer as the most visible current player of its guitars. In 1993, it officially recognised his importance by issuing a Brian Setzer model. It was based on that Friday guitar. Setzer had heard a whisper that Gretsch was making guitars again and tried to get in touch. When he didn't hear back, he started to court Yamaha and Guild. "I think Fred got wind of that eventually, and he said oh no, no, no: Setzer's a Gretsch guy. And all of a sudden it was full on. But I kind of had to nudge them a little bit."

The Setzer models had a thinner neck and tapered heel, a tune-o-matic style bridge, Sperzel locking tuners, alnico-magnet Filter'Trons, optional dice-pattern square knobs, and a choice of finishes (regular polyurethane $2,900; "vintage correct" lacquer $3,350). "I was begging them to try and make them like they did in the 50s," Setzer remembers. "I never really got an answer. They weren't that together: it was oh, we don't have those old machines any more, or something like that."[115] A second Setzer line, the stripped-down fancy-finish Hot Rods, first appeared in 1999, but as we'll discover later, Setzer had to wait until Gretsch's alliance with Fender for improvements to some important details of his signature guitars.

Meanwhile, in 1999, Gretsch bought the Bigsby Accessories company, owned since the mid 60s by ex-Gibson boss Ted McCarty. This seemed like a natural move: the basic wang-bar had first become associated with Gretsch when Chet Atkins insisted that it be included on the 6120, and since then many players have found a little bit of gentle arm to be an important part of the Gretsch sound.

In the late 90s, Gretsch first issued its Korean-made Electromatic-brand guitars with Gretsch-like features as a line exclusively for sale by the US Guitar Center stores. They included the perfectly named Mini Diddley model, a smaller rectangle for diminutive Bo fans. Similar lines with Synchromatic and Historic brands, for sale by other dealers through distributor Midco, came along in 2000. The Historic brand would be dropped

1999 NASHVILLE BRIAN SETZER HOT ROD 6120SHB

1997 *NASHVILLE 6120-6/12*

■ Brian Setzer (opposite, with his original 6120) headed a rockabilly revival in the 80s, and the reawakened Gretsch soon hooked up with him for some signature models. The second type was the Hot Rod series (above), new for 1999, with simple volume-and-selector controls and car-crazy colours. Duane Eddy had his first signature Gretsch, too (opposite), in 1997, and the remarkable rectangular-body Bo Diddley guitar appeared, aptly captured in Gretsch's almost identically-shaped 2000 ad (opposite). As well as artist models, Gretsch investigated the vintage reissue, one of the first of which was the 6120-1960 of 1992 (postcard, opposite). There was also room for a 6120-based double-neck (right) and a baritone Spectra Sonic (below).

2002 *SPECTRA SONIC C MELODY BARITONE 6144*

106   THE GRETSCH ELECTRIC GUITAR BOOK

SETZER IN HOT ROD HEAVEN

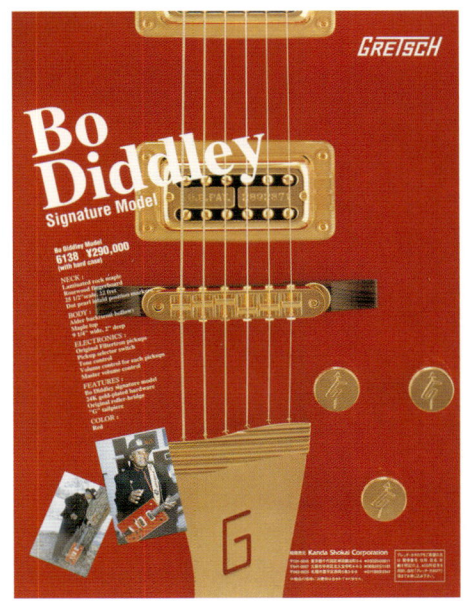

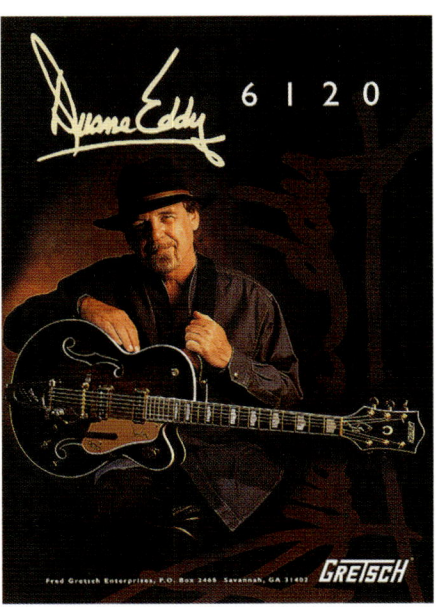

1960 6120 Nashville Reissue

The Nashville is often considered to be the most popular Gretsch electric guitar. Introduced in 1954, the Nashville has become standard issue for generations of country, rockabilly, and rock'n'roll players. This reintroduced 1960 model Nashville optimizes the design, playability, and sound of the first generation 6120.

Bo Diddley Signature Model

Duane Eddy 6120

THE GRETSCH ELECTRIC GUITAR BOOK

and the Synchromatic models gradually phased out, leaving from around 2004 the Electromatics as Gretsch's reworked and now generally-available budget line – made in Korea (by SPG) or China (Yako/Reliance) and complete with a proper Gretsch logo on the headstock and "Electromatic" underneath. The Synchromatic name would be revived in 2010 for an old-style hollowbody with floating pickup, and at the time of writing a plan was in place to issue a new line of budget guitars, below the Electromatics, using another old Gretsch-related name: Streamliner.

Gretsch made moves toward an alliance with Fender during 2002, officially registered with a press statement in August that declared "Fender & Gretsch join forces". The two companies said they were proud to announce an agreement where, effective January 1 2003, Fender Musical Instruments Corporation was granted the exclusive rights to "develop, produce, market, and distribute" Gretsch guitars worldwide. Gretsch was keen to explain that this was not a buy-out. "We looked at Fender as number one in the world, with great resources," Fred Gretsch recalled later. "Their proposal was: let us take over the distribution and manufacturing worldwide and we'll really build this business together. And that's what's happened. We still own and control the brand, and they do the marketing, manufacturing, and distribution."[116]

Fender made a complete overhaul of the line, overseen by Mike Lewis, who'd worked at Fender since the early 90s and now became Gretsch's newly-appointed marketing manager. He changed virtually every specification of every model. The alliance also introduced a number of new models and revamped the Brian Setzer line. To help decide exactly what to change, Fender went and bought some vintage Gretsch guitars (just as it had when devising the first proper Fender reissues in the early 80s). George Blanda in Fender R&D already owned a '55 Country Club, which also served for single-cut Falcon specs. Fender bought a single-cut '61 6120, a '64 Anniversary, and a '59 6121 Solid Body, and borrowed a '55 White Falcon and a '55 6120 from Gretsch nut Randy Bachman as the basis for two Custom Shop models. "Our guys completely reverse-engineered them," Lewis says.[117] He means they copied them, very accurately.

As a result, the Fender-era Gretsches – the regular Japanese-made Professional Series, rejigged in 2003, as well as the high-end US Custom Shop instruments, begun in '04 – have accurate body and headstock shapes and dead-on neck profiles. The guitars have authentically thinner three-ply body tops and backs. The pickups are closer to the old specs. The horseshoes are in the right place, thank goodness. Fender today insists that it's got it all right, and it's hard to disagree.

We've seen how the revived Gretsch operation issued the first Brian Setzer signature guitars in the early 90s but that Setzer wanted some of the details to be more like the originals. Most important of these was trestle bracing. "When Fender stepped in there, Mike Lewis said screw it, I'm gonna get to the bottom of this," Setzer recalls. "I thought it had just been a bunch of guys from New York on a Monday morning cutting pieces of wood and throwing them in that guitar. It wasn't. It's a very tricky little thing to put in."[118]

FRED & FENDER

Setzer's famous old Stray Cat 6120 was made during a relatively brief period when the body featured a new type of bracing inside the body, devised to allow the top and back to vibrate more sympathetically with one another, giving it more sustain, making it less susceptible to feedback, and adding mass that, in turn, provides a different (and for some players better) sound. Two parallel tone bars, or braces, ran the length of the body, and the pickups were screwed to them. From about 1958 to '62, two twin-leg trestles were added to each bar, and each trestle had one leg near the bridge and one near the neck, effectively and solidly connecting the guitar's top to its back at four points.

Lewis recalls a meeting with Setzer soon after Fender took over, probably in 2003. Setzer's mood for change coincided with the blanket upgrade to all models that Lewis was working on. Lewis took the vintage 6120 Fender had bought – Setzer played it at the meeting and deemed it a good one – and asked his colleague Ritchie Fliegler if he knew anyone with something that might let them see inside its body. Fliegler called some friends at Scottsdale Medical Imaging, who just happened to be guitar nuts, and they agreed to run the old 6120 through a CT scanner. "They gave us back this disc with all these images," Lewis says. "We got cross-sections of the body and the bracing and the neck joint and the heel and everything. I put those in Photoshop and created drawings for the factory, and they adapted them to their system. And we got trestle bracing!"

One element of the original bracing was not adopted. A little later in the original late-50s trestle-bracing period, Brooklyn workers would add a pile of tiny wood shims to fill in gaps between the "feet" of the trestles and the curve of the guitar's back. "We eliminated that, because with a CNC router we were able to match the radius of the inside of the back to the bottom of the brace," Lewis says. "Our method was much more refined and consistent, whereas the old ones we saw were pretty inconsistent."[119] The new-style trestle bracing was adopted for the Setzer models, and then it was added as appropriate to a few (vintage-relevant) models in the revised Gretsch line. A simpler trestle bracing, named ML for its developers, Masao Terada and Mike Lewis, with connecting legs only at the bridge, appeared on a couple of modern Anniversary models, beginning in 2008.

Lewis did a similar thing with the old 6121 Solid Body that Fender had bought, so that he and his team could see how the original Jet-style guitars were made. At first he peered into the guitar as much as he could himself, checking out the control cavity and the (empty) pickup routs. "I could see, hey, there's like a lot of open space in here," Lewis recalls with a chuckle. Then he sent the 6121 to the Japanese factory for a closer examination. "Short of tearing the guitar apart, they came up with a really close facsimile of how it was routed out. And it was virtually hollow!"

By the start of 2005, everything was well in place from the new alliance, and the pricelist of January that year showed 18 electric models, including a good variety of options and a selection of lefties. There were seven basic hollowbodys: Anniversary $2,275–$2,925; Tennessee Rose (Tennessean) $2,625–$2,725; Nashville (6120) $2,925–$3,900 (Reverend Horton Heat $4,125; Brian Setzer $3,850–$4,350; Keith Scott

Gretsch made an important and successful alliance with Fender in 2003. A new path opened, but the brand's illustrious past still offered much inspiration as the decade progressed. The White Penguin (main guitar) was the semi-solid model launched in the 50s as a companion to the White Falcon, and so unpopular that it would become a rare collectable. New versions began to appear in 1993 and again in 2003. Chet Atkins had absconded to Gibson, so his name was absent from models such as this Nashville Classic (top), in fact a reissue of the original Atkins Country Gent. Vintage re-creations improved, like the 6120DSW on the 2004 catalogue (opposite) and the Country Clubs in the 2006 catalogue (top). The '05 "Billy Bo" Jupiter Thunderbird (right) came about when Billy Gibbons was inspired by Bo Diddley's weird creations, while a 2003 ad (right) summed up the Gretsch vibe.

THE GRETSCH ELECTRIC GUITAR BOOK

A CLUBFUL OF COOL

2003 *NASHVILLE CLASSIC 6122-1959*

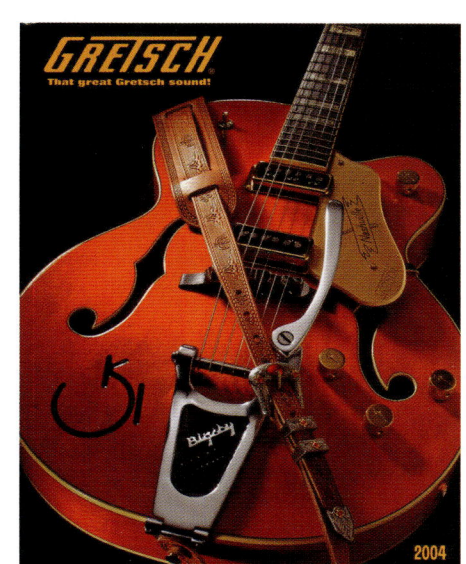

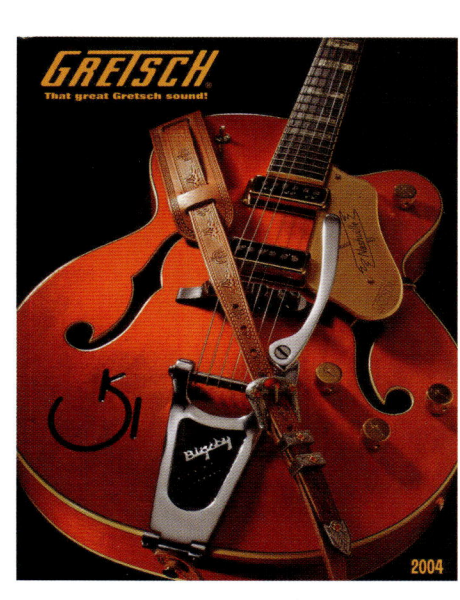

2003 *WHITE PENGUIN 6134*

2005 *"BILLY-BO" JUPITER THUNDERBIRD 6199*

THE GRETSCH ELECTRIC GUITAR BOOK

111

$4,025; Double Neck $5,375; US Custom Shop $9,000); Country Classic (Country Gentleman) $3,025–$3,875; Setzer Hot Rod $3,125–$3,375; Country Club $3,425-$3,625; White Falcon $4,025-$4,175 (Stephen Stills $4,825; US Custom Shop $11,000). There were eleven basic solids and semi-solids: Malcolm Young $1,975-$2,275; Duo Jet $2,425-$3,375 (Double Neck $4,850); Jet Firebird $2,425-$2,575; Spectra Sonic $2,500; Silver Jet $2,525-$3,075; Sparkle Jet $2,675; Bo Diddley $2,825; Roundup $2,925; Elliot Easton $3,075; Nashville Solid Body $3,250; White Penguin $3,975. There was also a line of ten Electromatic models, including three signature models.

Three Custom USA models were first shown at a trade show in 1995, intended to be made not in the regular Japanese factory but at home in the States, at Gretsch plants in Ridgeland, South Carolina, and in Arkansas. "We are looking at a true Custom Shop mentality," Fred said in a press release.[120] The three 1955-style models first appeared on a '96 pricelist: Country Club 6196-1955, White Falcon 6136-1955, and Nashville Custom 6120-1955, joined the following year by the G-brand Western Nashville Custom 6120W-1955. This attempt at American manufacture didn't last long: production stopped in 1998, if indeed many were made at all, and the models were gone from the pricelist by 2000.

Gretsch's Custom Shop had its proper launch in 2004, following the Fender alliance. While Terada in Japan continued to handle the bulk of Gretsch production for Fender, it seemed a good idea to develop an exclusive US-made Custom Shop line. Chris Fleming had joined Fender's Custom Shop in 2000 as a guitar builder, soon specialising in Guild models (Fender had acquired the brand in the 90s). With his experience in making hollowbodys, Fleming worked with George Blanda to build Gretsch prototypes ready for the '04 NAMM show.

"The team that I put together to build Guild built those first Gretsch archtops," Fleming remembers, "a 6120 and a White Falcon. We then made the first 25 or so Custom Shop Gretsches – I think about 12 or 13 6120s, and the rest were White Falcons – so there's only about 25 instruments that have my label on them, they're pretty rare. Then I handed it over to Stephen Stern."

Stephen Stern had started at Fender's Custom Shop in 1993, following some guitar-building experience with Charvel, before which he was a cabinet-maker building high-end office furniture. At Fender, he soon took responsibility for the D'Aquisto hollowbodys, which had been moved from Japanese production to the Custom Shop. "So that kind of made me the archtop guy," Stern recalls with a smile. "We also started making the Benedetto guitars." When Bob Benedetto moved to his own shop again, Stern was the obvious candidate to take over Gretsch Custom Shop production. One of his earliest new projects was a limited edition of 20 relic'd White Falcons, in 2006.

The Shop's first "Tribute" Gretsch was the Brian Setzer 6120SSC of 2007. The idea with the Tributes has been to reproduce an original historically-important guitar as accurately as possible, with relic'd (in other words aged) finish and hardware, and reproducing any other peculiarities of the instrument in question. There followed a

Silver Jet for Billy Zoom in 2008 and Eddie Cochran's famous 6120 in 2010. In order to spec the Cochran guitar, Stern travelled to the Rock & Roll Hall Of Fame in Cleveland, Ohio, where the instrument resides on loan from Cochran's relatives. Armed with his callipers and radius gauges and templates, Stern logged all the dimensions and wear patterns and dings.

"It had some really unusual wear on the back of the neck, a lot of dents in the middle," Stern noticed. "Maybe Eddie had some rings on his thumb or something?" The pickup routing for the P-90 that Cochran added at the neck was an interesting area for investigation. "I was surprised how cleanly that was routed, it was really cut out for a perfect fit." It seemed that Cochran probably had the work done by someone else. "Someone with good woodworking chops," Stern agrees.

A high spot for Stern was the Tribute model the Custom Shop made in 2011 based on George Harrison's '57 Duo Jet. The original came to the Shop for several days – it enjoyed a first-class round trip from London Heathrow to Los Angeles LAX – and Stern was able to examine the instrument in great detail and from every angle. "It was nerve-wracking to have it there and think about the part it played with the most popular rock band ever," Stern says, "the gigs that George played with it at the Cavern and how he used it for the very first album. Also, everybody in the shop wanted to come by and look at it. I was like: Go away, leave me alone! You have to switch over to what you have to do, your job at hand. And that thing was beat to crap, man." It didn't take long to notice that Harrison had got someone to refinish the already black-topped guitar with black paint. "It was on the back, the neck, and everything," Stern says. "When we took the back cover off, to see the serial number, even the label was painted over. Fortunately, Gretsch inscribe the number on the backplate, so I was able to get the serial number from that."

The new Gretsch Custom Shop really started to take off around 2008, according to Stern. "A lot of it was the right timing, I think. We did a mini summer NAMM show here at the factory, they converted an upstairs training room into a showroom, displayed a lot of Fenders, and we had a big area for Gretsch. I had made some Penguins and some Duo Jets. It really was the hit of the show, and it grew from there. We started making the Penguins in custom colours, showing them at the NAMM shows, and we started getting a good reputation."

Over the years, Stern has gradually inched the Custom Shop guitars closer and closer to what he calls vintage-correct. A major area for study and better imitation has been the interior routing of the Jet-style guitars, as well as the hollowbodys, and more recently Stern and his team have worked hard to improve their re-creations of the old parts: strap knobs, bridge bases, thumb wheels, even the felt under the pickguard. At the time of writing, Stern manages a crew of five: Antony Corona, who specialises in buffing and relic'ing; Andrew Hicks, for fret dress, assembly, and set-up; Chad Henrichsen, the newest member of the team, currently working on necks; Gonzalo Madrigal, Stern's longest-standing colleague, who works on bodies, necks, sanding, and more; and Vincent

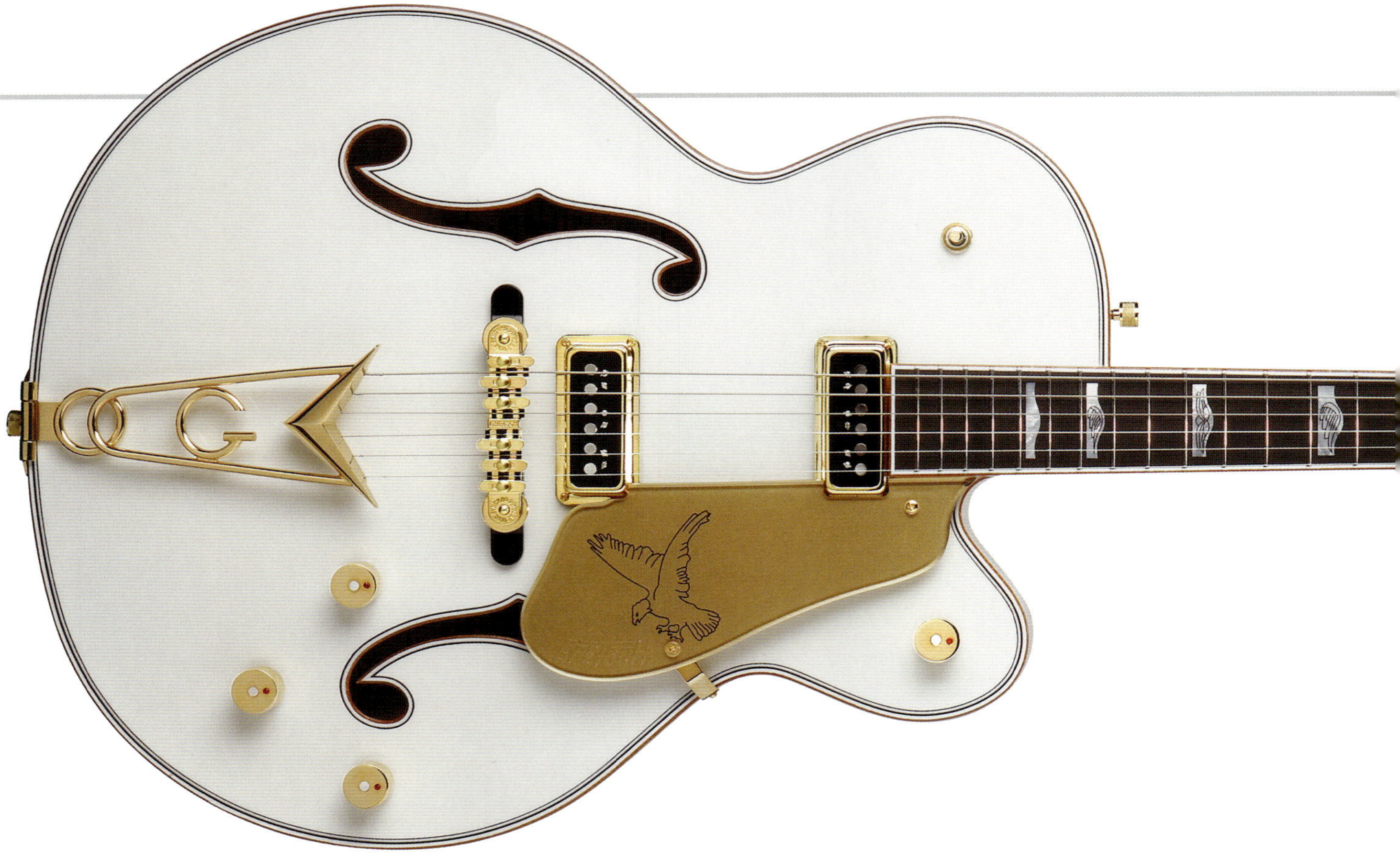

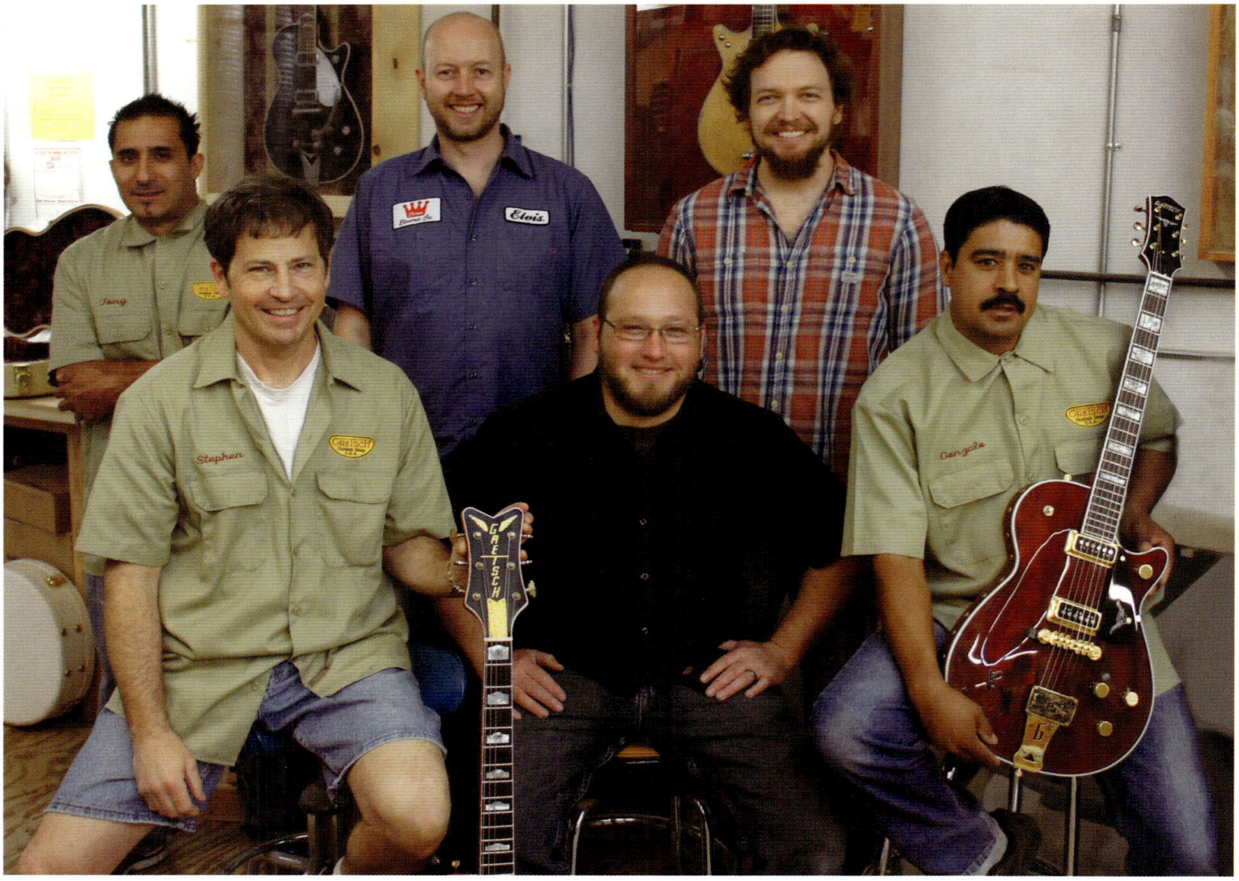
Elvis
Stephen
GRETSCH

CUSTOM MADE IN THE USA

2011 *WHITE FALCON 6136CST*

■ Gretsch's US Custom Shop got going properly in 2004, and its dazzling output has included "catalogue" items like this upscale White Falcon re-creation (main guitar) as well as one-offs that have included this pair of Chartreuse Sparkle Jets (below left: '55 left, '57 right) and a Lake Placid Blue Falcon and Penguin (below right). The 2014 Custom Shop team (left to right, opposite): Tony Corona, Stephen Stern, Vincent Van Trigt, Chad Henrichsen, Andy Hicks, and Gonzalo Madrigal. The Custom Shop produced an interesting hybrid for Darrel Higham (right) of Imelda May's band, where a Cochran-style 6120 meets a moody Falcon – a model whose future remains to be seen.

THE GRETSCH ELECTRIC GUITAR BOOK

Van Trigt, who is Stern's assistant for all the behind-the-scenes jobs. "I'm very fortunate to have this well trained and dedicated crew," Stern says.[121]

When Fender teamed up with Gretsch in 2003, a troubling omission from the brand was the Chet Atkins name along with the associated model names. But as Mike Lewis remembers, a change was not long in coming, and in fact it happened very simply. A mutual acquaintance mentioned casually one day that he thought Atkins's estate – Atkins had died in 2001 – might be interested in Gretsch regaining the names. "So I contacted them," Lewis says, "and it just sort of went like that. We'd talked about it a lot here and with Fred Gretsch, but it turned out it was a good time ... and it happened."[x]

The news was made public right at the start of 2007. "It is with great pleasure that Gretsch Guitars announces the return of the legendary Chet Atkins name to the iconic guitars he created and popularized throughout his storied multi-decade musical career," the press release declared. "We were already making these guitars," Lewis says, "so there was very little that needed to be done to change them, other than the name on the guitar. To us it just seemed the right thing to happen, and all our fans felt the same way, too."[122]

The renamed models, which would be offered in a number of different styles and levels, were the Chet Atkins Hollow Body 6120 (previously the Nashville) and the Chet Atkins Country Gentleman 6122 (previously Country Classic). Also, the Chet Atkins name was restored to the Solid Body 6121. The Chet Atkins Tennessee Rose 6119 was the only model that kept the newer name, because Gibson still owned a trademark for the original name, the Tennessean.

Meanwhile in Britain, many heard Dublin-born singer Imelda May for the first time in 2008 when she appeared on Jools Holland's TV show with a band that included her husband, Darrel Higham, on guitar. A couple of years later she enjoyed a rather bigger TV audience when she performed 'How High The Moon' with Jeff Beck at the Grammy Awards in part of a tribute to Les Paul, who had died in 2009. Working with Beck gave Higham the opportunity to acquire an exquisite Custom Shop 6120 – but this was hardly his first taste of the addictive flavours of Gretsch.

Darrel Higham had already established firm rock'n'roll credentials in the UK with his own band, The Enforcers, and through his work with the likes of Shakin' Stevens and Chrissie Hynde. And as we've seen, Higham's prime influence was Eddie Cochran. He recalls that as a youngster he first spotted a copy of Cochran's album *Singing To My Baby* in his parents' record collection, complete with its classic cover that includes a shot of Cochran and 6120. "It was just the most brilliant, beautiful guitar I'd ever seen in my life," Higham says. He's been hooked ever since. He got his first 6120 in 1990, as soon as he got wind of the revived Gretsch operation. Of course, he modified it with a P-90, fixed-arm Bigsby, and headstock steer's head. That guitar lasted until the late 90s, when it was stolen – ironically, while he was on a theatre tour portraying Eddie Cochran. May joked that it was Cochran's way of telling him to stop being a copycat. "It didn't soften the blow," Higham remembers, smiling, "but it did make me rethink things."

He made a deal with Peavey and co-designed the Rockingham model, more or less a White Falcon body with a 6120 neck, and he played that guitar for ten years or so. Then came the Beck moment. "I was in his house one day and I noticed this white guitar case sitting in the hallway," Higham says. "Lo and behold, inside was a 2008 6120 Custom Shop, made by Stephen Stern for the 125th anniversary. Just beautiful! Jeff said yeah, Fender sent it through to me because I was thinking about buying one, but to be honest I would only ever use it on the odd song and I can't justify owning it. He said he'd probably send it back. I said would you mind if I bought it? He said no, not at all – and I'll get the same deal for you as I would have got, which was really good of him. So that became the next guitar. I was always a bit leery about using it on stage, because it's a very precious guitar: you really don't want to trash it. It gets used all the time in the studio, and recently I've started using it on stage, too, simply because I love playing it so much."

Higham secured an endorsement deal with Gretsch, and at the time of writing he was trying out on tour with Imelda May a new guitar that Stern had built for him. "It's my dream guitar. It has the Falcon headstock – so you know it's a Falcon – then the 6120 scale length, neck wise, and then the body of a Falcon but with 6120 markings and colouring – I do want that Eddie Cochran influence to be there always." He feels great being back with Gretsch. Now it remains to be seen if the Higham guitar becomes a production model. Whatever happens, he's always been impressed by the versatility of a Gretsch. "They're not a rockabilly guitar: you can play anything on a guitar, doesn't matter what make it is. You can play anything on anything. But certain brands get labelled for what they are, through association."

And rockabilly itself seems set to go on forever in whatever contemporary guise it adopts. "With pop music becoming so bland as each year passes," Higham says, "there's generations of teenagers that are disillusioned, and they're going on the internet and discovering there are other types of music out there. Rockabilly is one of the genres that's benefitting from youngsters who want to hear a bit of fire and passion in the music, a bit of rawness. Rockabilly is passionate music – it's like blues, in that sense. You don't have to be a great player or a great singer to play it, as long as you play it like you mean it. Same with blues. When I started out, you were almost ashamed to say you played rockabilly, because nobody wanted to hear it. I think it's much more widely respected now."[123]

We met Chris Fleming a little earlier, when in 2004 he helped build the prototypes and then the first proper examples from Gretsch's new Custom Shop. After that, he concentrated on Fender models and became a Senior Master Builder. Next, he was production manager of Fender's Jackson/Charvel/EVH brands in the Shop, and then he moved to R&D to look after "specialty brands" (in other words, anything not Fender, and therefore including Gretsch). That's where we met him at the time of writing, as chief engineer of guitar development. Fleming says that the recent plan with Gretsch has been to steadily upgrade the line with new parts, new pickups, and new colours. The first big

2010 ELECTROMATIC PATRICK VAUGHN STUMP SIGNATURE "STUMP-O-MATIC" 5135CVT-PS

2012 CHET ATKINS HOLLOW BODY 6120DSW

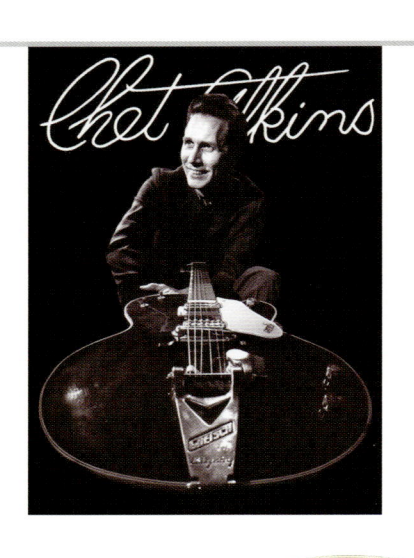

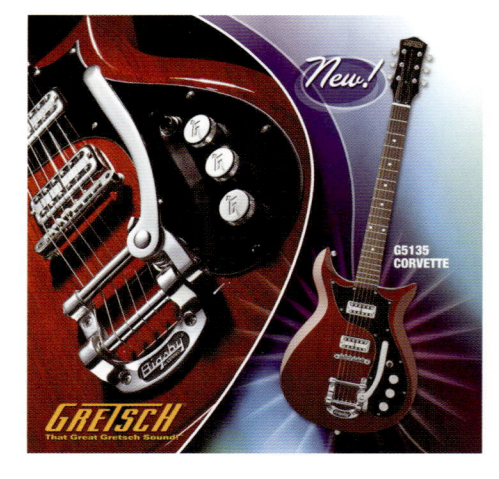

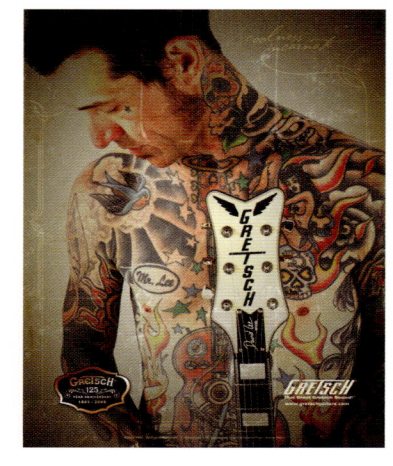

■ In the seventh decade of electric guitar making, the Gretsch story is far from over – yet ours must end around here. Chet Atkins's name was returned to the Gretsch lines in 2007 (catalogue, top left; renamed 6120, main guitar), and the White Falcon's continuing popularity was reflected in contemporary ads (near left). Old designs were giving new ideas to today's Gretsch designers (Corvette ad, far left), and there are fresh takes on construction, such as this Panther (right), which has a body with an internal centre-block. Of course, musicians continue to inspire development, with signature models such as the twisted Corvette-like Stump-o-Matic (top) for Fall Out Boy's Patrick Stump, and this striking hollowbody for Rancid's Tim Armstrong (opposite), both in Gretsch's less expensive Electromatic line. Whatever next?

THE GRETSCH ELECTRIC GUITAR BOOK

HERE COMES TOMORROW

2013 *ELECTROMATIC TIM ARMSTRONG HOLLOW BODY 5191TMS*

2014 *PANTHER 6137TCB*

project for Fleming when he started with Gretsch was a Tim Armstrong signature model, based to some extent on the Rancid frontman's '71 Country Club but updated and finished in handsome black. "I reverse-engineered the pickups, the hardware, the knobs, and the tailpiece," Fleming says, "and since then we've started filtering some of that stuff, like the black-top Filter'Tron pickups and the 'harp' tailpiece, out into the rest of the Electromatic line."

A further addition to Gretsch's lines came in 2013 with the Center-Block models, in the regular Professional series as well as the second-tier Electromatics. The Center-Blocks have a solid spruce block running the entire length of the body (although it's chambered at the lower bout to reduce weight), in a similar fashion to a Gibson ES-335. Somewhere, Chet Atkins is probably smiling. "The idea was to have a guitar that – and I hate to say it – is more Gibson-y," Fleming confirms. He talks about an idea in the planning stage at the time of writing that will develop this scheme to create a guitar that plays more like a modern semi-hollow centre-block instrument, working with an increased neck pitch, lower fingerboard-to-body height, and a tune-o-matic bridge fixed into the body. Another idea in planning is to use the old Corvette solidbody designs as a basis from which to devise some modern solidbodys. Fleming mentions the recent Patrick Stump signature model, based on a Corvette. "I like the way the Corvette looks, the way it feels, plus it's a goofy guitar," he says. "It's ripe for having fun with. So that's going to be our solidbody hop-off point. We'll see what happens."[124]

Patrick Stump from Fall Out Boy might be better known as a songwriter and frontman, and may have been a drummer before he switched to guitar, but he's a keen guitarist and collector (70-plus at the time of writing) and he knows his six-strings. "Once you get paid and you can afford a few things, some people go cars and drugs," Stump says. "I went gear every time." For a while he borrowed SGs from bandmate Joe Trohman, but then he spotted a bright orange 6120 Junior in a store. "I picked it up and it just clicked – I fell in love with that thing." Gretsch noticed this, and also that the band's second album, *Cork Tree* from 2005, was doing great business. Gretsch tried to get Stump to play one of its new solidbodys, around the same time that Stump stumbled on an early-60s Corvette Twist, the one with the whacky striped pickguard.

A signature model seemed in order. It had to have racing stripes, of course. Seriously, though? "Rhythm guitar is my everything," Stump says. "I wanted to have something where I could take only one guitar on the road – I'm very practical. I wanted a guitar capable of distorting in the darker range, in that area where SGs excel, since that became kind of a signature of my sound. But also I wanted to be able to get that kind of Fender brightness." The result was the gloriously-named Gretsch Stump-o-Matic, launched in 2010 as a further model in the mid-level Electromatic line and harking back to the 60s and the Corvette and shortlived variants such as the Twist and the Princess. Stump got the three pickups he wanted, a kill switch, some minimal controls, and strings-through-the-body for extra resonance. "They had me go to NAMM to show off the guitar," he recalls. "I get there, I play … and I realise about half way through the set that, you know, I'm not worthy of this thing. This is a really good guitar, and I'm not showing off enough of what it can do. That forced me to learn a lot more and practice a lot harder. This guitar is so good that I want to be a better player to warrant it. I have this special relationship with it. It's like dating a supermodel – and then you have to figure out how not to be grumpy in the mornings." Stump pauses, and then adds: "I'm assuming."[125]

Meanwhile, Chris Fleming at Fender sees an interesting future for the Gretsch brand. "This is a business and we have to grow it," he says. "The tricky part now is to appeal to younger players, without turning it into something that it isn't. That's super-hard. So our goal is to start using traditional Gretsch ideas to reinvent Gretsch. If Gretsch could have been run by the same company, the same creative people, for 60 or 80 years, what would it be like?"[126] Perhaps Gretsch staff today have to imagine that they're a Jimmie Webster or a Ray Butts, but – of course – surrounded by all the advantages and disadvantages of the 21st century.

So what's the continuing attraction of Gretsch electrics, all these years later? At their best, they're magical. Or maybe there's a better word? Mike Lewis remembers a guitarist he met once in Germany. "He mentioned that the Gretsch always sounds charming. No matter what kind of music you're playing or how you have your amp set, there's always a charming quality to the sound. The word 'charming' he used was so perfect. You can hear that: it doesn't get lost in the band; it always floats to the top."[127]

Joe Carducci, who took over from Mike Lewis at Gretsch in 2007, says the brand and its guitars are, quite simply, unique. "There is a heritage and there are some very iconic platforms that we build on," he explains. "Certainly we don't need to be in a position to chase other people or other ideas. We have our own thing, and it's our own identity."[128] Brian Setzer is a little more concise in his summary. "I think this is Gretsch's second golden age. I really do."[129]

And Fred Gretsch doesn't hesitate to offer his answer. "If you want a one-word reply, it's cool. But in the end, it comes down to the music that you create with our instruments, music that you really can't create on anything else. There's the cool factor and there's the music factor – and I think the music comes first. The cool is just a nice plus."[130]

ENDNOTES

1. *The Music Trades* February 1958
2. *Music Trade Review* May 24 1902
3. *Brooklyn Daily Eagle* September 2 1925
4. *Music Trade Review* September 24 1927
5. *Music Trade Review* August 1931
6. Author's interview March 20 1995
7. Author's interview August 2 1995
8. *Your Gretsch Guitar Guide* c.1952
9. *The Music Trades* February 1951
10. *Binghamton Press* July 11 1941
11. Author's interview April 1 1995
12. Author's interview August 2 1995
13. *Miami News* February 1 1957
14. *Guitar Player* Vol. 1 No. 1 1967
15. *Your Gretsch Guitar Guide* c.1952
16. Author's interview February 10 1992
17. Author's interview October 27 1992
18. Author's interview March 20 1995
19. *Down Beat* June 4 1952
20. Author's interview August 2 1995
21. *The Music Trades* March 1956
22. Author's interview August 2 1995
23. Author's interview April 10 & May 30 1995
24. Author's conversation with Ann Butts April 8 1995
25. Author's interview April 10 & May 30 1995
26. Author's interview March 20 1995
27. Author's interview April 10 & May 30 1995
28. *The Music Trades* December 1954
29. Author's interview April 10 & May 30 1995
30. *Musical Merchandise* November 1925
31. Author's interview April 10 & May 30 1995
32. Author's interview August 2 1995
33. Author's interview April 1 1995
34. Author's interview April 1 1995
35. Author's interview April 1 1995
36. Author's interview March 20 1995
37. Author's interview August 2 1995
38. Author's interview February 10 1992
39. Author's interview March 20 1995
40. Author's interview September 5 1995
41. Author's interview April 28 2014
42. *Town Hall Party* February 7 1959
43. Author's interview April 6 1995
44. Author's interview April 10 & May 30 1995
45. Author's interview April 6 1995
46. *Guitar Player* December 1983
47. Jeff Beck *Rock'n'Roll Party* DVD 2011
48. *Billboard* January 13 1958
49. *Guitar Player* February 1974
50. Jimmie Webster letter to Ray Butts July 14 1958
51. Author's interview April 8 1995
52. Author's interview April 10 & May 30 1995
53. Author's interview March 20 1995
54. Author's interview April 8 1995
55. Author's interview April 8 1995
56. Duffy *Inside The Gretsch Guitar Factory*
57. Author's interview April 8 1995
58. Letter from Harold Wood to Ray Butts August 12 1958
59. Atkins *Me And My Guitars*
60. Author's interview April 8 1995
61. Author's interview April 10 & May 30 1995
62. *The Music Trades* March 1959
63. Author's interview March 20 1995
64. Author's interview April 10 & May 30 1995
65. Author's interview March 20 1995
66. Author's interview September 5 1995
67. Author's interview September 5 1995
68. Author's interview July 25 1995
69. Author's interview March 20 1995
70. Author's interview March 20 1995
71. George Harrison letter c. October 1960
72. *Guitar Player* November 1987

ENDNOTES

73 Clarence LeBlanc *guitarworld.com* August 7 2014
74 *Guitar Player* November 1987
75 *The Music Trades* December 1964
76 Author's interview April 1 1995
77 GAMA conference report *The Music Trades* August 1967
78 *Brooklyn Daily Eagle* May 29 1932
79 Author's interview September 5 1995
80 *The Music Trades* January 1965
81 Author's interview March 20 1995
82 Author's interview August 2 1995
83 Author's interview July 12 & September 7 1995
84 *The Music Trades* June 1967
85 Author's interview March 20 1995
86 Author's interview July 25 1995
87 Author's interview August 2 1995
88 Author's interview July 12 & September 7 1995
89 Duffy *Inside The Gretsch Guitar Factory*
90 Author's interview July 25 1995
91 Author's interview April 10 & May 30 1995
92 Author's interview April 10 & May 30 1995
93 *Gretsch News* undated, c. August 1972
94 Author's interview April 10 & May 30 1995
95 *Gretsch News* undated, c. August 1972
96 Author's interview July 25 1995
97 *Guitar Player* October 1975
98 *Guitar Player* May/June 1972
99 *Guitar Player* April 1970
100 *Stephen Stills Talks Gretsch* Gretsch Guitars YouTube channel March 12 2013
101 *The Music Trades* February 1976
102 Letter from Duke Kramer to Butts July 16 1975
103 Author's interview April 8 1995
104 Author's interview March 20 1995
105 Author's interview March 20 1995
106 www.gretschslostweekend.com
107 Author's interview May 9 & September 30 2014
108 Author's interview July 25 1995
109 *Fort Scott Tribune* July 22 1982
110 Atkins *Me And My Guitars*
111 Author's interview July 12 & September 7 1995
112 Author's interview April 17 2014
113 Author's interview June 19 1995
114 Author's interview March 20 1995
115 Author's interview June 10 2014
116 Author's interview July 9 2004
117 Author's interview July 12 2004
118 Author's interview June 10 2014
119 Author's interview April 23 2014
120 Gretsch press release July 14 1995
121 Author's interview April 8 2014
122 Author's interview April 23 2014
123 Author's interview April 28 2014
124 Author's interview June 17 2014
125 Author's interview May 8 2014
126 Author's interview June 17 2014
127 Author's interview April 23 2014
128 Author's interview April 15 2014
129 Author's interview June 10 2014
130 Author's interview June 19 1995

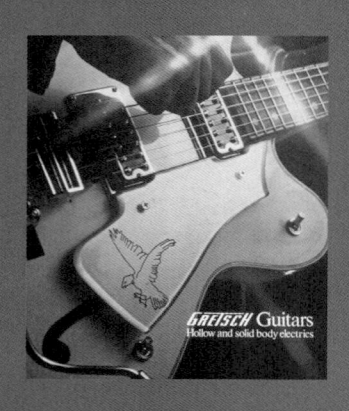

THE REFERENCE LISTING

WHAT'S HERE

We've designed this Reference Listing to help you find out more about Gretsch electric guitar models. First, here are a few notes to help you get the most from this section of the book. The Listing covers all the electric guitar models issued by Gretsch between 1939 and 2014. Bass guitars, acoustic guitars, and steel guitars are beyond the scope of this book.

WHAT'S WHERE?

The Listing is divided into three main parts:

- MODELS A-to-Z
- MODEL TIMELINE
- DATING & SERIALS

The **MODELS A-TO-Z** part has a section for each model name, in alphabetical order of model name, with a single entry or a series of entries for each individual model underneath, usually in chronological order (we've said so if they're in alphanumerical order). Signature models are listed in alphabetical order of the forename, not surname: so you'll find Brian Setzer, for example, under B, not S.

The **MODEL TIMELINE** lists the electric models produced by Gretsch from 1939 to 2014 in chronological order of the year of introduction.

The **DATING & SERIALS** part provides information to help you date a Gretsch guitar, by features and by serial number.

WHAT'S IT GOT?

Each entry under the main section name has a **heading with the model name** (and, for more recent models, the Gretsch model number) in bold type, and sometimes a version number or other identifier. This is followed by a **date or range of dates** showing the production period of the instrument. These dates and any others here are as accurate as possible, but they are approximate. As with any other guitar company, there is rarely a foolproof method to pinpoint exact periods of Gretsch manufacturing. All dates should be considered as a guide, not gospel. A "c." in front of a year or years stands for circa, which means "about".

For some models, usually those that exist in different versions, there may be a sentence below this, reading "Similar to ... , except: ... ". This will refer to another model listing, and the description that follows lists any major differences between the two.

The main information is presented in a **list of bullet points** that relate to the particular model's specifications and other features. In order, they refer to the following, where relevant:

- Neck, fingerboard; position markers; frets; truss-rod adjuster; headstock.
- Body; finish (with related Gretsch model number[s]).
- Pickup(s).
- Controls; output jack.
- Pickguard.
- Bridge, tailpiece (including vibrato).
- Metalwork finish.

Of course, not every model will need all seven points, and to avoid too much repetition we've considered **a number of features** to be **common to most Gretsch guitars**. They are:

- Glued-in neck, unless stated.
- Headstock with three tuners each side, unless stated.
- All controls on body front, unless stated.
- Side-mounted jack, unless stated.
- Pickguard present, unless stated.
- Metal bridge saddle(s) with wooden or metal base, unless stated.
- Nickel- or chrome-plated hardware, unless stated.

Any other **general comments**, *in italics*, are listed after the specification points. Some models were/are made in a number of variations, and where relevant these are are also listed here, in similar fashion – but be aware that we have not been able to record every single special-order option.

WHAT ELSE?

We've simplified the names of colour finishes. Where Gretsch often gave or gives a posh name, we tell you the real colour, for ease of identification. For example, Gretsch says Jaguar Tan; we say gold. Also, what Gretsch calls a string damper we call a string-mute. And we've ignored Gretsch's habit of putting a G in front of its model numbers: for example, Gretsch says G6120; we say 6120.

Production was in the USA until the early 80s and has been primarily in Japan since the late 80s. A US Custom Shop was started briefly in the mid 90s and has run permanently from 2004. Gretsch has used and uses other Asian sources for its Historic Series, Electromatic, and Synchromatic lines.

SHALL WE GET GOING?

All the detail in the Reference Listing that follows is designed to tell you more about your Gretsch electric guitar. When you combine the background story and the illustrations from earlier in the book with the data presented here, you should be able to put together some useful information about any Gretsch instrument.

ANNIVERSARY

■ ANNIVERSARY
Mono models here; for stereo model see next section.

ORIGINALS

ANNIVERSARY 1958–72
- Unbound ebony fingerboard (rosewood from c.1960), thumbnail markers; 22 frets (21 from c.1959); truss-rod adjuster at headstock; model nameplate on headstock.
- Hollow single-cutaway bound body (15.5in wide) with f-holes; sunburst (6124), light/dark green (6125), light/dark brown (6125).
- One humbucker at neck (one single-coil from c.1960).
- One knob (volume) and one selector (tone).
- Six-saddle bridge, separate G-cutout flat tailpiece; clip-on vibrato lever c.1962–65.

DOUBLE ANNIVERSARY first version 1958–72
- Unbound (bound from c.1962) ebony fingerboard (rosewood from c.1960), thumbnail markers; 22 frets (21 from c.1959; 21 plus zero fret from c.1968; some examples with 20 frets); truss-rod adjuster at headstock; model nameplate on headstock.
- Hollow single-cutaway bound body (15.5in wide) with f-holes; sunburst (6117), light/dark green (6118), light/dark brown (6118).
- Two humbuckers (two single-coils from c.1960).
- Three knobs (volume) and two selectors (tone, pickups).
- Six-saddle bridge, separate G-cutout flat tailpiece; clip-on vibrato lever c.1962–65.

DOUBLE ANNIVERSARY second version 1972–74
Similar to first version, except:
- Bound rosewood fingerboard, thumbnail markers; 22 frets plus zero fret; truss-rod adjuster at neck heel; no model nameplate on headstock.
- Sunburst (7560).

DOUBLE ANNIVERSARY third version 1974–77
Similar to second version, except:
- Block markers.
- Three knobs (two volume, one tone) and one selector (pickups).
- Anniversary logo on pickguard.
- Six-saddle bridge, separate frame-type tailpiece.

REISSUES

ANNIVERSARY 1993–98
- Bound ebony fingerboard, thumbnail markers; 22 frets; truss-rod adjuster at headstock; model nameplate on headstock.
- Hollow single-cutaway bound body with f-holes; sunburst (6124), light/dark green (6125).
- One humbucker at neck.
- One control (volume) and one selector (tone).
- Six-saddle bridge, separate G-cutout flat tailpiece.

(DOUBLE) ANNIVERSARY 1993–current
- Bound ebony fingerboard (unbound from c.2003), thumbnail markers; 22 frets; truss-rod adjuster at headstock; model nameplate on headstock.
- Hollow single-cutaway bound body with f-holes; sunburst (6117), light/dark green (6118).
- Two humbuckers.
- Three knobs (volume) and two selectors (tone, pickups).
- Six-saddle bridge, separate G-cutout flat tailpiece or vibrato tailpiece.
* *ANNIVERSARY 6117HT sunburst, two single-coils, 2003–current.*
* *ANNIVERSARY 6117THT sunburst, two single-coils, separate vibrato tailpiece, 2005–current.*
* *ANNIVERSARY 6118T/6118T-LTV light/dark green, separate vibrato tailpiece, 2007–08.*
* *120th ANNIVERSARY 6118T-120 yellow/brown, "1883–2003" on headstock, separate vibrato tailpiece, 2003–07.*
* *125th ANNIVERSARY 6118T-LTV light/dark green, "1883–2008" on headstock, separate vibrato tailpiece, 2008–12.*
* *130th ANNIVERSARY 6118T gold/black, "130 Gretsch Years 1883 2013" on headstock, separate vibrato tailpiece, Custom Shop limited edition of 30, 2013.*

ANNIVERSARY JUNIOR 6118JR 2002–08
- Bound ebony fingerboard, thumbnail markers, 22 frets; truss-rod adjuster at headstock; model nameplate on headstock.
- Hollow single-cutaway bound body with f-holes (14in wide); light/dark green (6118JR).
- Two humbuckers.
- Three knobs (volume) and two selectors (tone, pickups).
- Six-saddle bridge, separate G-cutout flat tailpiece.
* *ANNIVERSARY JUNIOR 6118TJR separate vibrato tailpiece, 2004–09.*
* *130th ANNIVERSARY JR 6118T-LTV gold/black, separate vibrato tailpiece, 2013–current.*

■ ANNIVERSARY STEREO

ANNIVERSARY STEREO 1961–63
- Unbound rosewood fingerboard, thumbnail markers; 21 frets; truss-rod adjuster at headstock; model nameplate on headstock.
- Hollow single-cutaway bound body with f-holes; sunburst (6111), light/dark green (6112).
- Two split-polepiece single-coils (close-spaced: one at neck, one central).
- Two knobs (volume) and three selectors (two tone, one pickups).
- Six-saddle bridge, separate G-cutout flat tailpiece.

■ ASTRO-JET

ASTRO-JET 1963–67
- Bound ebony fingerboard, thumbnail markers; 22 frets plus zero fret; truss-rod adjuster at headstock; four and two tuners-per-side headstock.
- Solid double-cutaway body; model nameplate on front; red/black (6126).
- Two humbuckers.
- Three knobs (volume) and three selectors (standby, tone, pickups), all on pickguard.
- Six-saddle bridge, separate vibrato tailpiece.
* *Some examples with 21 frets; some with single-saddle bridge; some with string-tension bar.*

BILLY ZOOM

■ ATKINS AXE

ATKINS AXE 1977–80
- Bound ebony fingerboard, small position markers; 22 frets plus zero fret; truss-rod adjuster at neck heel.
- Solid single-cutaway bound body with angled-in upper bout; dark grey or black (7685), red (7686).
- Two humbuckers.
- Four knobs (two volume, two tone) and one selector (pickups).
- Six-saddle wrapover bridge/tailpiece.

■ AXE

AXE 1995–2001
- Bound rosewood fingerboard, dice-type block markers; 22 frets; truss-rod adjuster at headstock.
- Solid single-cutaway bound body with angled-in upper bout; brown (7685), dark red (7686).
- Two humbuckers.
- Four knobs (two volume, two tone) and one selector (pickups).
- Six-saddle wrapover bridge/tailpiece.

■ BEAST
In alphanumerical order.

BEAST BST-1000 first version 1979–81
- Bolt-on neck with unbound rosewood fingerboard, dot markers; 24 frets plus zero fret; truss-rod adjuster at headstock; horizontal logo on headstock.
- Solid single-cutaway body with angled-in upper bout; brown (8210), red (8211).
- Two humbuckers.
- Two knobs (volume, tone), one selector (pickups), and jack, all on pickguard.
- Six-saddle bridge/tailpiece with through-body stringing.

BEAST BST-1000 second version 1979–81
- Bolt-on neck with unbound rosewood fingerboard, dot markers; 24 frets plus zero fret; truss-rod adjuster at headstock; vertical logo on headstock.
- Solid single-cutaway body with angled-in upper bout; brown (8215), red (8216).
- Two coverless humbuckers.
- Two knobs (volume, tone), one selector (pickups), and jack, all on pickguard.
- Six-saddle bridge/tailpiece with through-body stringing.

BEAST BST-1500 1979–81
Similar to BEAST BST-1000 second version, except:
- Brown (8217).

BEAST BST-2000 1980–81
- Bolt-on neck with unbound rosewood fingerboard, dot markers; 22 frets plus zero fret; truss-rod adjuster at headstock.
- Solid double-cutaway body; brown (8220), red (8221).
- Two humbuckers.
- Two knobs (volume, tone), one selector (pickups), one mini-switch (coil-split), and jack, all on pickguard.
- Six-saddle bridge/tailpiece with through-body stringing.

BEAST BST-5000 1979–81
- Laminated through-neck with bound rosewood fingerboard, dot markers; 24 frets plus zero fret; truss-rod adjuster at neck heel.
- Solid double-cutaway carved-edge body; brown (8250).
- Two humbuckers.
- Four knobs (two volume, two tone), one selector (pickups), one mini switch (coil-split).
- No pickguard.
- Six-saddle bridge, separate bar tailpiece.

■ BIKINI

BIKINI 1961
- Unbound maple fingerboard, dot markers; 22 frets; truss-rod adjuster at body.
- Double-cutaway body with solid rectangular centre section, detachable slide-on hinged back; black (6023).
- One single-coil.
- Two knobs (volume, tone) mounted on edge of body centre section.
- No pickguard.
- Wooden single-saddle bridge, separate trapeze tailpiece.
* Some examples with zero fret; some with model name on headstock; some with coloured plastic pickguard.
* Also guitar/bass double-neck (6025).

■ "BILLY BO" See under Bo Diddley.

■ BILLY DUFFY

BILLY DUFFY FALCON 7593T 2013–current
- Bound ebony fingerboard, block markers; 22 frets plus zero fret; truss-rod adjuster at headstock; signature on truss-rod cover.
- Hollow single-cutaway bound body with f-holes; white (7593T).
- Two humbuckers (differing types).
- Three knobs (volume) and two selectors (tone, pickups).
- No pickguard.
- Six-saddle bridge, separate vibrato tailpiece.

■ BILLY GIBBONS See "BILLY BO" entry in Bo Diddley section.

■ BILLY ZOOM

BILLY ZOOM TRIBUTE SILVER JET 6129BZT 2008–11
- Bound rosewood fingerboard, block markers; 22 frets; truss-rod adjuster at headstock; custom neck shape.
- Semi-solid single-cutaway bound body; silver sparkle relic (6129BZT).
- Two single-coils.
- Four knobs (three volume, one tone) and one selector (pickups).
- No pickguard.
- Six-saddle bridge, separate vibrato tailpiece.
- Relic nickel-plated hardware.
* Custom Shop relic'd reproduction of Zoom's '55 Duo Jet, with package of repro memorabilia, in a limited edition of 50. Serial-numbered 15697 XXX, where XXX is the edition number, from 072 to 112.

THE GRETSCH ELECTRIC GUITAR BOOK

BLACK HAWK

■ **BLACK FALCON** See various entries under White Falcon.

■ BLACK HAWK

BLACK HAWK 1967–70
- Bound rosewood fingerboard, thumbnail markers with dot markers from 15th fret; 22 frets plus zero fret; truss-rod adjuster at headstock; model nameplate on headstock.
- Hollow double-cutaway bound body with f-holes; sunburst (6100), black (6101).
- Two humbuckers.
- Three knobs (volume) and three selectors (standby, tone, pickups).
- Bar-frame Floating Sound unit plus six-saddle bridge, separate G-cutout flat tailpiece.

■ **BLACK PANTHER** See Panther.

■ **BLACK PENGUIN** See WHITE PENGUIN 6134 under White Penguin: Reissues.

■ **BLACK PHOENIX** See under Brian Setzer.

■ **BLACK PRINCE** See CORVETTE solidbody third version under Corvette.

■ BONO

BONO "IRISH FALCON" 6136I 2005–current
- Bound ebony fingerboard, hump-top block markers with Bono's signature engraved on the 12th fret; 22 frets; truss-rod adjuster at headstock with gold-sparkle cover; vertical gold-sparkle Gretsch logo on headstock.
- Hollow single-cutaway bound body with f-holes; green (6136I).
- Two humbuckers.
- Three knobs (volume) and two selectors (tone, pickups).
- The Goal Is Soul graphic logo on pickguard.
- Single-saddle bridge, separate G-logo tubular frame-type tailpiece.
- Gold-plated hardware.

BONO RED See CENTER-BLOCK BONO RED under Electromatic: Later.

■ BO DIDDLEY In alphanumerical order.

"BILLY-BO" JUPITER THUNDERBIRD 6199 2005–current
- Bound rosewood fingerboard, thumbnail markers, 22 frets; truss-rod adjuster at headstock.
- Semi-solid bound body, irregular and slightly waisted, concave cutouts at rear; red (6199).
- Two humbuckers.
- Four knobs (three volume, one tone) and one selector (pickups).
- Six-saddle bridge, separate G-cutout flat tailpiece.

BO DIDDLEY 6138 2000–current
- Unbound rosewood fingerboard, dot markers, 22 frets; truss-rod adjuster at headstock; Bo Diddley signature on truss-rod cover.
- Semi-solid bound rectangular body; red (6138).
- Two humbuckers.
- Four knobs (three volume, one tone) and one selector (pickups).
- No pickguard.
- Six-saddle bridge, separate G-cutout flat tailpiece.
- Gold-plated hardware.

ELECTROMATIC BO DIDDLEY 5810 2000–14
- Bolt-on neck with unbound rosewood fingerboard, dot markers; 22 frets; truss-rod adjuster at headstock; "Gretsch" on truss-rod cover; "Electromatic" on headstock.
- Semi-solid rectangular body; red (5810).
- Two humbuckers.
- Four knobs (three volume, one tone) and one selector (pickups).
- No pickguard.
- Six-saddle wrapover bridge/tailpiece.
* *Model number changed to 5810 from c.2004.*
* *ELECTROMATIC MINI DIDDLEY 5850 smaller, single humbucker, 2006–09.*
* *SYNCHROMATIC BO DIDDLEY 1810 "Synchromatic" on headstock, red, 2000–03.*

■ BRIAN SETZER

NASHVILLE BRIAN SETZER 6120 1993–current
- Bound ebony fingerboard, thumbnail markers; 22 frets; Brian Setzer on truss-rod cover at headstock; horseshoe on headstock.
- Hollow single-cutaway bound body (16in wide, 2.75in deep) with f-holes; urethane finish: orange (6120SSU), green (6120SSUGR); vintage-style cellulose lacquer: orange (6120SSL); 'vintage orange' (6120SSLVO).
- Two humbuckers.
- Three knobs (volume; two with optional dice-style knobs) and two selectors (tone, pickups).
- Brian Setzer signature and model name on pickguard.
- Six-saddle bridge, separate vibrato tailpiece.
- Gold-plated hardware (except vibrato).

NASHVILLE BRIAN SETZER HOT ROD 6120 1999–current
- Bound ebony fingerboard, thumbnail markers; 22 frets; "Brian Setzer Hot Rod" on headstock.
- Hollow single-cutaway bound body (16in wide, 2.5in deep) with f-holes; black (6120SHBK), blue (6120SHB), red (6120SHA), 'lime gold' (6120SHL), purple (6120SHP), tangerine (6120SHT); also with TV Jones pickups, adds "TV" to model number.
- Two humbuckers.
- One knob (volume) and one selector (pickups).
- Hot Rod logo on pickguard (early models without logo).
- Six-saddle bridge, separate vibrato tailpiece.

BRIAN SETZER BLACK PHOENIX 6136SLBP 2005–current
- Bound ebony fingerboard, thumbnail markers; 22 frets; silver-sparkle vertical Gretsch logo on headstock.
- Hollow single-cutaway bound body (17in wide, 2.75in deep) with f-holes; black (6136SLBP).
- Two humbuckers.
- One knob (volume) and one selector (pickups).
- Phoenix logo on pickguard.
- Six-saddle bridge, separate vibrato tailpiece.

BRIAN SETZER TRIBUTE NASHVILLE 6120SSC
2007–09
- Bound ebony fingerboard, thumbnail markers; 22 frets; graphic on headstock; custom neck shape.
- Hollow single-cutaway bound body (15.75in wide, 2.75in deep) with f-holes; orange relic (6120SSC), graphics.
- Two humbuckers.
- Three knobs (volume; two with dice-style knobs) and one selector (pickups), with "hole" for tone switch.
- Six-saddle bridge, separate vibrato tailpiece.
- Relic gold-plated hardware (except vibrato).
* Custom Shop relic'd reproduction of Setzer's Stray Cats c.'59 6120, with package of repro memorabilia, in a limited edition of 59. Serial-numbered 33024 XX, where XX is the edition number, from 26 to 85 (number 59 was not used).

■ BROADKASTER: SEMI-HOLLOW

BROADKASTER semi-hollow body first version
1974–77
- Unbound rosewood fingerboard, dot markers; 22 frets plus zero fret; truss-rod adjuster at headstock.
- Semi-hollow double-cutaway bound body (16in wide) with f-holes; natural (7603, 7607), sunburst (7604, 7608).
- Two humbuckers.
- Three knobs (volume) and two selectors (tone, pickups).
- Six-saddle bridge/tailpiece (7607, 7608); six-saddle bridge and separate vibrato tailpiece (7603, 7604).
* Finish at first red-to-black sunburst; tobacco sunburst from 1975.

BROADKASTER semi-hollow body second version
1977–79
Similar to first version, except:
- Red (7609).
- Five knobs (three volume, two tone) and one selector (pickups).
- Six-saddle wrapover bridge/tailpiece.

■ BROADKASTER: SOLIDBODY

BROADKASTER solidbody 1974–77
- Bolt-on neck with unbound maple fingerboard, dot markers; 22 frets; truss-rod adjuster at headstock.
- Solid double-cutaway body; natural (7600), sunburst (7601).
- Two humbuckers.
- Two controls (volume), two selectors (tone, pickups), and jack, all on pickguard.
- Six-saddle bridge/tailpiece.

■ CAT'S-EYE CUSTOM

"CAT'S-EYE CUSTOM" 6117 1964–67
- Bound rosewood fingerboard, thumbnail markers; 22 frets plus zero fret; truss-rod adjuster at headstock.
- Hollow single-cutaway bound body with cat's-eye soundholes; various colours (6117).
- Two single-coils.
- Four knobs (two volume, two tone) and one selector (pickups).
- Six-saddle bridge, separate G-cutout flat tailpiece.

* Some examples with 21 frets.
* Custom order for Sam Ash stores.

■ **CHET ATKINS** See Chet Atkins entries under: Country Gentleman; Solid Body; Tennessean; 6120.

■ CLIPPER

CLIPPER first version 1956–57
- Unbound rosewood fingerboard, dot markers; 21 frets; truss-rod adjuster at headstock; early examples with "Electromatic" on headstock.
- Hollow bound body (16in wide) with f-holes; sunburst (6186), cream/grey (6187).
- One single-coil at neck.
- Two knobs (volume, tone).
- Single-saddle wooden bridge, separate G-cutout flat tailpiece.

CLIPPER second version 1957–72
- Unbound rosewood fingerboard, dot markers; 22 frets; truss-rod adjuster on headstock.
- Hollow single-cutaway bound body (15.75in wide 2.75in deep to c.1959; 1.75in deep from c.1959) with f-holes; sunburst (6186), cream/grey (6187).
- One single-coil at neck.
- Two knobs (volume, tone).
- Single-saddle wooden bridge, separate G-cutout flat tailpiece (some with trapeze tailpiece).

CLIPPER third version 1972–74
- Bound rosewood fingerboard, thumbnail markers; 22 frets plus zero fret; truss-rod adjuster at neck heel.
- Hollow single-cutaway bound body (16in wide 1.75in deep) with f-holes; sunburst/black (7555).
- Two single-coils.
- Three knobs (volume) and two selectors (tone, pickups).
- Six-saddle bridge, separate trapeze tailpiece.

■ COMMITTEE

COMMITTEE 1977–81
- Laminated through-neck with bound rosewood fingerboard, dot markers; 22 frets; truss-rod adjuster at neck heel.
- Solid double-cutaway body; brown (7628/7628D).
- Two humbuckers (7628D coverless).
- Four knobs (two volume, two tone) and one selector (pickups).
- Clear plastic pickguard.
- Six-saddle bridge/tailpiece with through-body stringing.
* Some examples with black plastic pickguard.

■ CONVERTIBLE

CONVERTIBLE 1955–59
- Bound rosewood fingerboard (ebony from c.1958), hump-top block markers (thumbnail from c.1957); 21 frets; truss-rod adjuster at headstock.
- Hollow single-cutaway bound body with f-holes; cream/brown (6199).

CORVETTE

- One single-coil, attached to pickguard.
- Two knobs (volume, tone) mounted on pickguard.
- Single-saddle wooden bridge, separate G-cutout flat tailpiece.
- Gold-plated hardware.
* *Some sunburst; some yellow/brown (6199) from c.1958.*
* *Known as SAL SALVADOR from c.1959; see under Sal Salvador.*

■ CORVETTE: HOLLOWBODY

CORVETTE 1953–56
- Unbound rosewood fingerboard, dot markers; 20 frets; "Electromatic" on headstock; truss-rod adjuster at headstock (from c.1954).
- Hollow bound body (16in wide) with f-holes; sunburst (6182 or 6182-3), natural (6183 or 6182-3), gold (6184).
- One single-coil at neck.
- Two controls (volume, tone).
- Single-saddle wooden bridge, separate trapeze tailpiece.
* *Previously known as ELECTROMATIC SPANISH (second version); see under Electromatic: Early.*

■ CORVETTE: SOLIDBODY

CORVETTE first version 1961–62
- Unbound rosewood fingerboard, dot markers; 21 frets; truss-rod adjuster at body.
- Solid double-cutaway slab body; dark brown (6132), grey (6133).
- One single-coil at bridge.
- Two controls (volume, tone) on pickguard.
- Single-saddle wooden bridge, separate trapeze tailpiece.

CORVETTE second version 1962–65
- Unbound rosewood fingerboard, dot markers; 21 frets; truss-rod adjuster at body (truss-rod adjuster at headstock from c.1962).
- Solid double-cutaway bevelled-edge body; dark red (6132, 6134, 6135).
- One single-coil at bridge (6132, 6134); two-single-coils (6135).
- Two knobs (volume, tone) on pickguard (6132, 6134); three knobs (two volume, one tone) and one selector (pickups) all on pickguard (6135).
- Bar bridge; separate trapeze tailpiece (6132), separate vibrato tailpiece (6134, 6135).

CORVETTE third version 1965–70
- Unbound rosewood fingerboard, dot markers; 21 frets; truss-rod adjuster at headstock; two and four tuners-per-side headstock.
- Solid double-cutaway bevelled-edge body; red sunburst (6132, 6134).
- One single-coil (6132, 6134); two single-coils (6135).
- Two knobs (volume, tone) on pickguard (6132, 6134); three knobs (two volume, one tone) and one selector (pickups), all on pickguard (6135, to c.1968); three knobs (two volume, one tone) and two selectors (pickups, treble-boost), all on pickguard (6135, from c.1968).
- Bar bridge; separate trapeze tailpiece (6132), separate vibrato tailpiece (6134, 6135).
* *Some 6135 examples in gold or silver metallic finish, known as GOLD DUKE and SILVER DUKE, 1966.*
* *PRINCE 6141 bound ebony fingerboard, two humbuckers, gold-plated hardware, 1968–70; also known as BLACK PRINCE.*

CORVETTE fourth version 1971–73
- Bound rosewood fingerboard, dot markers; 21 frets plus zero fret; truss-rod adjuster at headstock; two and four tuners-per-side headstock.
- Solid double-cutaway body; dark red (7623).
- Two humbuckers.
- Three knobs (volume, tone, treble, distortion blend) and two selectors (pickups, distortion), all on pickguard; active circuit.
- Six-saddle bridge, separate vibrato tailpiece.

CORVETTE II 1976–77
- Unbound rosewood fingerboard, dot markers; 21 frets plus zero fret; truss-rod adjuster at headstock; two and four tuners-per-side headstock.
- Solid double-cutaway body; dark red (7630).
- Two humbuckers.
- Two knobs (volume, tone) and one selector (pickups) on pickguard.
- Six-saddle wrapover bridge/tailpiece.

CVT See under Electromatic: Later.

DELUXE CORVETTE two versions 1976–77
- Bound rosewood fingerboard, dot markers; 21 frets plus zero fret; truss-rod adjuster at headstock; two and four tuners-per-side headstock.
- Solid double-cutaway body; green-ish black (7632).
- Two humbuckers.
- Version 1: Three knobs (one volume, two tone) and three selectors (pickups, treble boost, distortion) on elliptical plate. Version 2: Four knobs (one volume, two pickup tone; one distortion blend) and two selectors (pickups, distortion).
- Metal control plate as well as pickguard.
- Six-saddle wrapover bridge/tailpiece.

■ *COUNTRY CLASSIC* See COUNTRY CLASSIC entries under Country Gentleman / Country Classic.

■ COUNTRY CLUB
Mono models here; for stereo models see next section.

ORIGINALS

COUNTRY CLUB first version 1953–58
- Bound rosewood fingerboard, block markers (hump-top block from c.1955); 21 frets; truss-rod adjuster at headstock.
- Hollow single-cutaway bound body (17in wide 3.25in deep to c.1955; 2.75in deep from c.1955) with f-holes; sunburst (6192), natural (6193), green (6196), light/dark grey (6196).
- Two single-coils.
- Four knobs (three volume, one tone) and one selector (pickups).
- Six-saddle bridge, separate G-cutout flat tailpiece.
- Gold-plated hardware.
* *Some examples in other colours.*
* *Previously known as ELECTRO II (second version), see under Electro II.*

COUNTRY CLUB second version 1958–72
Similar to first version, except:
- Bound ebony fingerboard, thumbnail markers; 21 frets (plus zero fret from c.1959).

COUNTRY GENTLEMAN

- Body 2.75in deep to c.1960, 1.75in c.1960–63, 2.75in from c.1963; pad on body back c.1962–63; sunburst (6192), natural (6193), green (6196).
- Two humbuckers.
- Three knobs (volume) and two selectors (tone, pickups) to c.1962; three knobs (volume) and three selectors (standby, tone, pickups) from c.1962, plus one string-mute control c.1962–65.
* Some examples c.1959 2.25in deep.

COUNTRY CLUB third version 1972–74
Similar to second version, except:
- Truss-rod adjuster at neck heel.
- Sunburst (7575), natural (7576).

COUNTRY CLUB fourth version 1974–81
Similar to third version, except:
- Block markers; 22 frets.
- Sunburst (7575), natural (7576), brown (7577).
- Five knobs (three volume, two tone) and one selector (pickups).
- Separate frame-type tailpiece with model nameplate overlay.

REISSUES

COUNTRY CLUB 1955 CUSTOM 6196-1955 1995–99
"Custom USA" reissue based on 1955-period natural-finish original but with bound ebony fingerboard. Also blue sunburst, green, 1997–99.

COUNTRY CLUB single-coils 2001–13
- Bound ebony or rosewood fingerboard, block or hump-top block markers; 22 frets; truss-rod adjuster at headstock.
- Hollow single-cutaway bound body with f-holes; sunburst (6192), natural (6193), green (6196), yellow/brown (6196TSP-BY), light/dark grey (6196TSP-2G).
- Two single-coils.
- Four controls (three volume, one tone) and one selector (pickups).
- Six-saddle bridge, separate G-cutout flat tailpiece or separate vibrato tailpiece.
- Gold or chrome-plated hardware.
* Some examples with thumbnail markers.

COUNTRY CLUB humbuckers 2004–current
Similar to first version, except:
- Bound ebony fingerboard, thumbnail markers.
- Amber (6193T), green (6196T).
- Two humbuckers.
- Three controls (volume) and three selectors (standby, tone, pickups).
- Separate vibrato tailpiece.

■ COUNTRY CLUB STEREO

COUNTRY CLUB PROJECT-O-SONIC (STEREO) first version 1958–60
- Bound ebony fingerboard, thumbnail markers; 21 frets (plus zero fret from c.1959); truss-rod adjuster at headstock.
- Hollow single-cutaway bound body with f-holes; sunburst (6101), natural (6102), green (6103).
- Two split-polepiece humbuckers (close-spaced: one at neck; one in central position).
- Two knobs (volume) and three selectors (two tone, one pickups).
- Six-saddle bridge, separate G-cutout flat tailpiece.
- Gold-plated hardware.
* Some examples with regular humbuckers (not split-polepiece); some with model numbers as COUNTRY CLUB second version.

COUNTRY CLUB STEREO second version 1960–65
Similar to first version, except:
- Pad on body back c.1962–64.
- Two humbuckers (regular position).
- Two knobs (volume) and five selectors (one standby, four tone/pickups), plus one string-mute control c.1962–64.

■ COUNTRY GENTLEMAN / COUNTRY CLASSIC

SINGLE-CUTAWAY ORIGINAL

CHET ATKINS COUNTRY GENTLEMAN 1958–61
- Bound ebony fingerboard, thumbnail markers; 22 frets (plus zero fret from c.1959); metal nut (c.1958); truss-rod adjuster at headstock; model nameplate on headstock.
- Hollow sealed single-cutaway bound body (17in wide 2.25in deep) with fake f-holes; dark brown (6122).
- Two humbuckers.
- Three knobs (volume) and two selectors (tone, pickups).
- Bar bridge, separate vibrato tailpiece.
- Gold-plated hardware.
* Some examples with f-holes.
* Some examples with Chet Atkins logo on pickguard.

SINGLE-CUTAWAY REISSUES

COUNTRY CLASSIC I 6122S 1989–2003
- Bound ebony fingerboard, thumbnail markers; 22 frets; truss-rod adjuster at headstock; model nameplate on headstock.
- Hollow single-cutaway bound body with real f-holes; dark brown (6122S).
- Two humbuckers.
- Four knobs (three volume, one tone) and one selector (pickups).
- Model name on pickguard.
- Six-saddle bridge, separate vibrato tailpiece.
- Gold-plated hardware.

COUNTRY CLASSIC 6122-1958 1997–2006
- Bound ebony fingerboard, thumbnail markers; 22 frets; shorter scale-length; truss-rod adjuster at headstock; model nameplate on headstock.
- Hollow sealed single-cutaway bound body with fake f-holes; dark brown (6122-1958).
- Two humbuckers.
- Three knobs (volume) and two selectors (tone, pickups).
- Bar bridge, separate vibrato tailpiece.
- Gold-plated hardware (except vibrato tailpiece).

CHET ATKINS COUNTRY GENTLEMAN 6122-1958 2007–current
Similar to COUNTRY CLASSIC 6122-1958 except:

COUNTRY GENTLEMAN

- New model name on headstock plate.
- Aged binding.
- Model name on pickguard.

NASHVILLE CLASSIC 6122-1959 2003–08
- Bound ebony fingerboard, thumbnail markers; 21 frets plus zero fret; truss-rod adjuster at headstock; model nameplate on headstock.
- Hollow sealed single-cutaway bound body with fake f-holes; dark brown (6122-1959).
- Two humbuckers (differing types).
- Three knobs (two volume, one tone) and one selector (pickups).
- Bar bridge, separate vibrato tailpiece.
- Gold-plated hardware.

CHET ATKINS COUNTRY GENTLEMAN 6122-1959 2009–current
Similar to NASHVILLE CLASSIC 6122-1959, except:
- New model name on headstock plate.

DOUBLE-CUTAWAY ORIGINALS

CHET ATKINS COUNTRY GENTLEMAN double-cutaway first version 1961–72
- Bound ebony fingerboard, thumbnail markers; 22 frets plus zero fret; truss-rod adjuster at headstock; model nameplate on headstock.
- Hollow sealed double-cutaway bound body with fake f-holes; pad on body back; dark brown (6122).
- Two humbuckers.
- Three knobs (volume) and three selectors (standby, tone, pickups), plus two string-mute controls (one from c.1966).
- Model name on pickguard from c.1967.
- Bar bridge, separate vibrato tailpiece; two string-mutes (one from c.1966).
- Gold-plated hardware.
* Some examples in black c.1967; some with real f-holes.

CHET ATKINS COUNTRY GENTLEMAN double-cutaway second version 1972–81
Similar to first version, except:
- Truss-rod adjuster at neck heel; no model nameplate on headstock.
- Hollow double-cutaway bound body with real f-holes; no pad on body back; brown (7670).
- Three knobs (volume) and two selectors (tone, pickups) from c.1978; no string-mute controls.
- Six-saddle bridge; no string mutes.
* Name changed to COUNTRY SQUIRE (7676) c.1981, then SOUTHERN BELLE (7176 or 7676) c.1982–83. Southern Belle models have small plaque on rear indicating "Assembled in Mexico".

DOUBLE-CUTAWAY REISSUES

COUNTRY CLASSIC 6122 1989–2006
- Bound ebony fingerboard, thumbnail markers; 22 frets; truss-rod adjuster at headstock; model nameplate on headstock.
- Hollow double-cutaway bound body with real f-holes; dark brown (6122).
- Two humbuckers.
- Four knobs (three volume, one tone) and one selector (pickups) to 2003; three knobs (volume) and two selectors (tone, pickups) from 2003.
- Model name on pickguard.
- Six-saddle bridge, separate vibrato tailpiece.
- Gold-plated hardware.
* Also known as Country Classic II 6122.

COUNTRY CLASSIC 6122-1962 1993–2006
- Bound ebony fingerboard, thumbnail markers; 22 frets plus zero fret; truss-rod adjuster at headstock; model nameplate on headstock.
- Hollow sealed double-cutaway bound body with fake f-holes; dark brown (6122).
- Two humbuckers.
- Three knobs (volume) and three selectors (standby, tone, pickups).
- Six-saddle bridge, separate vibrato tailpiece.
- Gold-plated hardware.
* Also known as COUNTRY CLASSIC II 6122-1962.
* COUNTRY CLASSIC SPECIAL 6122SP two string-mutes and controls, pad on body back, 2005.
* COUNTRY CLASSIC 6122-12 12-string natural, separate G-cutout tailpiece, 1996–2001.

COUNTRY CLASSIC JUNIOR 6122R 1998–2004
- Bound ebony or rosewood fingerboard, thumbnail markers; 22 frets; truss-rod adjuster at headstock.
- Small bodied twin-shallow-cutaway hollow archtop, with binding; two large f-holes; dark brown, black, orange.
- Two humbuckers.
- Four controls (three volume, one tone) and one selector.
- Six-saddle bridge, separate vibrato tailpiece.
- Gold-plated hardware.

COUNTRY CLASSIC 12-STRING 6122-12 / CHET ATKINS COUNTRY GENTLEMAN 12-STRING 6122-12 2006–2014
- Bound ebony fingerboard, thumbnail markers, 22 frets; truss-rod adjuster at headstock; model nameplate on headstock (not early models).
- Hollow sealed double-cutaway bound body with fake f-holes; dark brown (6122-12).
- Two humbuckers.
- Three knobs (volume) and three selectors (standby, tone, pickups).
- Six-saddle bridge, separate G-cutout flat tailpiece.
- Gold-plated hardware.
* For earlier 12-string model, see COUNTRY CLASSIC 6122-1962 entry above.

CHET ATKINS COUNTRY GENTLEMAN 6122-1962 2007–current
- Bound ebony fingerboard, thumbnail markers; 22 frets plus zero fret; truss-rod adjuster at headstock; model nameplate on headstock.
- Hollow sealed double-cutaway bound body with fake f-holes; pad on body back; dark brown (6122).
- Two humbuckers.
- Three knobs (volume) and three selectors (standby, tone, pickups), plus two string-mute controls.
- Bar bridge, separate vibrato tailpiece; two string-mutes.
- Gold-plated hardware.

CHET ATKINS COUNTRY GENTLEMAN 6122II
2007–current
- Bound ebony fingerboard, thumbnail markers, 22 frets; truss-rod adjuster at headstock; model nameplate on headstock.
- Hollow double-cutaway bound body with real f-holes; dark brown (6122II).
- Two humbuckers.
- Three knobs (volume) and two selectors (tone, pickups).
- Six-saddle bridge, separate vibrato tailpiece.
- Gold-plated hardware.

■ **COUNTRY ROC** See under Roc.

■ **COUNTRY SQUIRE** See CHET ATKINS COUNTRY GENTLEMAN double-cutaway second version under Country Gentleman/Country Classic.

■ DAVID LEE

DAVID LEE 6136DL 2008
- Unbound fingerboard, block markers; 22 frets; truss-rod adjuster at headstock with black cover; black vertical Gretsch logo on headstock.
- Hollow single-cutaway bound body with f-holes; white (6136DL).
- Two humbuckers.
- Three knobs (two volume, one tone) and one selector (pickups).
- No pickguard.
- Bar bridge, separate vibrato tailpiece.

■ DELUXE CHET

DELUXE CHET 1972–73
- Bound ebony fingerboard, thumbnail markers; 22 frets plus zero fret; truss-rod adjuster at neck heel.
- Hollow single-cutaway bound body with angled-in upper bout and f-holes; dark red (7680), dark brown (7681).
- Two humbuckers.
- Five knobs (three volume, two tone) and one selector (pickups).
- Chet Atkins name on pickguard.
- Six-saddle bridge, separate vibrato tailpiece.
- Gold-plated hardware.
* Continued briefly as Skinny Chet, 1974.

■ **DELUXE CORVETTE**
See under Corvette.

■ **DOUBLE ANNIVERSARY**
See under Anniversary.

■ **DOUBLE JET**
See under Electromatic: Later and Synchromatic.

■ DUANE EDDY

DUANE EDDY 6120DE/DEO 1997–2003
- Bound ebony fingerboard, hump-top block markers; 22 frets; truss-rod adjuster at headstock; Duane Eddy signature on truss-rod cover; brass nut.
- Hollow single-cutaway bound body with f-holes; black sunburst (6120DE), orange (6120DEO).
- Two single-coils.
- Four knobs (three volume, one tone) and one selector (pickups).
- Duane Eddy signature on pickguard.
- Six-saddle bridge, separate vibrato tailpiece.
- Gold-plated hardware (except vibrato tailpiece).

DUANE EDDY SIGNATURE HOLLOW BODY 6120DE
2012–current
- Bound rosewood fingerboard, hump-top block markers; 22 frets; truss-rod adjuster at headstock.
- Hollow single-cutaway bound body with f-holes; orange (6120DE).
- Two single-coils.
- Four knobs (three volume, one tone) and one selector (pickups).
- Duane Eddy signature on pickguard.
- Bar bridge, separate vibrato tailpiece.
- Gold-plated hardware (except vibrato tailpiece).

■ DUO JET

ORIGINALS

DUO JET first version 1953–61
- Bound rosewood fingerboard (ebony from c.1958), block markers (hump-top block from c.1957, thumbnail from c.1958); 22 frets (plus zero fret from c.1960); truss-rod adjuster at headstock.
- Semi-solid single-cutaway bound body (13.5in wide); black (6128).
- Two single-coils (two humbuckers from c.1959).
- Four knobs (three volume, one tone) and one selector (pickups) to c.1959; three knobs (volume) and two selectors (tone, pickups) from c.1959.
- Six-saddle bridge, separate G-cutout flat tailpiece or vibrato tailpiece.
* Some examples c.1957/58 with green body-front, gold-plated hardware, and (sometimes) metal banjo-style arm-rest.

DUO JET second version 1961–69
- Bound rosewood fingerboard, thumbnail markers; 22 frets plus zero fret; truss-rod adjuster at headstock.
- Semi-solid double-cutaway bound body; black (6128).
- Two humbuckers.
- Three knobs (volume) and two selectors (tone, pickups) to c.1962; three knobs (volume) and three selectors (standby, tone, pickups) c.1962–68; four knobs (three volume, one treble-boost) and three selectors (standby, tone, pickups) from c.1968.
- Six-saddle bridge, separate vibrato tailpiece.
- Gold-plated hardware from c.1962.
* Some examples with G-cutout flat tailpiece.
* Colour-sparkle options from c.1963; see also SILVER JET second version under Silver Jet.

REISSUES

DUO JET 6128/6128T first version 1989–2003
- Bound rosewood fingerboard, hump-top block markers; 22 frets; truss-rod adjuster at headstock; horseshoe on headstock.

DUO JET

- Semi-solid single-cutaway bound body; black (6128/6128T).
- Two humbuckers.
- Four knobs (three volume, one tone) and one selector (pickups).
- Six-saddle bridge, separate G-cutout flat tailpiece (6128) or vibrato tailpiece (6128T).

DUO JET 6128-1957/6128T-1957 1994–2006
- Bound rosewood fingerboard, hump-top block markers; 22 frets; truss-rod adjuster at headstock.
- Semi-solid single-cutaway bound body; black (6128-1957/6128T-1957).
- Two single-coils.
- Four knobs (three volume, one tone) and one selector (pickups).
- Six-saddle bridge, separate G-cutout flat tailpiece (6128-1957) or vibrato tailpiece (6128T-1957).
* *DUO JET CUSTOM EDITION 6128TSP Harrison-style, bar bridge, aged markers and binding, 2005–06.*
* *DUO JET 6128T-DSV block markers, fixed-arm vibrato, 2005–14.*
* *DUO JET 6128TCG green finish, aged markers and binding, gold-plated hardware, 2005–current.*

DUO JET 6128T-1962 2001–current
- Bound ebony fingerboard, thumbnail markers, 22 frets plus zero fret; truss-rod adjuster at headstock.
- Semi-solid double-cutaway bound body; black (6128T-62).
- Two humbuckers.
- Three knobs (volume) and two selectors (tone, pickups).
- Six-saddle bridge, separate vibrato tailpiece.
* *DUO JET 6128T-DCM dark cherry, four knobs and one selector, 2013–14.*

DUO JET 6128/6128T second version 2003–current
- Bound ebony fingerboard, thumbnail markers; 22 frets; truss-rod adjuster at headstock.
- Semi-solid single-cutaway bound body; black (6128, 6128T).
- Two humbuckers.
- Three knobs (volume) and two selectors (tone, pickups).
- Six-saddle bridge, separate G-cutout flat tailpiece (6128) or vibrato tailpiece (6128T).

DUO JET 6128DS/6128TDS 2007–10
- Bound rosewood fingerboard, aged hump-top block markers; 22 frets; truss-rod adjuster at headstock.
- Semi-solid single-cutaway aged-bound body; black (6128DS/6128TDS).
- Two single-coils.
- Four knobs (three volume, one tone) and one selector (pickups).
- Bar bridge, separate G-cutout flat tailpiece (6128DS) or vibrato tailpiece (6128TDS).

OTHERS alphanumeric order

DUO JET RELIC 6128TDS-R 2008
- Bound rosewood fingerboard, aged hump-top block markers; 22 frets; truss-rod adjuster at headstock.
- Semi-solid single-cutaway aged-bound body; relic black (6128TDS-R).
- Two single-coils.
- Four knobs (three volume, one tone) and one selector (pickups).
- Bar bridge, separate vibrato tailpiece.
* *Custom Shop limited edition of 75.*

DUO JET 6128T-6/12 double-neck 1998–2007
- 12-string and 6-string necks, each with bound ebony fingerboard, hump-top block markers, 22 frets; truss-rod adjuster at headstock; horseshoe on headstock.
- Semi-solid single-cutaway bound body (17in wide); black (6128T-6/12).
- Two humbuckers per neck.
- Two knobs (one volume, one tone) and two selectors (necks, pickups).
- Six-saddle bridge per neck, separate G-cutout flat tailpiece (12-string neck), separate vibrato tailpiece (6-string neck).

GEORGE HARRISON See under George Harrison.

POWER JET 6128TVP/6128T-TVP 2006–current
- Bound ebony fingerboard, thumbnail markers; 22 frets; truss-rod adjuster at headstock.
- Semi-solid single-cutaway bound body; black (6128TVP/6128T-TVP).
- Two humbuckers.
- Three knobs (volume) and two selectors (tone, pickups).
- Six-saddle bridge, separate G-cutout flat tailpiece (6128TVP), separate vibrato tailpiece (6128T-TVP).

10th ANNIVERSARY DUO JET NOS 2014
- Bound ebony fingerboard, hump-top block markers; 22 frets; truss-rod adjuster at headstock.
- Semi-solid single-cutaway bound body; red sparkle.
- Two single-coils.
- Four knobs (three volume, one tone) and one selector (pickups).
- Custom Shop 10th Anniversary logo on pickguard.
- Six-saddle bridge, separate G-logo tubular frame-type tailpiece.
* *Custom Shop limited edition of 10 to mark the Shop's tenth anniversary.*

■ EDDIE COCHRAN

EDDIE COCHRAN TRIBUTE HOLLOW BODY 6120EC 2010
- Bound rosewood fingerboard, engraved block markers; 22 frets; truss-rod adjuster at headstock; steer head on headstock; custom neck shape.
- Hollow single-cutaway bound body with f-holes; G-brand on front; relic orange (6120EC).
- Two single-coils (differing types).
- Four knobs (three volume, one tone) and one selector (pickups).
- Clear plastic pickguard.
- Single-saddle bridge, separate vibrato tailpiece.
- Relic gold-plated hardware.
* *Custom Shop relic'd reproduction of Cochran's '55 6120, with package of repro memorabilia, in a limited edition of 25. Serial-numbered 16942 XXXX, where XXXX is the edition number, from (numbers) 1963 to 2013.*
* *See also NASHVILLE WESTERN 6120W-1957 under 6120.*

EDDIE COCHRAN SIGNATURE HOLLOW BODY 6120 2011–current
- Bound rosewood fingerboard, engraved block markers; 22 frets; truss-rod adjuster at headstock; signature on truss-rod cover; steer head on headstock.
- Hollow single-cutaway bound body with f-holes; G-brand on

ELECTROMATIC

front; orange (6120).
- Two single-coils (differing types).
- Four knobs (three volume, one tone) and one selector (pickups).
- Clear plastic pickguard.
- Single-saddle bridge, separate vibrato tailpiece.
- Gold-plated hardware.

■ ELECTRO II

ELECTRO II non-cutaway 1951–53
- Bound rosewood fingerboard, block markers; 20 frets; "Electromatic" on headstock.
- Hollow bound body (16in wide) with f-holes; sunburst (6187 or 6187-8), natural (6188 or 6187-8).
- Two single-coils.
- Three knobs (two volume, one tone) to c.1952; four knobs (three volume, one tone) from c.1952.
- Single-saddle wooden bridge, separate trapeze tailpiece.

ELECTRO II single-cutaway 1951–53
- Bound rosewood fingerboard, block markers; 21 frets; truss-rod adjuster at body end of neck; "Synchromatic" on headstock.
- Hollow single-cutaway bound body (17in) with f-holes; sunburst (6192), natural (6193).
- Two single-coils.
- Three controls (two volume, one tone) to c.1952; four controls (two volume, two tone) from c.1952.
- Single-saddle wooden bridge (six-saddle bridge from c.1951), separate harp-frame tailpiece or G-cutout flat tailpiece.
- Gold-plated hardware.
* Some examples with 19 frets.
* Known as COUNTRY CLUB (first version) from 1953: see under Country Club.

■ ELECTROMATIC: EARLY

ELECTROMATIC SPANISH first version 1939–42
- Hollow body with f-holes; sunburst.
- One single-coil.
- Two knobs (volume, tone).
* No other information available.

ELECTROMATIC SPANISH second version 1949–53
- Unbound rosewood fingerboard, dot markers; 20 frets; "Electromatic" on headstock.
- Hollow bound body (16in wide) with f-holes; sunburst (6185 or 6185-6), natural (6185N or 6185-6).
- One single-coil at neck.
- Two knobs (volume, tone).
- Single-saddle wooden bridge, separate trapeze tailpiece.
* Known as CORVETTE (hollowbody) from 1953; see under Corvette.

ELECTROMATIC 1951–54
- Bound rosewood fingerboard, block markers; 21 frets; "Electromatic" on headstock.
- Hollow single-cutaway bound body (16in wide) with f-holes; sunburst (6190), natural (6191).
- One single-coil at neck.
- Two knobs (volume, tone).
- Six-saddle bridge, separate trapeze tailpiece.
* Some examples with two single-coils (6189).
* Known as STREAMLINER (single-cutaway) from 1954; see under Streamliner.

■ ELECTROMATIC: LATER
With "Electromatic" on headstock. In alphanumerical order and in simplified format.

BO DIDDLEY See under Bo Diddley.

CENTER-BLOCK BONO RED 2014–current
Double-cut hollow, two humbuckers, Bono "Red" logo on pickguard, red (5623-CB).

CORVETTE/CVT 5135 2006–current
Double-cut solid, two humbuckers, cherry (5135).

CVT III 2012–13
Double-cut solid, three humbuckers, cherry (5103), black (5105).

DOUBLE CUTAWAY HOLLOW BODY first version 2010–12
Double-cut hollow, two humbuckers, black or brown (5122DC).

DOUBLE CUTAWAY HOLLOW BODY second version 2012–current
Double-cut hollow, two humbuckers, black, brown, red, white, or cherry (5422TDC), 12-string black (5422DC-12).

DOUBLE JET first version 2000–03
Double-cut semi-solid, bolt-on neck, two humbuckers, natural (2910), black (2921), silver sparkle (2922), silver sparkle with vibrato (2922T), red (2923).

DOUBLE JET second version 2004–current
Double-cut semi-solid, vibrato, two humbuckers, black (5245T), silver sparkle (5246T), gold sparkle (5248T), red (5441T), gold (5441T).

ELLIOT EASTON See under Elliot Easton.

G. LOVE See under G. Love.

HOLLOW BODY first version 2004–08
Single-cut hollow, two single-coils, black (5125), silver sparkle (5126), light blue (5127), gold sparkle (5128), red (5129).

HOLLOW BODY second version 2006–12
Single-cut hollow, two humbuckers, orange (5120), black (5120B), sunburst (5120SB).

HOLLOW BODY third version 2012–current
Single-cut hollow, two humbuckers, black, green, sunburst, or orange (all 5420T).

HOLLOW BODY CENTER-BLOCK 2014–current
Single-cut hollow centre-block, two humbuckers, cat's-eye soundholes, black, red, or green (5620T-CB); three humbuckers, black, red, or green (5622T-CB).

ELECTROMATIC

JET BARITONE 2004–current
Single-cut semi-solid, extended scale-length, bolt-on neck, two humbuckers, black sparkle (5265).

JET CLUB 2000–current
Single-cut semi-solid, bolt-on neck, two humbuckers, sunburst (2403), red (5421), black (5425), silver (5426).

JET DOUBLE NECK 2004–current
Baritone and 6-string necks on one single-cut body, silver sparkle (5566, 5265).

JET PRO 2000–03
Single-cut semi-solid, two humbuckers, figured sunburst (2504), same with vibrato (2554).

JET SPARKLE 2000–03
Single-cut semi-solid, bolt-on neck, two humbuckers, black (2610), black sparkle (2615), silver sparkle (2616), blue sparkle (2617), gold sparkle (2618), red sparkle (2619).

JET SPARKLE F/HOLE 2000–03
Single-cut semi-solid with one f-hole, bolt-on neck, two humbuckers, black (2620), black sparkle (2625), silver sparkle (2626), blue sparkle (2627), gold sparkle (2628), red sparkle (2629).

JET II 2000–03
Single-cut solid, two humbuckers, red sunburst (2305).

JUNIOR JET 2000–03
Single-cut solid, one single-coil, sunburst (2101).

JUNIOR JET / JUNIOR JET II 2004–10
Single-cut solid, one mini-humbucker (Junior Jet) or two mini-humbuckers (Junior Jet II), sunburst (5210, 5220), black (5215, 5225).

PATRICK VAUGHN STUMP See under Patrick Stump.

PRO JET 2004–current
Single-cut semi-solid, two humbuckers, black (5235, 5435), silver sparkle (5236, 5439), gold sparkle (5238, 5438), with vibrato add T.

SPECIAL JET first version 2004–07
Single-cut semi-solid, two single-coils, sunburst (5250), black (5255), dark red (5259).

SPECIAL JET second version 2012–13
Single-cut solid, bolt-on neck, two humbuckers, sunburst (5410), black (5415).

TIM ARMSTRONG See under Tim Armstrong.

5655T-CB 2104–current
Double-cut semi-solid centre-block, two humbuckers, black, red, or green (5655T-CB).

■ ELLIOT EASTON

ELLIOT EASTON 6128 2000–05
- Bound ebony fingerboard, thumbnail markers; 22 frets; truss-rod adjuster at headstock; Elliot Easton signature on truss-rod cover; longer scale length.
- Semi-solid single-cutaway bound body; green (6128TEE), red (6128TREE), black (6128TBEE).
- Two humbuckers.
- Three knobs (volume) and two selectors (tone, pickups).
- Elliot Easton signature on pickguard.
- Six-saddle bridge, separate vibrato tailpiece.
- Gold-plated hardware.

ELECTROMATIC ELLIOT EASTON 5570 2004–05
- Bound rosewood fingerboard, thumbnail markers; 22 frets; truss-rod adjuster at headstock; Elliot Easton on truss-rod cover; small Electromatic logo on headstock.
- Semi-solid single-cutaway bound body; green (5570).
- Two humbuckers.
- Three knobs (volume) and one selector (pickups).
- Six-saddle bridge, separate vibrato tailpiece.
* *SYNCHROMATIC ELLIOT EASTON 1570 "Synchromatic" on headstock, 2002–03.*

■ G. LOVE

ELECTROMATIC G. LOVE CORVETTE 5135 2008–10
- Unbound rosewood fingerboard, dot markers; 21 frets; truss-rod adjuster at headstock with "G" logo on cover.
- Solid double-cutaway body; green with white stripe (5135).
- Two humbuckers.
- Three controls (two volume, one tone) and one selector (pickups) on pickguard.
- Six-saddle bridge, separate vibrato tailpiece.

■ GEORGE HARRISON

GEORGE HARRISON TRIBUTE DUO JET 6128T-GH 2011–current
- Bound rosewood fingerboard, hump-top block markers; 22 frets; truss-rod adjuster at headstock; custom neck shape.
- Semi-solid single-cutaway bound body; relic black (6128T-GH).
- Two single-coils.
- Four knobs (three volume, one tone) and one selector (pickups).
- Single-saddle bridge, separate vibrato tailpiece.
- Relic chrome-plated hardware.
* *Custom Shop relic'd reproduction of Harrison's '57 Duo Jet, with package of repro memorabilia, in a limited edition of 62. Serial-numbered 21179 XXX, where XXX is the edition number, from 048 to 110.*
* *See also DUO JET CUSTOM EDITION 6128TSP under Duo Jet.*

GEORGE HARRISON SIGNATURE DUO JET 6128T-GH 2011–current
- Bound rosewood fingerboard, hump-top block markers; 22 frets; truss-rod adjuster at headstock; signature on truss-rod cover.
- Semi-solid single-cutaway bound body; black (6128T-GH).
- Two single-coils.
- Four knobs (three volume, one tone) and one selector (pickups).
- Single-saddle bridge, separate vibrato tailpiece.
* *See also DUO JET CUSTOM EDITION 6128TSP under Duo Jet.*

■ **GOLD DUKE** See CORVETTE solidbody third version under Corvette.

■ **HI ROLLER** See SUPER AXE entry under Super Axe.

■ **HISTORIC SERIES** See under Streamliner single-cutaway; Synchromatic.

■ **HOLLOW BODY** See under 6120.

■ **HOT ROD** See under Brian Setzer.

■ **JET CLUB** See under Electromatic: Later and Synchromatic.

■ JET FIRE BIRD
ORIGINALS

JET FIRE BIRD first version 1955–61
- Bound rosewood fingerboard (ebony from c.1959), block markers (hump-top block from c.1957; thumbnail from c.1959); 22 frets (plus zero fret from c.1960); truss-rod adjuster at headstock.
- Semi-solid single-cutaway bound body (13.5in wide); red (6131).
- Two single-coils (two humbuckers from c.1958).
- Four knobs (three volume, one tone) and one selector (pickups) to c.1959; three knobs (volume) and two selectors (tone, pickups) from c.1959.
- Six-saddle bridge, separate G-cutout flat tailpiece or vibrato tailpiece.
* Some examples with 21 frets.

JET FIRE BIRD second version 1961–69
- Bound rosewood fingerboard, thumbnail markers; 22 frets plus zero fret; truss-rod adjuster at headstock.
- Semi-solid double-cutaway bound body; red (6131).
- Two humbuckers.
- Three knobs (volume) and two selectors (tone, pickups) to c.1962; three knobs (volume) and three selectors (standby, tone, pickups) c.1962–68; four knobs (three volume, one treble-boost) and three selectors (standby, tone, pickups) from c.1968.
- Six-saddle bridge, separate vibrato tailpiece.
- Gold-plated hardware from c.1962.
* Some examples with G-cutout flat tailpiece.
* Some examples with 21 frets.

REISSUES

JET FIREBIRD 6131 1989–2003
- Bound rosewood fingerboard, hump-top block markers; 22 frets; truss-rod adjuster at headstock; horseshoe on headstock.
- Semi-solid single-cutaway bound body; red (6131).
- Two humbuckers.
- Four knobs (three volume, one tone) and one selector (pickups).
- Six-saddle bridge, separate G-cutout flat tailpiece.

JET FIREBIRD 6131/6131T 2003–09
- Bound ebony fingerboard, thumbnail markers; 22 frets; truss-rod adjuster at headstock.
- Semi-solid single-cutaway bound body; silver sparkle (6131/6131T).
- Two humbuckers.
- Three knobs (volume) and two selectors (tone, pickups).
- Six-saddle bridge, separate G-cutout flat tailpiece (6131) or vibrato tailpiece (6131T).

JET FIREBIRD 6131TDS 2005–09
- Bound rosewood fingerboard, aged hump-top block markers; 22 frets; truss-rod adjuster at headstock.
- Semi-solid single-cutaway aged-bound body; red (6131TDS).
- Two single-coils.
- Four knobs (three volume, one tone) and one selector (pickups).
- Six-saddle bridge, separate vibrato tailpiece.

OTHERS

POWER JET FIREBIRD 6131-TVP/6131T-TVP 2006–current
- Bound ebony fingerboard, thumbnail markers; 22 frets; truss-rod adjuster at headstock.
- Semi-solid single-cutaway bound body; red (6131-TVP/6131T-TVP).
- Two humbuckers.
- Three knobs (volume) and two selectors (tone, pickups).
- Six-saddle bridge, separate G-cutout flat tailpiece (6131-TVP), separate vibrato tailpiece (6131T-TVP).

■ **JET PRO**
See under Electromatic: Later and Synchromatic.

■ **JUNIOR JET**
See under Electromatic: Later and Synchromatic.

■ KEITH SCOTT

NASHVILLE KEITH SCOTT 6120KS 1999–2012
- Bound ebony fingerboard, hump-top block markers; 22 frets; truss-rod adjuster at headstock; Keith Scott signature on truss-rod cover; horseshoe on headstock.
- Hollow single-cutaway bound body with f-holes; gold (6120KS).
- Two single-coils.
- Four knobs (three volume, one tone) and one selector (pickups).
- Keith Scott signature and model name on pickguard.
- Six-saddle bridge, separate vibrato tailpiece.
- Gold-plated hardware.

■ MALCOLM YOUNG

MALCOLM YOUNG I 6131 1996–2011
- Bound ebony or rosewood fingerboard, thumbnail markers; 22 frets; truss-rod adjuster at headstock; Malcolm Young signature on truss-rod cover.
- Semi-solid double-cutaway bound body; natural (6131SMY), red (6131SMYR), flame maple (6131SMYF).
- One humbucker.
- Two knobs (one volume, one tone).
- No pickguard.
- Six-saddle wrapover bridge/tailpiece.

MALCOLM YOUNG II 6131 1996–2011
Similar to MALCOLM YOUNG I 6131, except:

MONKEES

- Natural (6131MY), red (6131MYR), flame maple (6131MYF).
- Two humbuckers.
- Three knobs (volume) and two selectors (tone, pickups).

■ MONKEES

MONKEES 6123 1966–67
- Bound rosewood fingerboard, left and right thumbnail markers; 22 frets plus zero fret; truss-rod adjuster at headstock; model nameplate on headstock; Monkees logo on truss-rod cover.
- Hollow double-cutaway bound body with f-holes; red (6123).
- Two humbuckers.
- Three knobs (volume) and three selectors (standby, tone, pickups).
- Monkees logo on pickguard.
- Single-saddle bridge, separate vibrato tailpiece.

■ *NASHVILLE* See under Brian Setzer; Country Gentleman/Country Classic; Keith Scott; Solid Body; 6120.

■ NEW JET

NEW JET 6114 2002–03
- Bound ebony fingerboard, hump-top block markers; 22 frets; truss-rod adjuster at headstock.
- Semi-solid single-cutaway bound body; flame maple front in black (6114B), natural (6114A), or red (6114R).
- Two humbuckers.
- Four controls (three volume, one tone) and one selector (pickups).
- Six-saddle bridge, separate G-cutout flat tailpiece.

■ PANTHER

PANTHER 6137TCB 2013–current
- Bound ebony fingerboard, thumbnail markers; 22 frets; truss-rod adjuster at headstock.
- Hollow double-cutaway bound with f-holes and internal centre-block; white, red, or black.
- Two humbuckers.
- Four knobs (three volume, one tone) and one selector (pickups); jack on body front.
- Panther logo on pickguard.
- Six-saddle bridge, separate vibrato tailpiece.
* White version also known as White Panther; black version as Black Panther.

■ PATRICK STUMP

ELECTROMATIC PATRICK VAUGHN STUMP SIGNATURE "STUMP-O-MATIC" 5135CVT-PS 2010–current
- Unbound rosewood fingerboard, dot markers; 21 frets; truss-rod adjuster at headstock with vertical Electromatic logo on headstock.
- Small bodied twin-offset-horned solid, no binding; silver with black stripes (to 2012); white with silver stripes (from 2013).
- Three humbuckers.
- Three knobs (volume, tone, series/parallel) and two selectors (pickups, kill switch) on pickguard.

- Six-saddle bridge with through-body stringing.

■ *POWER JET*
See under Duo Jet.

■ *PRINCE*
See CORVETTE solidbody third version under Corvette.

■ PRINCESS

PRINCESS 1962–63
- Unbound rosewood fingerboard, dot markers; 21 frets; truss-rod adjuster at headstock.
- Solid double-cutaway bevelled-edge body; pad on body back; blue, pink, or white (6106).
- One single-coil at bridge.
- Two knobs (volume, tone) on pickguard.
- Model name on coloured pickguard.
- Bar bridge; separate trapeze tailpiece; clip-on vibrato lever.
* Some examples with no model name on pickguard.

■ *PRO JET* See under Electromatic: Later.

■ *PROJECT-O-SONIC* See COUNTRY CLUB STEREO under Country Club; and WHITE FALCON STEREO entries under White Falcon Stereo.

■ RALLY

RALLY 1967–68
- Bound rosewood fingerboard, thumbnail markers with dot markers from 15th fret; 22 frets plus zero fret; truss-rod adjuster at headstock; diagonal stripes on truss-rod cover.
- Hollow double-cutaway bound body with f-holes; green (6104), yellow/brown (6105).
- Two single-coils.
- Four knobs (three volume, tone) and three selectors (standby, pickups, treble boost); active circuit.
- Diagonal stripes on pickguard.
- Single-saddle bridge, separate vibrato tailpiece.
* Some examples with six-saddle bridge.
* See also SAL FEBBRAIO.

■ RAMBLER

RAMBLER first version 1957–59
- Unbound rosewood fingerboard, dot markers; 20 frets; truss-rod adjuster at headstock.
- Hollow single-pointed-cutaway bound body (13in wide) with f-holes; cream/black (6115).
- One single-coil at neck.
- Two knobs (volume, tone).
- Single-saddle wooden bridge, separate G-cutout flat tailpiece.
* Some examples in cream/green (6115).

RAMBLER second version 1959–62
Similar to first version, except:
- Hollow single-rounded-cutaway bound body with f-holes.

ROUND UP

■ RANCHER

RANCHER 6022CV 1992–99
- Bound ebony fingerboard, block markers; 20 frets; truss-rod adjuster at headstock; steer head on headstock.
- Hollow single-cutaway bound flat-top body with triangular soundhole; orange (6022CV).
- One single-coil at neck.
- Two knobs (volume, tone) mounted on body side.
- Six-saddle bridge, separate vibrato tailpiece.

■ REVEREND HORTON HEAT

REVEREND HORTON HEAT G6120RHH
2005–current
- Aged bound ebony fingerboard, Western-motif block markers; 22 frets plus zero fret; truss-rod adjuster at headstock.
- Hollow single-cutaway bound body with f-holes; G-brand on body front; orange (6120RHH).
- Two humbuckers.
- Three knobs (volume) and two selectors (tone, pickups).
- Clear plastic pickguard.
- Six-saddle bridge, separate vibrato tailpiece.

■ ROC

ROC JET first version 1969–72
- Bound ebony fingerboard, thumbnail markers; 22 frets plus zero fret; truss-rod adjuster at headstock; model nameplate on headstock.
- Semi-solid single-cutaway bound body; orange (6127), black (6130).
- Two humbuckers.
- Five knobs (three volume, two tone) and one selector (pickups).
- Six-saddle bridge, separate G-cutout flat tailpiece.

ROC JET second version 1972–79
Similar to ROC JET first version, except:
- Bound rosewood fingerboard from c.1977; truss-rod adjuster at neck heel; no model nameplate on headstock.
- Orange (7611), black (7610), red (7611, 7612), brown (7613, 7619).
- Six-saddle wrapover bridge/tailpiece from c.1977.

ROC II 1973–74
- Bound ebony fingerboard, thumbnail markers; 22 frets plus zero fret; truss-rod adjuster at neck heel; locking bar on nut.
- Solid single-cutaway bound body; dark red (7621).
- Two humbuckers.
- Four knobs (volume, tone, treble, "Supersound" blend) and one selector (pickups) on elliptical plate; active circuit.
- Six-saddle wrapover bridge/tailpiece.

COUNTRY ROC 1973–79
- Bound ebony fingerboard, western-motif block markers; 22 frets plus zero fret; truss-rod adjuster at neck heel; horseshoe on headstock.
- Semi-solid single-cutaway bound body; G-brand on front; studded leather around sides; orange (7620).
- Two humbuckers.
- Five knobs (three volume, two tone) and one selector (pickups).
- Six-saddle bridge, separate G-cutout tailpiece with western-style belt buckle.
- Gold-plated hardware.

ROC I 1976–77
- Rosewood fingerboard, small block markers; 22 frets; truss-rod adjuster at headstock.
- Solid single-cutaway bound body; brown (7635).
- Two humbuckers.
- Four knobs (two volume, two tone) and one selector (pickups).
- Clear plastic pickguard.
- Six-saddle bridge/tailpiece.

SUPER ROC two versions 1976–77
- Bound ebony fingerboard, small block markers; 22 frets plus zero fret; truss-rod adjuster at neck heel.
- Solid single-cutaway bound body; black (7640).
- Two humbuckers.
- Version 1: Three knobs (one volume, two tone) and three selectors (pickups, treble boost, distortion) on elliptical plate.
 Version 2: Four knobs (one volume, two pickup tone, one distortion blend) and two selectors (pickups, distortion).
- Six-saddle wrapover bridge/tailpiece.

■ RONNY LEE

RONNY LEE 1962–63
- Bound rosewood fingerboard, left and right thumbnail markers; 22 frets plus zero fret; truss-rod adjuster at headstock; model nameplate on headstock.
- Hollow sealed double-cutaway bound body with fake f-holes; sunburst or brown.
- Two single-coils.
- Three knobs (all volume) and three selectors (standby, tone, pickups).
- Six-saddle bridge, separate vibrato tailpiece.
* *Some examples with single-saddle bridge.*
* *Not an artist signature model; made for New York teacher Ronny Lee.*

■ ROUND UP

ORIGINAL

ROUND UP 1954–58
- Bound rosewood fingerboard, engraved block markers (hump-top from c.1955); 22 frets; truss-rod adjuster at headstock; steer head on headstock (horseshoe from c.1957).
- Semi-solid single-cutaway bound body (13.5in wide); G-brand on front (no G-brand from c.1957); studded leather around sides; orange (6130).
- Two single-coils.
- Four knobs (three volume, one tone) and one selector (pickups).
- Steer head logo on pickguard.
- Six-saddle bridge, separate G-cutout flat tailpiece with western-style belt buckle.
- Gold-plated hardware.

THE GRETSCH ELECTRIC GUITAR BOOK

ROUND UP

* *Some c.1958 examples reported with thumbnail markers, humbuckers, three knobs and two selectors.*
* *Colours vary from orange through red and walnut.*

REISSUES

ROUND UP 6121 1989–2003
- Bound rosewood fingerboard, Western motif block markers; 22 frets; truss-rod adjuster at headstock; horseshoe on headstock.
- Semi-solid single-cutaway bound body; G-logo on front; orange (6121).
- Two humbuckers.
- Four knobs (three volume, one tone) and one selector (pickups).
- Six-saddle bridge, separate vibrato tailpiece.
- Gold-plated hardware.

ROUND UP 6121W 2003–05
Similar to ROUND UP 6121, except:
- Steer head on headstock.
- G-brand on body front.
- Two single-coils.
- Bar bridge.
- Gold-plated hardware (except vibrato tailpiece).

ROUND UP 6130 2006
- Bound rosewood fingerboard, engraved block markers; 22 frets; truss-rod adjuster at headstock; steer head on headstock.
- Semi-solid single-cutaway bound body; G-brand on front; studded leather around sides; orange (6130).
- Two single-coils.
- Four knobs (three volume, one tone) and one selector (pickups).
- Six-saddle bridge, separate vibrato tailpiece.
- Gold-plated hardware.

KNOTTY PINE WESTERN ROUNDUP 6130KPW 2009–10
- Bound rosewood fingerboard, engraved block markers; 22 frets; truss-rod adjuster at headstock; steer head on headstock.
- Semi-solid single-cutaway bound body; G-brand on front; studded leather around sides; figured orange (6130KPW).
- Two single-coils.
- Four knobs (three volume, one tone) and one selector (pickups).
- Steer head logo on pickguard.
- Six-saddle bridge, separate G-cutout flat tailpiece with western-style belt buckle.
- Gold-plated hardware.

ROUND UP 6130CS NOS 2012–current
- Bound rosewood fingerboard, engraved block markers; 22 frets; truss-rod adjuster at headstock; steer head on headstock.
- Semi-solid single-cutaway bound body; G-brand on front; studded leather around sides; figured orange (6130).
- Two single-coils.
- Four knobs (three volume, one tone) and one selector (pickups).
- Six-saddle bridge, separate G-cutout flat tailpiece with western-style belt buckle.
- Gold-plated hardware.
* *Custom Shop production with NOS ageing.*
* *ROUND UP 6130CS RELIC As 6130CS NOS but Relic ageing, 2012–current.*

■ SAL FEBBRAIO

SAL FEBBRAIO c.1967
- Bound rosewood fingerboard, thumbnail markers with dot markers from 15th fret; 22 frets plus zero fret; truss-rod adjuster at headstock.
- Hollow double-cutaway bound body with cat's-eye soundholes; sunburst (6105/6116).
- Two single-coils.
- Four knobs (three volume, tone) and three selectors (standby, pickups, treble boost); active circuit.
- Six-saddle bridge, separate vibrato tailpiece.
* *Not an artist signature model; version of Rally with cat's-eye soundholes made for Sal Febbraio school, New York.*

■ SAL SALVADOR

SAL SALVADOR 6199 1959–66
- Bound ebony fingerboard, thumbnail markers (block from c.1964); 21 frets (plus zero fret from c.1960); truss-rod adjuster at headstock.
- Hollow single-cutaway body (17in wide) with f-holes; sunburst (6199).
- One humbucker (one single-coil from c.1962) attached to pickguard (mounted on body from c.1964).
- Two knobs (volume, tone) mounted on pickguard (mounted on body from c.1964).
- Single-saddle wooden bridge, separate G-cutout flat tailpiece.
- Gold-plated hardware.
* *Previously known as CONVERTIBLE; see under Convertible.*

■ SAM GOODY

SAM GOODY 1967
- Bound rosewood fingerboard, thumbnail markers with dot markers from 15th fret; 22 frets plus zero fret; truss-rod adjuster at headstock; model nameplate on headstock.
- Hollow double-cutaway bound body with G-shape soundholes; sunburst (6106).
- Two single-coils.
- Three knobs (volume) and three selectors (standby, tone, pickups).
- Single-saddle bridge, separate vibrato tailpiece.
* *Not a signature model: made for Sam Goody music stores. Also known as 7-11 Songbird.*

■ **SILVER DUKE** See CORVETTE solidbody third version under Corvette.

■ **SILVER FALCON** See various entries under White Falcon.

■ SILVER JET

ORIGINALS

SILVER JET first version 1954–61
- Bound rosewood fingerboard (ebony from c.1958), block markers (hump-top block from c.1957, thumbnail from c.1958);

SOLID BODY

- 22 frets (plus zero fret from c.1960); truss-rod adjuster at headstock.
- Semi-solid single-cutaway bound body (13.5in wide); silver sparkle (6129).
- Two single-coils (two humbuckers from c.1959).
- Four knobs (three volume, one tone) and one selector (pickups) to c.1959; three knobs (volume) and two selectors (tone, pickups) from c.1959.
- Six-saddle bridge, separate G-cutout flat tailpiece or vibrato tailpiece.

SILVER JET second version 1961–63
- Bound rosewood fingerboard, thumbnail markers; 22 frets plus zero fret; truss-rod adjuster at headstock.
- Semi-solid double-cutaway bound body; silver sparkle (6129).
- Two humbuckers.
- Three knobs (volume) and two selectors (tone, pickups) to c.1962; three knobs (volume) and three selectors (standby, tone, pickups) c.1962–63.
- Six-saddle bridge, separate vibrato tailpiece.
- Gold-plated hardware from c.1962.
* Colour-sparkle options from c.1962.
* Known as DUO JET (second version) with colour-sparkle finish from c.1963; see under Duo Jet.

REISSUES

SILVER JET 6129/6129T first version 1989–2003
- Bound rosewood fingerboard, hump-top block markers; 22 frets; truss-rod adjuster at headstock; horseshoe on headstock.
- Semi-solid single-cutaway bound body; silver sparkle (6129/6129T).
- Two humbuckers.
- Four knobs (three volume, one tone) and one selector (pickups).
- Six-saddle bridge, separate G-cutout flat tailpiece (6129) or vibrato tailpiece (6129T).
* SPARKLE JET 6129T colour-sparkle finishes (black, blue, champagne, gold, green, or red), 1995–current.

SILVER JET 6129/6129T second version 2003–current
- Bound ebony fingerboard, thumbnail markers; 22 frets; truss-rod adjuster at headstock.
- Semi-solid single-cutaway bound body; silver sparkle (6129/6129T).
- Two humbuckers.
- Three knobs (volume) and two selectors (tone, pickups).
- Coloured plastic pickguard.
- Six-saddle bridge, separate G-cutout flat tailpiece (6129) or vibrato tailpiece (6129T).
* 6129T known as SPARKLE JET (with silver finish) from 2013.

SILVER JET 6129-1957/6129T-1957 1994–current
- Bound rosewood fingerboard, hump-top block markers; 22 frets; truss-rod adjuster at headstock.
- Semi-solid single-cutaway bound body; silver sparkle (6129-1957/6129T-1957).
- Two single-coils.
- Four knobs (three volume, one tone) and one selector (pickups).
- Six-saddle bridge, separate G-cutout flat tailpiece (6129-1957) or vibrato tailpiece (6129T-1957).
* SPARKLE JET colour-sparkle finishes, 6129AU-1957 (gold), 6129G-1957 (green), 1996–2002.

SILVER JET 6129T-1962 1996–2009
- Bound ebony fingerboard, thumbnail markers, 22 frets plus zero fret; truss-rod adjuster at headstock.
- Semi-solid double-cutaway bound body; silver sparkle (6129T-62).
- Two humbuckers.
- Three knobs (volume) and two selectors (tone, pickups).
- Six-saddle bridge, separate vibrato tailpiece.
* SPARKLE JET 6129TC-1962 champagne colour-sparkle finish, 2003.

BILLY ZOOM See under Billy Zoom.

■ *SKINNY CHET* See DELUXE CHET entry under Deluxe Chet.

■ SOLID BODY
ORIGINALS

CHET ATKINS SOLID BODY first version 1955–61
- Bound rosewood fingerboard (ebony from c.1958), engraved block markers (plain block from c.1956; hump-top block from c.1957; thumbnail from c.1958); 22 frets (plus zero fret from c.1959); truss-rod adjuster at headstock; steer head on headstock (horseshoe from c.1957).
- Semi-solid single-cutaway bound body (13.5in wide); G-brand on front (no G-brand from c.1957); studded leather around sides (c.1955–56); orange (6121).
- Two single-coils (two humbuckers from c.1958).
- Four knobs (three volume, one tone) and one selector (pickups) to c.1958; three knobs (volume) and two selectors (tone, pickups) from c.1958.
- Chet Atkins logo on pickguard.
- Single-saddle bridge, separate vibrato tailpiece.
- Gold-plated hardware.

CHET ATKINS SOLID BODY second version 1962
- Bound ebony fingerboard, thumbnail markers; 22 frets plus zero fret; truss-rod adjuster at headstock; horseshoe on headstock.
- Semi-solid double-cutaway bound body; orange (6121).
- Two humbuckers.
- Three knobs (volume) and three selectors (standby, tone, pickups).
- Chet Atkins logo on pickguard.
- Single-saddle bridge, separate vibrato tailpiece.
- Gold-plated hardware.

REISSUES

ROUND UP 6121 and 6121W See under Round Up section.

NASHVILLE SOLID BODY 6121 2005–06
- Bound ebony fingerboard, thumbnail markers; 22 frets plus zero fret; truss-rod adjuster at headstock; horseshoe on headstock.
- Semi-solid single-cutaway bound body; orange (6121).
- Two humbuckers.

SOLID BODY

- Three knobs (volume) and two selectors (tone, pickups).
- Nashville logo on pickguard.
- Single-saddle bridge, separate vibrato tailpiece.

CHET ATKINS SOLID BODY 6121/6121-1959
2007–current
- Bound ebony fingerboard, thumbnail markers; 22 frets plus zero fret; truss-rod adjuster at headstock; horseshoe on headstock.
- Semi-solid single-cutaway bound body; orange (6121).
- Two humbuckers.
- Three knobs (volume) and two selectors (tone, pickups).
- Chet Atkins name on pickguard.
- Single-saddle bridge, separate vibrato tailpiece.
* Known as CHET ATKINS SOLID BODY 6121-1959, 2008–current.
* CHET ATKINS SOLID BODY 6121-1955 with engraved block markers, G-brand on body front, studded leather around sides, two single-coils; four controls & one selector, 2007–current.

■ **SONGBIRD** See Sam Goody.

■ **SOUTHERN BELLE** See CHET ATKINS COUNTRY GENTLEMAN double-cutaway second version under Country Gentleman/Country Classic.

■ **SPARKLE JET** See under Silver Jet; Synchromatic.

■ **SPECIAL JET** See under Electromatic: Later.

■ SPECTRA SONIC

SPECTRA SONIC LEAD 6143 2002–07
- Unbound padouk fingerboard, dot markers, 22 frets; truss-rod adjuster at headstock; "Spectra Sonic" on truss-rod cover.
- Semi-solid single-cutaway body (bound from c.2005); black (6143).
- Two humbuckers.
- Two controls (one volume, one tone) and one selector (pickups).
- Six-saddle bridge, separate vibrato tailpiece.

SPECTRA SONIC C MELODY BARITONE 6144
2002–07
Similar to SPECTRA SONIC LEAD, except:
- Extended scale length neck; black (6144).

■ STEPHEN STILLS

WHITE FALCON STEPHEN STILLS 6136-1958
2000–current
- Bound ebony fingerboard, thumbnail markers; 22 frets; truss-rod adjuster at headstock; horizontal Gretsch logo on headstock; Stephen Stills signature on fingerboard.
- Hollow single-cutaway bound body with f-holes; aged white (6136-1958).
- Two humbuckers.
- Three knobs (volume) and two selectors (tone, pickups).
- No pickguard.
- Six-saddle bridge, separate vibrato tailpiece.
- Gold-plated hardware.

■ STREAMLINER: SINGLE-CUT
For double-cutaway Streamliners, see next section.

STREAMLINER 1954–58
- Bound rosewood fingerboard, block markers (hump-top block markers from c.1955; thumbnail markers from c.1958); 21 frets; truss-rod adjuster at headstock; "Electromatic" on headstock until c.1957.
- Hollow single-cutaway bound body (15.5in wide) with f-holes; sunburst (6190), gold (6189), yellow/brown (6189), natural (6191).
- One single-coil at neck (one humbucker from c.1958).
- Two knobs (volume, tone) to c.1957; one knob (volume) and one selector (tone) from c.1958.
- Six-saddle bridge, separate G-cutout flat tailpiece.
* Previously known as ELECTROMATIC; see under Electromatic: Early.

HISTORIC SERIES STREAMLINER 1999–2003
- Bound rosewood fingerboard, thumbnail markers; 22 frets; truss-rod adjuster at headstock; "Historic Series" on truss-rod cover; arrow-through-G on headstock.
- Hollow single-cutaway bound body with cat's-eye soundholes; red (3150), black (3151).
- Two single-coils.
- Three knobs (two volume, one tone) and one selector (pickups).
- Six-saddle bridge, separate G-cutout flat tailpiece.
* Also with separate vibrato tailpiece, gold-plated hardware; red (3155), white (3156).

■ STREAMLINER: DOUBLE-CUT
For single-cutaway Streamliners, see previous section.

STREAMLINER first version 1967–72
- Bound rosewood fingerboard, thumbnail markers with dot markers from 15th fret; 22 frets plus zero fret; truss-rod adjuster at headstock; model nameplate on headstock.
- Hollow double-cutaway bound body with f-holes; sunburst (6102), red (6103).
- Two humbuckers.
- Three knobs (volume) and three selectors (standby, tone, pickups).
- Six-saddle bridge, separate G-cutout flat tailpiece.

STREAMLINER second version 1972–75
Similar to STREAMLINER first version, except:
- All thumbnail markers; truss-rod adjuster at neck heel; no model nameplate on headstock.
- Sunburst (7565), red (7566).

STREAMLINER II 1973–75
Similar to STREAMLINER first version, except:
- All thumbnail markers; truss-rod adjuster at neck heel; no model nameplate on headstock.
- Red (7667).
- Four knobs (volume, tone, treble, "Supersound" blend) and one selector (pickups) on elliptical metal plate; active circuit.
- No pickguard.

■ **STUMP-O-MATIC** See under Patrick Stump.

TENNESSEAN

■ SUPER AXE

SUPER AXE 1977–81
- Bound ebony fingerboard, small block markers; 22 frets plus zero fret; truss-rod adjuster at neck heel.
- Solid single-cutaway bound body with angled-in upper bout; red (7680), dark grey or black (7681), sunburst (7682).
- Two humbuckers.
- Five knobs (volume, tone, sustain, phaser blend, phaser rate), two selectors (phaser on/off, compressor on/off) and jack, all on elliptical plate; one selector (pickups) on body; active circuit.
- Six-saddle wrapover bridge/tailpiece, or six-saddle bridge with separate vibrato tailpiece.
* Known briefly as Hi Roller.

■ SUPER CHET

SUPER CHET 1972–80
- Bound ebony fingerboard, floral-style markers; 22 frets plus zero fret; truss-rod adjuster at neck heel; floral-style inlay on headstock.
- Hollow single-cutaway bound body with angled-in upper bout and f-holes; dark red (7690), dark brown (7691).
- Two humbuckers.
- Five knobs (three volume, two tone) all mounted along edge of pickguard and one selector (pickups).
- Model name on pickguard.
- Six-saddle bridge, separate frame-type tailpiece with floral-style insert (separate vibrato tailpiece option from c.1977).
- Gold-plated hardware.

■ SUPER GRETSCH

SUPER GRETSCH 7690 1998–2002
- Bound ebony fingerboard, floral-style markers, 22 frets; truss-rod adjuster at headstock; floral-style inlay on headstock.
- Hollow single-cutaway bound body with f-holes; sunburst (7690).
- Two humbuckers.
- Four knobs (three volume, one tone) and one selector (pickups).
- Six-saddle bridge, separate vibrato tailpiece.
- Gold-plated hardware.

■ *SUPER ROC* See under Roc.

■ SYNCHROMATIC
In alphanumerical order and in simplified format.

BO DIDDLEY See under Bo Diddley.

CUTAWAY 2010–current
Single-cut hollow with f-holes, one floating single-coil, black or natural (100CE).

DOUBLE JET 2000–03
Double-cut solid, two humbuckers, natural (1910), black (1921), silver sparkle (1922), red (1923).

ELLIOT EASTON See under Elliot Easton.

HISTORIC SERIES SYNCHROMATIC 1999–2003
Single-cut hollow, two single-coils, sunburst (3110).

HISTORIC SERIES SYNCHROMATIC JR 2001–03
Non-cutaway hollow, one single-coil, sunburst (3900, 3905), gold (3967).

HISTORIC SERIES THINLINE SYNCHROMATIC 1999–2003
Single-cut hollow, two single-coils, orange (3140), black (3141).

JET BARITONE 2002–03
Single-cut semi-solid, extended scale-length, bolt-on neck, two humbuckers, black sparkle (1255).

JET CLUB 2000–03
Single-cut semi-solid, bolt-on neck, two humbuckers, sunburst (1413).

JET PRO 2000–03
Single-cut semi-solid, two humbuckers, black (1511), silver sparkle (1512), sunburst (1514), sunburst with vibrato (1554).

JET II 2000–03
Single-cut solid, two mini-humbuckers, redburst (1315).

JUNIOR JET 2000–03
Single-cut solid, one mini-humbucker, sunburst (1121), black (1122), red (1125), blue (1126), orange (1127), purple (1128).

SPARKLE JET 2000–04
Single-cut semi-solid, bolt-on neck, two humbuckers, black sparkle (1615), black sparkle with vibrato (1615T), silver sparkle (1616), blue sparkle (1617), gold sparkle (1618), red sparkle (1619).

SPARKLE JET DOUBLE-NECK 2002–03
Baritone and 6-string necks on one single-cut body, silver sparkle (1566).

SPARKLE JET F/HOLE 2000–04
Single-cut semi-solid with one f-hole, bolt-on neck, two humbuckers, black sparkle (1625), silver sparkle (1626), silver sparkle with vibrato (1626T), blue sparkle (1627), gold sparkle (1628), red sparkle (1629).

400/6040 1992–2001
Single-cutaway hollow, one humbucker, sunburst (400CV), natural (400MCV), with separate harp-frame tailpiece (6040MC-SS).

■ TENNESSEAN / TENNESSEE ROSE

ORIGINALS

CHET ATKINS TENNESSEAN first version 1958–61
- Unbound ebony fingerboard, thumbnail markers; 22 frets plus zero fret (earliest examples without zero fret); truss-rod adjuster at headstock; brass nut.
- Hollow single-cutaway bound body (15.5in wide, 2.75in deep; 2.5in deep from c.1960) with real f-holes; dark red (6119).

TENNESSEAN

- One humbucker near bridge.
- One knob (volume) and one selector (tone).
- Chet Atkins logo on pickguard.
- Bar bridge, separate vibrato tailpiece.
* *Some examples with 21 frets.*

CHET ATKINS TENNESSEAN second version
1961–72
Similar to first version, except:
- Bound rosewood fingerboard; model nameplate on headstock (c.1967–71).
- Hollow sealed single-cutaway bound body with fake f-holes; dark red or dark brown (6119).
- Two single-coils.
- Three knobs (volume) and three selectors (standby, tone, pickups).
- Coloured plastic pickguard with model name.

CHET ATKINS TENNESSEAN third version 1972–80
Similar to second version, except:
- Truss-rod adjuster at neck heel; no model nameplate on headstock.
- Real f-holes; dark red (7655).
- Three knobs (volume) and two selectors (tone, pickups) from c.1978.
- Six-saddle bridge.

REISSUES

TENNESSEE ROSE 6119 1989–2006
- Bound rosewood fingerboard, thumbnail markers; 22 frets; truss-rod adjuster at headstock.
- Hollow single-cutaway bound body with real f-holes; dark red (6119).
- Two humbuckers.
- Four knobs (three volume, one tone) and one selector (pickups).
- Model name on pickguard.
- Six-saddle bridge, separate vibrato tailpiece.
* *Renamed in 2007; see CHET ATKINS TENNESSEE ROSE 6119 entry here.*

TENNESSEE ROSE 6119-1962FT 1993–2006
Similar to TENNESSEE ROSE 6119, except:
- 22 frets plus zero fret.
- Hollow sealed single-cutaway bound body with fake f-holes; brown (6119-1962).
- Three controls (volume) and three selectors (standby, tone, pickups).
- Bar bridge.
* *Renamed in 2007; see CHET ATKINS TENNESSEE ROSE 6119-1962FT entry here.*

TENNESSEE ROSE 6119-1962HT 1999–2006
Similar to TENNESSEE ROSE 6119-1962FT, except:
- Two single-coils.
* *Harrison-style, renamed in 2007; see CHET ATKINS TENNESSEE ROSE 6119-1962HT entry here.*

TENNESSEE SPECIAL 6119SP 2003–06
Similar to TENNESSEE ROSE 6119, except:
- Body 2.5in deep.
- Unbound ebony fingerboard; 22 frets plus zero fret.
- Dark red (6119SP).

- Two humbuckers.
- Three knobs (volume) and two selectors (tone, pickups).

CHET ATKINS TENNESSEE ROSE 6119
2007–current
- Bound rosewood fingerboard, thumbnail markers; 22 frets; truss-rod adjuster at headstock.
- Hollow single-cutaway bound body with real f-holes; dark red (6119).
- Two humbuckers.
- Four knobs (three volume, one tone) and one selector (pickups).
- Chet Atkins logo and model name on pickguard.
- Six-saddle bridge, separate vibrato tailpiece.

CHET ATKINS TENNESSEE ROSE 6119-1962FT
2007–current
Similar to CHET ATKINS TENNESSEE ROSE 6119 except:
- 22 frets plus zero fret.
- Hollow sealed single-cutaway bound body with fake f-holes; brown (6119-1962FT).
- Three controls (volume) and three selectors (standby, tone, pickups).
- Bar bridge from c.2007.

CHET ATKINS TENNESSEE ROSE 6119-1962HT
2007–current
Similar to CHET ATKINS TENNESSEE ROSE 6119-1962FT except:
- Two single-coils.
* *Harrison-style.*

CHET ATKINS TENNESSEE ROSE 6119-1959
2008–14
Similar to CHET ATKINS TENNESSEE ROSE 6119 except:
- Unbound ebony fingerboard; 22 frets plus zero fret.
- Body 2.5in deep.
- One humbucker.
- One knob (volume) and one selector (tone).

■ TIM ARMSTRONG

ELECTROMATIC TIM ARMSTRONG HOLLOW BODY 5191BK 2010–current
- Bound rosewood fingerboard, block markers; 21 frets; truss-rod adjuster at headstock; Vertical Electromatic logo on headstock.
- Hollow single-cutaway bound body with f-holes; black (5191BK), pink (5191MS).
- Two humbuckers.
- Five knobs (three volume, two tone) and one selector (pickups).
- No pickguard.
- Six-saddle bridge, separate harp-style tailpiece.
- Gold-plated hardware.
* *ELECTROMATIC TIM ARMSTRONG HOLLOW BODY 5191TMS with six-saddle bridge, separate vibrato tailpiece, pink, 2012–14.*

■ TK 300

TK 300 1977–81
- Bolt-on neck with unbound rosewood fingerboard, dot markers (no markers c.1977); 22 frets (plus zero fret 1977–78); truss-

rod adjuster at neck heel; six tuners-in-line headstock with long Gretsch logo.
- Solid double-cutaway body; red (7624), natural (7625).
- Two humbuckers.
- Two controls (volume, tone) and one selector (pickups), all on pickguard.
- Six-saddle wrapover bridge/tailpiece.

■ TRAVELING WILBURYS

TW (TRAVELING WILBURYS) 1989–90
TW-100 One single-coil, three-saddle bridge/tailpiece.
TW-100T Similar to TW-100, except six-saddle bridge/vibrato unit.
TW-200 Similar to TW-100, except two single-coils.
TW-300 One humbucker, six-saddle bridge/vibrato unit.
TW-500 Two single-coils, six-saddle bridge/tailpiece.
TW-600 Similar to TW-500, except six-saddle bridge/vibrato unit.

* *Inexpensive Korean-made solidbody models issued as a marketing tie-in with The Traveling Wilburys supergroup and featuring the Wilbury-alias autographs of members Bob Dylan, George Harrison, Jeff Lynne, Roy Orbison and Tom Petty. No Gretsch markings.*

■ TWIST

TWIST 1962–63
- Unbound rosewood fingerboard, dot markers; 21 frets; truss-rod adjuster at headstock or body.
- Solid double-cutaway bevelled-edge body; red (6109, 6110).
- One single-coil at bridge.
- Two knobs (volume, tone) on pickguard.
- Stripes on pickguard.
- Bar bridge; separate trapeze tailpiece and clip-on vibrato lever (6109) or separate vibrato tailpiece (6110).

* *Some examples in yellow.*

■ VAN EPS

VAN EPS seven-string first version 1968–72
- Bound ebony fingerboard, thumbnail markers; 21 frets plus zero fret; truss-rod adjuster at headstock; model nameplate on headstock; four and three tuners-per-side asymmetric headstock.
- Hollow single-cutaway bound body with f-holes; sunburst (6079), brown (6080).
- Two humbuckers.
- Three knobs (volume) and three selectors (standby, tone, pickups).
- Bar-frame Floating Sound unit plus single-saddle wooden bridge, separate G-cutout flat tailpiece.
- Gold-plated hardware.

* *Six-string version, sunburst (6081), brown (6082), 1968–72.*

VAN EPS seven-string second version 1972–78
Similar to first version, except:
- Truss-rod adjuster at neck heel; no model nameplate on headstock.
- Sunburst (7580), brown (7581).
- Bar-frame Floating Sound unit plus six-saddle bridge.

* *Some late examples with three knobs (volume) and two selectors; no 'Floating Sound' unit; single-saddle wooden bridge; chrome-plated hardware.*

■ VIKING

VIKING first version 1964–72
- Bound ebony fingerboard, thumbnail markers with offset dot markers from 15th fret; 21 frets plus zero fret; truss-rod adjuster at headstock; model nameplate on headstock.
- Hollow double-cutaway bound body with f-holes; pad on body back; sunburst (6187), natural (6188), green (6189).
- Two humbuckers.
- Three knobs (volume) and three selectors (standby, tone, pickups), plus one string-mute control.
- Model name on pickguard.
- Six-saddle bridge (bar-frame Floating Sound unit plus six-saddle bridge from c.1966), separate vibrato tailpiece; one string-mute.
- Gold-plated hardware.

* *Some early examples with Viking ship logo and model name on pickguard.*

VIKING second version 1972–75
Similar to first version, except:
- Truss-rod adjuster at neck heel; no model nameplate on headstock.
- No pad on body back; sunburst (7585), natural (7586).
- No string-mute control.
- Six-saddle bridge from c.1973; no string-mute.

VIKING third version 1975
Similar to second version, except:
- Flower-shape markers; 22 frets plus zero fret.
- Sunburst (7588).
- Five knobs (three volume, two tone) and one selector (pickups).
- No model name on pickguard.
- Six-saddle bridge, separate frame-style tailpiece.

■ WHITE FALCON
Mono models here; for stereo models see next section.

SINGLE-CUTAWAY ORIGINALS

WHITE FALCON single-cutaway first version 1955–60
- Bound ebony fingerboard, engraved hump-top block markers (thumbnail from c.1958); 21 frets (plus zero fret from c.1959); truss-rod adjuster at headstock; vertical Gretsch logo on headstock (horizontal logo from c.1958; model nameplate from c.1959).
- Hollow single-cutaway bound body (17in wide, 2.75in deep; 2.25in deep from c.1959) with f-holes; pad on body back from c.1960; white (6136).
- Two single-coils (two humbuckers from 1958).
- Four knobs (three volume, one tone) and one selector (pickups) to c.1958; three knobs (volume) and two selectors (tone, pickups) c.1958–59; three knobs (volume) and three selectors (standby, tone, pickups), plus two string-mute controls c.1960.
- Falcon logo on pickguard.
- Six-saddle bridge, separate G-logo tubular frame-type tailpiece; two string-mutes from 1960.

WHITE FALCON

- Gold-plated hardware.
* Some examples with 22 frets; some in black; some with optional separate vibrato tailpiece.
* Replaced by double-cutaway version: see later entry here.

WHITE FALCON single-cutaway second version 1975–80
- Bound ebony fingerboard, block markers; 21 frets plus zero fret; truss-rod adjuster at neck heel.
- Hollow single-cutaway bound body with f-holes; white (7593).
- Two humbuckers.
- Three knobs (volume) and two selectors (tone, pickups).
- Falcon logo on pickguard.
- Six-saddle bridge, separate vibrato tailpiece.
- Gold-plated hardware.
* Some examples with separate frame-type tailpiece.
* "Special order" from 1979.

SINGLE-CUTAWAY REISSUES

WHITE FALCON 6136 1989–2006
- Bound ebony fingerboard, hump-top block markers; 22 frets; truss-rod adjuster at headstock; vertical Gretsch logo on headstock.
- Hollow single-cutaway bound body with f-holes; white (6136).
- Two humbuckers.
- Four knobs (three volume, one tone) and one selector (pickups) to c.2002; three knobs (volume) and two selectors (tone, pickups) from c.2003.
- Falcon logo on pickguard.
- Six-saddle bridge, separate G-logo tubular frame-type tailpiece.
- Gold-plated hardware.
* Some early examples with block markers, horizontal Gretsch logo on headstock.
* BLACK FALCON 6136BK black, 1992–98, 2003–05.
* SILVER FALCON 6136SL black, chrome-plated hardware, 1995–2006.

WHITE FALCON 7593 1989–2012
- Bound ebony fingerboard, block markers; 22 frets; truss-rod adjuster at headstock; horizontal Gretsch logo on headstock.
- Hollow single-cutaway bound body with f-holes; white (7593).
- Two humbuckers.
- Three knobs (two volume, one tone) and one selector (pickups) to c.1997; four knobs (three volume, one tone) and one selector (pickups) c.1997–2002; three knobs (volume) and two selectors (tone, pickups) from c.2003.
- Falcon logo on pickguard.
- Six-saddle bridge, separate vibrato tailpiece.
- Gold-plated hardware.
* Also known as White Falcon I.
* BLACK FALCON 7593BK black, 1992–98, 2003–04.

WHITE FALCON 1955 CUSTOM 6136-1955 1995–99
"Custom USA" reissue based on 1955-period original, single-coils, hump-top markers, but 22 frets. No other information available.

WHITE FALCON 6136T 2004–current
- Bound ebony fingerboard, hump-top block markers (thumbnail from c.2006); 22 frets; truss-rod adjuster at headstock; vertical Gretsch logo on headstock (horizontal from c.2006).
- Hollow single-cutaway bound body with f-holes; white (6136T).
- Two humbuckers.
- Three knobs (volume) and two selectors (tone, pickups).
- Falcon logo on pickguard.
- Six-saddle bridge, separate vibrato tailpiece.
- Gold-plated hardware.
* BLACK FALCON 6136TBK black, 2004–current.
* SILVER FALCON 6136TSL black, chrome-plated hardware, 2004–current.
* WHITE FALCON 6136TLTV lacquer finish, 2008–current.
* WHITE FALCON STEPHEN STILLS 6136-1958 See under Stephen Stills.

WHITE FALCON 6136DS 2006–current
- Bound ebony fingerboard, hump-top block markers; 22 frets; truss-rod adjuster at headstock; vertical Gretsch logo on headstock.
- Hollow single-cutaway bound body with f-holes; white (6136DS).
- Two single-coils.
- Four knobs (three volume, one tone) and one selector (pickups).
- Falcon logo on pickguard.
- Six-saddle bridge, separate G-logo tubular frame-type tailpiece.
- Gold-plated hardware.
* BLACK FALCON 6136DSBK black, 2006–current.
* WHITE FALCON 6136CST Custom Shop, 21 frets, 2004–current.
* WHITE FALCON 6136CST-R relic finish, Custom Shop limited edition of 20, 2006.
* WHITE FALCON 6136TLDS lacquer finish, vibrato tailpiece, 2008–current.

WHITE FALCON 6139CB 2013–current
- Bound ebony fingerboard, thumbnail markers; 22 frets; truss-rod adjuster at headstock; vertical Gretsch logo on headstock.
- Hollow single-cutaway bound body with f-holes and internal centre-block; white or black (6139CB).
- Two humbuckers.
- Four knobs (three volume, one tone) and one selector (pickups).
- Falcon logo on pickguard.
- Six-saddle bridge, separate G-logo tubular frame-type tailpiece.
- Gold-plated hardware.
* BLACK FALCON 6139CBSL black, 2014–current.

BILLY DUFFY See under Billy Duffy.

BONO IRISH FALCON See under Bono.

DAVID LEE See under David Lee.

STEPHEN STILLS See under Stephen Stills.

DOUBLE-CUTAWAY ORIGINALS

WHITE FALCON double-cutaway first version 1960–72
- Bound ebony fingerboard, thumbnail markers (with offset dot markers from 15th fret c.1964); 21 frets plus zero fret; truss-rod adjuster at headstock; model nameplate on headstock.
- Hollow double-cutaway bound body with f-holes; pad on body back; white (6136).
- Two humbuckers.

WHITE FALCON STEREO

- Three knobs (volume) and three selectors (standby, tone, pickups), plus two string-mute controls.
- Falcon logo on pickguard.
- Six-saddle bridge (bar-frame Floating Sound unit plus six-saddle bridge from c.1966), separate G-logo tubular frame tailpiece (separate vibrato tailpiece from c.1964), two string-mutes.
- Gold-plated hardware.
* Some examples with three controls (volume) and two selectors (tone, pickups).
* Vibrato tailpiece option c.1960–64.
* Replaced single-cutaway version: see earlier entry here.

WHITE FALCON double-cutaway second version 1972–80
- Bound ebony fingerboard, thumbnail markers with offset dot markers from 15th fret (block from c.1974); 21 frets plus zero fret; truss-rod adjuster at neck heel.
- Hollow double-cutaway bound body with f-holes; white (7594).
- Two humbuckers.
- Three knobs (volume) and three selectors (standby, tone, pickups), plus two string-mute controls until c.1974; three knobs (volume) and two selectors (tone, pickups) from c.1978.
- Falcon logo on pickguard.
- Bar-frame Floating Sound unit plus six-saddle bridge (six-saddle bridge from c.1974), separate vibrato tailpiece, two string-mutes until c.1974.
- Gold-plated hardware.
* "Special order" from 1979.

DOUBLE-CUTAWAY REISSUES

WHITE FALCON 7594 1989–2005
- Bound ebony fingerboard, block markers; 22 frets; truss-rod adjuster at headstock.
- Hollow double-cutaway bound body with f-holes; white (7594).
- Two humbuckers.
- Four knobs (three volume, one tone) and one selector (pickups); three knobs (volume) and two selectors (tone pickups) from c.2003.
- Falcon logo on pickguard.
- Six-saddle bridge, separate vibrato tailpiece.
- Gold-plated hardware.
* Also known as White Falcon II.
* BLACK FALCON 7594BK black, 1992–98.
* SILVER FALCON 7594SL black, chrome-plated hardware, 1995–98.

WHITE FALCON JUNIOR 7594JR 1999–2002
- Bound ebony fingerboard, block markers, 22 frets; truss-rod adjuster at headstock.
- Hollow double-cutaway bound body (14in wide) with f-holes; white (7594JR).
- Two humbuckers.
- Four knobs (three volume, one tone) and one selector (pickups).
- Falcon logo on pickguard.
- Six-saddle bridge, separate vibrato tailpiece.
- Gold-plated hardware.

WHITE FALCON 6136DC 2006–current
- Bound ebony fingerboard, thumbnail markers; 22 frets; truss-rod adjuster at headstock; model nameplate on headstock.
- Hollow double-cutaway bound body with f-holes; white (6136DC).
- Two humbuckers.
- Three knobs (volume) and three selectors (standby, tone, pickups).
- Falcon logo on pickguard.
- Six-saddle bridge, separate vibrato tailpiece.
- Gold-plated hardware.

WHITE FALCON 6139T-CBDC 2013–current
- Bound ebony fingerboard, thumbnail markers; 22 frets; truss-rod adjuster at headstock; vertical Gretsch logo on headstock.
- Hollow single-cutaway bound body with f-holes and internal centre-block; white or black (6139T-CBDC).
- Two humbuckers.
- Four knobs (three volume, one tone) and one selector (pickups).
- Falcon logo on pickguard.
- Six-saddle bridge, separate vibrato tailpiece.
- Gold-plated hardware.
* BLACK FALCON 6139T-CBDCSL black, 2014–current.

■ WHITE FALCON STEREO

Listed by Gretsch as the White Falcon Super Project-O-Sonic model until c.1967, and from then until its demise around 1981 as the White Falcon Stereo model. For mono models, see previous section.

SINGLE-CUTAWAY

WHITE FALCON STEREO (SUPER PROJECT-O-SONIC) single-cutaway first version 1958–59
- Bound ebony fingerboard, engraved hump-top block markers (thumbnail from c.1958); 21 frets (plus zero fret from c.1959); truss-rod adjuster at headstock; vertical Gretsch logo on headstock (horizontal type plus model nameplate from c.1958).
- Hollow single-cutaway bound body with f-holes; white (6137).
- Two split-polepiece humbuckers (close-spaced: one at neck; one in central position).
- Two knobs (volume) and three selectors (two tone, one pickups).
- Falcon logo on pickguard.
- Six-saddle bridge, separate G-logo tubular frame-type tailpiece.
- Gold-plated hardware.
* Some examples with 22 frets; some with regular humbuckers (not split-polepiece); some with optional separate vibrato tailpiece.

WHITE FALCON STEREO (SUPER PROJECT-O-SONIC) single-cutaway second version 1959–60
- Bound ebony fingerboard, thumbnail markers; 21 frets plus zero fret; truss-rod adjuster at headstock; horizontal Gretsch logo on headstock plus model nameplate.
- Hollow single-cutaway bound body with f-holes; pad on body back from c.1960; white (6137).
- Two humbuckers (regular positions).
- Two knobs (volume) and five selectors (one standby, four tone/pickups), plus two string-mute controls from c.1960.
- Falcon logo on pickguard.
- Six-saddle bridge, separate G-logo tubular frame-type tailpiece; two string-mutes from c.1960.
- Gold-plated hardware.
* Replaced by double-cutaway version: see later entry here.

THE GRETSCH ELECTRIC GUITAR BOOK

WHITE FALCON STEREO

WHITE FALCON STEREO single-cutaway third version 1974–79
- Bound ebony fingerboard, block markers; 21 frets plus zero fret; truss-rod adjuster at neck heel.
- Hollow single-cutaway bound body with f-holes; white (7593).
- Two humbuckers.
- Two knobs (volume) and five selectors (one standby, four tone/pickups).
- Falcon logo on pickguard.
- Six-saddle bridge, separate vibrato tailpiece.
- Gold-plated hardware.

DOUBLE-CUTAWAY

WHITE FALCON STEREO/SUPER PROJECT-O-SONIC double-cutaway first version 1960–72
- Bound ebony fingerboard, thumbnail markers (offset dot markers from 15th fret from c.1964); 21 frets plus zero fret; pad on back; truss-rod adjuster at headstock; model nameplate on headstock.
- Hollow double-cutaway bound body with f-holes; white (6137).
- Two humbuckers.
- Two knobs (volume) and five selectors (one standby, four tone/pickups), with four selectors on top left bout, to c.1964; two knobs (volume) and five selectors (one standby, four tone/pickups), all on right side of body, c.1964–66; two knobs (volume) and six selectors (one standby, five tone/pickups), including one on lower left body front, from c.1966; plus two string-mute controls.
- Falcon logo on pickguard.
- Six-saddle bridge (bar-frame Floating Sound unit plus six-saddle bridge from c.1966), separate G-logo tubular frame tailpiece (separate vibrato tailpiece from c.1964); two string-mutes.
- Gold-plated hardware.
* Known as WHITE FALCON PROJECT-O-SONIC until c.1967; WHITE FALCON STEREO from c.1967.
* Vibrato tailpiece option c.1960–64.
* Replaced single-cutaway version: see earlier entry here.

WHITE FALCON STEREO double-cutaway second version 1972–81
Similar to first version, except:
- Block position markers from c.1974; truss-rod adjuster at neck heel; no model nameplate on headstock.
- White (7595).
- Two knobs (volume) and six selectors (one standby, five tone/pickups) to c.1977; two knobs (volume) and five selectors (one standby, four tone/pickups) from c.1978; plus two string-mute controls c.1972–74.
- Six-saddle bridge from c.1974; two string-mutes to c.1974.
* "Special order" from 1979.

■ *WHITE PANTHER* See Panther.

■ WHITE PENGUIN

ORIGINALS

WHITE PENGUIN first version 1956–61
- Bound ebony fingerboard, engraved hump-top block markers (thumbnail from c.1958); 22 frets; truss-rod adjuster at headstock; vertical Gretsch logo on headstock (horizontal logo from c.1958).
- Semi-solid single-cutaway bound body (13.5in wide); metal arm-rest (some without); white (6134).
- Two single-coils (two humbuckers from c.1958).
- Four knobs (three volume, one tone) and one selector (pickups) to c.1958; three knobs (volume) and two selectors (tone, pickups) from c.1958.
- Penguin logo on pickguard.
- Six-saddle bridge, separate G-logo tubular frame tailpiece.
- Gold-plated hardware.
* Some examples in black and white, or with gold-sparkle body front.
* Some examples with stereo circuitry.

WHITE PENGUIN second version 1961–62
- Bound ebony fingerboard, thumbnail markers; 22 frets plus zero fret; truss-rod adjuster at headstock.
- Semi-solid single-cutaway bound body; white (6134).
- Two humbuckers.
- Three knobs (volume) and two selectors (tone, pickups) to c.1962; three knobs (volume) and three selectors (standby, tone, pickups) from c.1962.
- Penguin logo on pickguard.
- Six-saddle bridge, separate vibrato tailpiece.
- Gold-plated hardware.
* Some examples without penguin logo on pickguard.

REISSUES

WHITE PENGUIN 6134 1993–94 2003–current
- Bound ebony fingerboard, feather motif hump-top block markers; 22 frets; truss-rod adjuster at headstock; vertical Gretsch logo on headstock.
- Semi-solid single-cutaway bound body; metal arm-rest from 2010; white (6134).
- Two single-coils.
- Four knobs (three volume, one tone) and one selector (pickups).
- Penguin logo on pickguard.
- Six-saddle bridge, separate G-logo tubular frame tailpiece.
- Gold-plated hardware.
* BLACK PENGUIN 6134B black, 2003–current.
* WHITE PENGUIN LIMITED RELEASE 6134T-LTV thumbnail markers, metal arm-rest, two humbuckers, three knobs & two selectors, vibrato tailpiece, lacquer finish, 2008.

■ *7/11 SONGBIRD* See Sam Goody.

■ 12-STRING

12-STRING 1966–70
- Bound rosewood or ebony fingerboard, triangle markers; 22 frets plus zero fret; truss-rod adjuster at headstock; 12-string headstock.
- Hollow double-cutaway bound body with f-holes; sunburst (6075), natural (6076).
- Two humbuckers.
- Three knobs (all volume) and three selectors (standby, tone, pickups).
- Single-saddle wooden bridge, separate G-cutout flat tailpiece.

6120

* Some examples with pad on body back; some with string-mute and control.

■ **400/6040** See under Synchromatic.

■ **5655** See under Electromatic: Later.

■ **6120**
Listed by Gretsch at first as the Chet Atkins Hollow Body model, but in 1967 the name was changed to the Chet Atkins Nashville. By the time the first reissues appeared in 1989, Gretsch had lost the Chet Atkins part of the name, but regained it in 2007 when the model once again became the Chet Atkins Hollow Body.

SINGLE-CUTAWAY ORIGINALS

CHET ATKINS HOLLOW BODY single-cutaway 1955–61
- Bound rosewood fingerboard (ebony from c.1958), engraved block markers (plain block from c.1956; hump-top block from c.1957; thumbnail from c.1958); 22 frets (earliest 1955 examples with 21 frets; 22 frets plus zero fret from c.1959); brass nut (bone from c.1959); truss-rod adjuster at headstock; steer head on headstock (horseshoe from c.1956).
- Hollow single-cutaway bound body (15.5in wide, 2.75in deep to c.1960; 2.5in deep c.1960; 2.25in deep c.1961) with f-holes and G-brand on front (no G-brand from c.1957); orange (6120).
- Two single-coils (two humbuckers from c.1958).
- Four knobs (three volume, one tone) and one selector (pickups) to c.1958; three knobs (volume) and two selectors (tone, pickups) c.1958–61; three knobs (volume) and three selectors (standby, tone, pickups) c.1961.
- Chet Atkins logo on pickguard.
- Single-saddle bridge, separate vibrato tailpiece (gold anodised 1955; silver colour with black infilled base from c.1956).
- Gold-plated hardware.
* Some examples in red.

SINGLE-CUTAWAY REISSUES

NASHVILLE 6120 1989–2006
- Bound rosewood fingerboard, block markers (thumbnail from 2003); 22 frets; truss-rod adjuster at headstock; horseshoe on headstock.
- Hollow single-cutaway bound body (16in wide, 2.75in deep) with f-holes; orange (6120, 6120TM), black (6120BK), blue (6120BS), green (6120GR), natural (6120AM).
- Two humbuckers.
- Four knobs (three volume, one tone) and one selector (pickups) to c.2003; three knobs (volume) and two selectors (tone, pickups) from c.2003.
- Nashville logo on pickguard.
- Six-saddle bridge, separate vibrato tailpiece.
- Gold-plated hardware.
* Renamed CHET ATKINS HOLLOWBODY 6120 from 2007; see later entry here.
* NASHVILLE JUNIOR 6120JR2 Small body (14in wide), thumbnail markers, horseshoe on headstock, orange, 1996–2004; NASHVILLE JUNIOR 6120JR with single humbucker 1996–98.
* NASHVILLE JUNIOR Center-Block LTD 2-Tone 6112TCB-JR, gold/brown finish, 2014–current.
* NASHVILLE 1955 CUSTOM 6120-1955 "Custom USA" reissue based on CHET ATKINS HOLLOW BODY (6120) 1955-period orange original (also in black) but with ebony fingerboard, 1995–99.
* NASHVILLE 1955 CUSTOM WESTERN 6120W-1955 "Custom USA" reissue based on CHET ATKINS HOLLOW BODY (6120) 1955-period orange original, western motif markers, G-brand on body front, 1997–99.
* NASHVILLE 6120-6/12 double-neck, 12-string and 6-string necks on one 17in-wide non-cutaway body, two humbuckers per neck, 1997–2007.
* NEW NASHVILLE 6120N sharp-pointed single cutaway hump-top markers, 2002–03.

NASHVILLE WESTERN 6120W 1989–2003
- Bound rosewood fingerboard, Western-motif block markers; 22 frets; truss-rod adjuster at headstock; horseshoe on headstock.
- Hollow single-cutaway bound body with f-holes; G-logo on front; orange (6120W).
- Two humbuckers.
- Four knobs (three volume, one tone) and one selector (pickups).
- Nashville logo on pickguard.
- Six-saddle bridge, separate vibrato tailpiece.
- Gold-plated hardware.

NASHVILLE 6120-1960 1992–2005
- Bound rosewood fingerboard, thumbnail markers; 22 frets plus zero fret; truss-rod adjuster at headstock; horseshoe on headstock.
- Hollow single-cutaway bound body with f-holes; orange (6120-1960).
- Two humbuckers.
- Three knobs (volume) and two selectors (tone, pickups).
- Nashville logo on pickguard.
- Single-saddle bridge, separate vibrato tailpiece.
- Gold-plated hardware (except vibrato).
* NASHVILLE GOLDEN ANNIVERSARY 6120GA gold body front, no zero fret, 2004–06.

NASHVILLE WESTERN 6120W-1957 2001–06
- Bound ebony fingerboard, Western-motif block markers; 22 frets; truss-rod adjuster at headstock; steer head on headstock.
- Hollow single-cutaway bound body with f-holes; G-logo on front; orange (6120W-1957).
- Two single-coils (differing types).
- Four knobs (three volume, one tone) and one selector (pickups).
- Nashville logo on pickguard.
- Six-saddle bridge, separate vibrato tailpiece.
- Gold-plated hardware.
* Based on Eddie Cochran's personally modified 50s 6120.

NASHVILLE WESTERN/ CHET ATKINS HOLLOW BODY 6120DSW 2003–current
- Bound rosewood fingerboard, Western-motif block markers; 22 frets; truss-rod adjuster at headstock; steer head on headstock.
- Hollow single-cutaway bound body with f-holes; G-brand on body front; orange (6120DSW).
- Two single-coils.
- Four knobs (three volume, one tone) and one selector (pickups).
- Nashville logo or Chet Atkins logo on pickguard.

6120

- Single-saddle bridge, separate vibrato tailpiece.
- Gold-plated hardware (except vibrato).
* Known as NASHVILLE WESTERN 6120DSW until c.2006, and CHET ATKINS HOLLOW BODY 6120DSW from c.2007.
* NASHVILLE 6120DS horseshoe on headstock, block markers, no G-brand on body, 2003–04.
* NASHVILLE 6120DSV horseshoe on headstock, hump-top markers, no G-brand on body, 2005–10.

NASHVILLE WESTERN/CHET ATKINS HOLLOW BODY 6120WCST 2004–08
- Bound rosewood fingerboard, Western-motif block markers; 22 frets; truss-rod adjuster at headstock; steer head on headstock.
- Hollow single-cutaway bound body with f-holes; G-brand on body front; orange (6120WCST).
- Two single-coils.
- Four knobs (three volume, one tone) and one selector (pickups).
- Nashville logo or Chet Atkins logo on pickguard.
- Single-saddle bridge, separate vibrato tailpiece.
- Gold-plated hardware (except vibrato tailpiece).
* Custom Shop production.
* Known as NASHVILLE WESTERN 6120WCST until c.2007, and CHET ATKINS HOLLOW BODY 6120WCST from c.2007.

CHET ATKINS HOLLOW BODY 6120 2007–current
- Bound ebony fingerboard, thumbnail markers, 22 frets; truss-rod adjuster at headstock; horseshoe on headstock.
- Hollow single-cutaway bound body with f-holes; orange (6120), black (6120BK), blue (6120BS).
- Two humbuckers.
- Three knobs (volume) and two selectors (tone, pickups).
- Chet Atkins name on pickguard.
- Six-saddle bridge, separate vibrato tailpiece.
- Gold-plated hardware.
* Previously named NASHVILLE 6120 until 2006; see earlier entry here.

CHET ATKINS HOLLOW BODY 6120-1959/1959LTV 2007–current
- Bound ebony fingerboard, thumbnail markers; 22 frets plus zero fret; truss-rod adjuster at headstock; horseshoe on headstock.
- Hollow single-cutaway bound body with f-holes; orange (6120-1959), lacquer finish (6120-1959LTV).
- Two humbuckers.
- Three knobs (volume) and two selectors (tone, pickups).
- Chet Atkins logo on pickguard.
- Single-saddle bridge, separate vibrato tailpiece.
- Gold-plated hardware (except vibrato).
* Known as NASHVILLE 6120-1959 and 6120-1959LTV, Nashville logo on pickguard, 2006.
* CHET ATKINS 6120-125 125th ANNIVERSARY LIMITED EDITION special finish transparent orange over gold-leaf, Custom Shop production of 25, 2008.

CHET ATKINS STEREO GUITAR 6120-CGP 2008–10
- Bound rosewood fingerboard, block markers, 22 frets; truss-rod adjuster at headstock; horseshoe on headstock.
- Hollow sealed single-cutaway bound body with fake f-holes; G-brand on body front; orange (6120-CGP).
- Two non-standard humbuckers.
- Three knobs (volume) and two selectors (mono/stereo, pickups); two jacks.
- Chet Atkins name on pickguard.
- Single-saddle bridge, separate vibrato tailpiece.
- Gold-and nickel-plated hardware.

BRIAN SETZER See under Brian Setzer.

DUANE EDDY See under Duane Eddy.

EDDIE COCHRAN See under Eddie Cochran.

KEITH SCOTT See under Keith Scott.

REVEREND HORTON HEAT See under Reverend Horton Heat.

DOUBLE-CUTAWAY ORIGINALS

CHET ATKINS HOLLOW BODY double-cutaway 1962–66
- Bound ebony fingerboard, thumbnail markers; 22 frets plus zero fret; truss-rod adjuster at headstock; horseshoe on headstock.
- Hollow sealed double-cutaway bound body (2in deep) with fake f-holes; pad on body back; orange (6120).
- Two humbuckers.
- Three knobs (volume) and three selectors (standby, tone, pickups), plus one string-mute control.
- Chet Atkins name on pickguard.
- Single-saddle bridge, separate vibrato tailpiece; one string-mute.
- Gold-plated hardware.

CHET ATKINS NASHVILLE double-cutaway first version 1966–72
- Bound ebony fingerboard, thumbnail markers; 22 frets plus zero fret; truss-rod adjuster at headstock; nameplate on headstock.
- Hollow sealed double-cutaway bound body with fake f-holes; pad on body back; orange (6120).
- Two humbuckers.
- Three knobs (volume) and three selectors (standby, tone, pickups), plus one string-mute control until c.1971.
- Chet Atkins name and model name on pickguard.
- Single-saddle bridge (six-saddle from c.1971), separate vibrato tailpiece; one string-mute until c.1971.
- Gold-plated hardware.
* Some examples with bound rosewood fingerboard.

CHET ATKINS NASHVILLE double-cutaway second version 1972–79
- Bound ebony fingerboard, thumbnail markers; 22 frets plus zero fret; truss-rod adjuster at neck heel.
- Hollow double-cutaway bound body with f-holes; red (7660).
- Two humbuckers.
- Three knobs (volume) and three selectors (standby, tone, pickups) to c.1976; three knobs (volume) and two selectors (tone, pickups) from c.1976.
- Chet Atkins name and model name on pickguard.
- Six-saddle bridge, separate vibrato tailpiece.
- Gold- or chrome-plated hardware.

MODEL TIMELINE

DOUBLE-CUTAWAY REISSUES

NASHVILLE/CHET ATKINS 6120DC 2003–current
- Bound ebony fingerboard, thumbnail markers; 22 frets plus zero fret; truss-rod adjuster at headstock; horseshoe on headstock.
- Hollow sealed double-cutaway bound body with fake f-holes; pad on body back; orange (6120DC).
- Two humbuckers.
- Three knobs (volume) and three selectors (standby, tone, pickups), plus string-mute control.
- Chet Atkins name on pickguard.
- Single-saddle bridge, separate vibrato tailpiece; one string-mute.
- Gold-plated hardware (except vibrato tailpiece).
* *Known as NASHVILLE DOUBLE CUTAWAY 6120DC until c.2006, and CHET ATKINS DOUBLE CUTAWAY HOLLOW BODY from c.2007.*

MODEL TIMELINE

Here are the electric models produced by Gretsch, listed in chronological order of the year of introduction.

1939
Electromatic Spanish 1st 1939–42

1949
Electromatic Spanish 2nd 1949–53

1951
Electro II non-cut 1951–53
Electro II single-cut 1951–53
Electromatic 1951–54

1953
Corvette hollow 1953–56
Country Club 1st, 2nd, 3rd, 4th 1953–81
Duo Jet 1st 1953–61

1954
Round Up 1954–58
Silver Jet 1st 1954–61
Streamliner single-cut 1954–58

1955
Chet Atkins Hollow Body 6120 1st 1955–61
Chet Atkins Solid Body single-cut 1955–61
Convertible 1955–59
Jet Fire Bird 1st 1955–61
White Falcon single-cut 1st 1955–60

1956
Clipper 1st 1956–57
White Penguin 1st 1956–61

1957
Clipper 2nd, 3rd 1957–74
Rambler 1st 1957–59

1958
Anniversary 1958–72
Chet Atkins Country Gentleman single-cut 1958–61
Chet Atkins Tennessean 1st, 2nd, 3rd 1958–80
Country Club Stereo 1st, 2nd 1958–65
Double Anniversary 1st, 2nd, 3rd 1958–77
White Falcon Stereo single-cut 1st, 2nd 1958–60

1959
Rambler 2nd version 1959–62
Sal Salvador 1959–66

1960
White Falcon double-cut 1st, 2nd 1960–80
White Falcon Stereo double-cut 1st, 2nd 1960–81

1961
Anniversary Stereo 1961–63
Bikini 1961
Chet Atkins Country Gentleman double-cut 1st, 2nd 1961–81
Corvette solid 1st 1961–62
Duo Jet 2nd 1961–69
Jet Fire Bird 2nd 1961–69
Silver Jet 2nd 1961–63
White Penguin 2nd 1961–62

1962
Chet Atkins Hollow Body 6120 double-cut 1962–66
Chet Atkins Solid Body 2nd 1962
Corvette solid 2nd 1962–65
Princess 1962–63
Ronny Lee 1962–63
Twist 1962–63

1963
Astro-Jet 1963–67

1964
"Cat's-Eye Custom" 1964–67
Viking 1st, 2nd, 3rd 1964–75

1965
Corvette solid 3rd 1965–70

1966
Chet Atkins Nashville 6120 double-cut 1st, 2nd 1966–79
Monkees 1966–67
12-string 1966–70

1967
Black Hawk 1967–70
Rally 1967–68
Sal Febbraio 1967
Sam Goody 1967
Streamliner double-cut 1st, 2nd 1967–75

1968
Prince 1968–70
Van Eps seven-string 1st, 2nd 1968–78
Van Eps six-string 1968–72

1969
Roc Jet 1st, 2nd 1969–79

1970
Deluxe Chet 1972–73
Super Chet 1972–80

1971
Corvette solid 4th 1971–73

1973
Country Roc 1973–79
Roc II 1973–74
Streamliner II double-cut 1973–75

1974
Broadkaster semi-hollow 1st, 2nd 1974–79
Broadkaster solid 1974–77
White Falcon Stereo single-cut 3rd 1974–79

1975
White Falcon single-cut 2nd 1975–80

1976
Corvette II 1976–77
Deluxe Corvette 1976–77
Roc I 1976–77
Super Roc 1976–77

1977
Atkins Axe 1977–80
Committee 1977–81

THE GRETSCH ELECTRIC GUITAR BOOK 151

MODEL TIMELINE

Super Axe 1977–81
TK300 1977–81

1979
Beast BST-1000/1500/5000 1979–81

1980
Beast BST-2000 1980–81

1981
Country Squire 1981

1982
Southern Belle 1982–83

1989
Country Classic 6122 1989–2006
Country Classic 6122S 1989-2003
Duo Jet 6128/6128T 1st 1989–2003
Jet Firebird 6131 1989–2003
Nashville 6120 1989–2006
Nashville Western 6120W 1989–2003
Round Up 6121 1989–2003
Silver Jet 6129/6129T 1st 1989–2003
Tennessee Rose 6119 1989–2006
Traveling Wilburys TW 1989–90
White Falcon 6136 1989–2006
White Falcon 7593 1989–2012
White Falcon 7594 1989–2005

1992
Black Falcon 6136BK 1992–98, 2003–05
Black Falcon 7593BK 1992–98, 2003–04
Black Falcon 7594BK 1992–98
Nashville 6120-1960 1992–2005
Rancher 6022CV 1992–99
Synchromatic 400/6040 1992-2001

1993
Anniversary 1993–98
(Double) Anniversary 1993–current
Country Classic 6122-1962 1993–2006
Nashville Brian Setzer 1993–current
Tennessee Rose 6119-1962FT 1993–2006
White Penguin 1993–94, 2003–current

1994
Duo Jet 6128(T)-1957 1994–2006
Silver Jet 6129(T)-1957 1994–current

1995
Axe 1995–2001
Country Club 1955 Custom 6196-1955 1995–99
Nashville 1955 Custom 6120-1955 1995–99
Silver Falcon 6136SL 1995–2006
Silver Falcon 7594SL 1995–98
Sparkle Jet 6129T 1995–current
White Falcon 1955 Custom 6136-1955 1995–99

1996
Country Classic 6122-12 12-string 1996-2001
Malcolm Young I/II 1996–2011
Nashville Junior 6120JR 1996–98
Nashville Junior 6120JR2 1996–2004
Silver Jet 6129T-1962 1996–2009
Sparkle Jet 6129-1957 1996-2002

1997
Country Classic 6122-1958 1997–2006
Duane Eddy 6120DE/DEO 1997–2003
Nashville 1955 Custom Western 6120W-1955 1997–99
Nashville 6120-6/12 double neck 1997–2007

1998
Country Classic Junior 6122R 1998–2004
Duo Jet 6128T-6/12 double neck 1998–2007
Super Gretsch 7690 1998-2002

1999
Historic Series Streamliner 1999-2003
Historic Series Synchromatic 1999-2003
Historic Series Thinline Synchromatic 1999-2003
Nashville Brian Setzer Hot Rod 1999–current
Nashville Keith Scott 6120KS 1999–2012
Tennessee Rose 6119-1962HT 1999–2006
White Falcon Junior 7594JR 1999-2002

2000
Bo Diddley 6138 2000–current
Electromatic Bo Diddley 2000–14
Electromatic Double Jet 1st 2000–03
Electromatic Jet Club 2000–current
Electromatic Jet Pro 2000–03
Electromatic Jet Sparkle 2000–03
Electromatic Jet Sparkle F/Hole 2000–03
Electromatic Junior Jet 2000–03
Electromatic Jet II 2000–03
Elliot Easton 6128 2000–05
Synchromatic Bo Diddley 2000–03
Synchromatic Double Jet 2000–03
Synchromatic Jet Club 2000–03
Synchromatic Jet Pro 2000–03
Synchromatic Jet II 2000–03
Synchromatic Junior Jet 2000–03
Synchromatic Sparkle Jet 2000–04
Synchromatic Sparkle Jet F/Hole 2000–04
White Falcon Stephen Stills 6136-1958 2000–current

2001
Country Club single-coils 2001–13
Duo Jet 6128T-1962 2001–current
Historic Series Synchromatic Jr 2001–03
Nashville Western 6120W-1957 2001–06

2002
Anniversary Junior 6118JR 2002–08
New Jet 6114 2002–03
New Nashville 6120N 2002–03
Spectra Sonic 2002–07
Synchromatic Elliot Easton 2002–03
Synchromatic Jet Baritone 2002–03
Synchromatic Sparkle Jet Double Neck 2002–03

2003
Anniversary 120th 6118T-120 2003–07
Anniversary 6117HT 2003–current
Black Penguin 6134B 2003–current
Duo Jet 6128/6128T 2nd 2003–current
Jet Firebird 6131/6131T 2003–09
Nashville Classic 6122-1959 2003–08
Nashville/Chet Atkins Double Cutaway 6120DC 2003–current
Nashville 6120DS 2003–04
Nashville Western/Chet Atkins Hollow Body 6120DSW 2003–current
Round Up 6121W 2003–05
Silver Jet 6129/6129T 2nd 2003–current
Sparkle Jet 6129TC-1962 2003
Tennessee Special 6119SP 2003–06

2004
Anniversary Junior 6118TJR 2004–09
Black Falcon 6136TBK 2004–current
Country Club humbuckers 2004–current
Electromatic Double Jet 2nd 2004–current
Electromatic Elliot Easton 2004–05
Electromatic Jet Baritone 2004–current
Electromatic Jet Double Neck 2004–current
Electromatic Junior Jet/Jet II 2004–10
Electromatic Hollow Body 1st 2004–08
Electromatic Pro Jet 2004–current
Electromatic Special Jet 1st 2004–07
Nashville Golden Anniversary 6120GA 2004–06
Nashville Western/Chet Atkins Hollow Body 6120WCST 2004–08
Silver Falcon 6136TSL 2004–current
White Falcon 6136CST 2004–current
White Falcon 6136T 2004–current

2005
Anniversary 6117THT 2005–current
"Billy-Bo" Jupiter Thunderbird 6199 2005–current
Bono "Irish Falcon" 6136I 2005–current
Brian Setzer Black Phoenix 6136SLBP 2005–current
Country Classic Special 6122SP 2005
Duo Jet Custom Edition 6128TSP 2005–06
Duo Jet 6128T-DSV 2005–14
Duo Jet 6128TCG 2005–current
Jet Firebird 6131TDS 2005–09
Nashville Solid Body 6121 2005–06
Nashville 6120DSV 2005–10

REFERENCE LISTING

MODEL TIMELINE

Reverend Horton Heat G6120RHH 2005–current

2006
Black Falcon 6136DSBK 2006–current
Electromatic Corvette/CVT 5135 2006–current
Electromatic Hollow Body 2nd 2006–12
Electromatic Mini Diddley 5850 2006–09
Country Classic/Chet Atkins Country Gentleman 12-String 6122-12 2006–14
Power Jet 6128TVP/6128T-TVP 2006–current
Power Jet Firebird 6131TVP/6131T-TVP 2006–current
White Falcon 6136CST-R 2006
White Falcon 6136DC 2006–current
White Falcon 6136DS 2006–current

2007
Anniversary 6118T/6118T-LTV 2007–08
Brian Setzer Tribute Nashville 6120SSC 2007–09
Chet Atkins Country Gentleman 6122-1958 2007–current
Chet Atkins Country Gentleman 6122-1962 2007–current
Chet Atkins Country Gentleman 6122II 2007–current
Chet Atkins Hollow Body 6120 2007–current
Chet Atkins Hollow Body 6120-1959/1959LTV 2007–current
Chet Atkins Solid Body 6121/6121-1959 2007–current
Chet Atkins Solid Body 6121-1955 2007–current
Chet Atkins Tennessee Rose 6119 2007–current
Chet Atkins Tennessee Rose 6119-1962FT/HT 2007–current

Duo Jet 6128DS/6128TDS 2007–10
Round Up 6130 2006

2008
Anniversary 125th 6118T-LTV 2008–12
Billy Zoom Tribute Silver Jet 6129BZT 2008–11
Chet Atkins Tennessee Rose 6119-1959 2008–14
Chet Atkins Stereo Guitar 6120-CGP 2008–10
Chet Atkins 6120-125 125th Anniversary Limited Edition 2008
David Lee 6136DL 2008
Duo Jet Relic 6228TDS-R 2008
Electromatic G. Love Corvette 5135 2008–10
White Falcon 6136TLTV 2008–current
White Falcon 6136TLDS 2008–current
White Penguin Limited Release 6134T-LTV 2008

2009
Chet Atkins Country Gentleman 6122-1959 2009–current
Knotty Pine Western Roundup 6130KPW 2009–10

2010
Eddie Cochran Tribute Hollow Body 6120EC 2010
Electromatic Double Cutaway Hollow Body 1st 2010–12
Electromatic Patrick Vaughn Stump Signature "Stump-O-Matic" 5135CVT-PS 2010–current
Electromatic Tim Armstrong Hollow Body 5191BK 2010–current
Synchromatic Cutaway 2010–current

2011
Eddie Cochran Signature Hollow Body 6120 2011–current
George Harrison Signature Duo Jet 6128T-GH 2011–current
George Harrison Tribute Duo Jet 6128T-GH 2011–current

2012
Duane Eddy Signature Hollow Body 6120DE 2012–current
Electromatic CVT III 2012–13
Electromatic Double Cutaway Hollow Body 2nd 2012–current
Electromatic Hollow Body 3rd 2012–current
Electromatic Special Jet 2nd 2012–13
Electromatic Tim Armstrong Hollow Body 5191TMS 2012–14

2013
Anniversary 130th 6118T 2013
Anniversary Jr 130th 6118T-LTV 2013–current
Billy Duffy Falcon 7593T 2013–current
Duo Jet 6128T-DCM 2013–14
Panther 6137TCB 2013–current
White Falcon 6139T-CBDC 2013–current
White Panther 6137TCB 2013–current

2014
Black Falcon 6139CBSL 2014–current
Electromatic Center-Block Bono Red 2014–current
Electromatic Hollow Body Center-Block 2014–current
Electromatic 5655T-CB 2014–current
Nashville Junior Center-Block LTD 6112TCB-JR 2014–current
10th Anniversary Duo Jet NOS 2014

DATING & SERIALS

First we'll clarify some terms and assumptions used in the main Listing, and then we'll find out how to date Gretsch guitars.

MODEL NAMES & NUMBERS
Some Gretsch models were given different names at various times in company literature and pricelists. We use the official names throughout this reference section, as shown on the nameplate or logo on the instruments themselves, as used consistently in Gretsch printed material, or both. Some models may be better known or equally well known by other names or numbers, and we've noted and cross-referenced these to the relevant listing.

FRET COUNT
Examples of the same model are occasionally seen with different numbers of frets. We've noted this in the listing when we know about it, but additional variations may well exist.

PICKUPS
Gretsch's use of single-coil or humbucking pickups at various times can give a clue to the instrument's period of production, and these two broad pickup types have therefore been identified within each entry in the listing. Gretsch has used various designs of single-coil and humbucker pickups over the years, but in the interests of clarity the differences have not been noted in the listing. There's often more detail in the main text. In general on Gretsch guitars, a single-coil pickup can be identified by the presence of one row of six equally-spaced polepieces. Humbuckers have dual coils, usually indicated by two rows of six equidistant polepieces. An exception is when a plated metal cover is fitted that allows only one row of six polepieces to be visible, as featured on models – for instance the TK 300 – from the mid to late 70s.

BRIDGES
Gretsch has used various bridge designs over the years. In the interests of space, they are not detailed in this listing. They include:

THE GRETSCH ELECTRIC GUITAR BOOK

SPEC CHANGES

Melita Synchro-Sonic (from about 1952), Bigsby compensated, partnering B6 tailpiece (from 1955), Space Control (from about 1957), a single metal "rocker" bar (from about 1957), Floating Sound (from about 1965), Adjustamatic (from about 1970), and Terminator (from about 1975), as well as a handful of single-saddle wooden varieties.

BIGSBY TAILPIECES
Many Gretsch guitars come with a separate vibrato tailpiece. Apart from a period during the early 60s when a British-designed Burns unit was used on the solidbody models, Gretsch favoured US-made Bigsby tailpieces and associated bridges. A Bigsby was sometimes listed as an option for certain models, although the Gretsch factory would fit one to virtually any guitar if requested. The Bigsby vibrato tailpiece was equally easy to retro-fit, and often Gretsches turn up with a Bigsby retrofitted by the owner after purchase. In view of all this, the presence of a separate vibrato tailpiece has only been noted when it was officially offered in Gretsch literature. Various different types of Bigsby units were used by Gretsch, but in the interests of clarity these differences are not mentioned in the listing, although again there is some detail on this in the main text.

DATING GRETSCH GUITARS
Establishing the age of an instrument is important for most owners, especially those lucky enough to own vintage guitars, because age usually has a direct relationship with value. Many Gretsch models from the 50s and 60s have long been elevated to collectable status, thanks as much to their image and associations with famous players as to their inherent quality. Serial numbers can help. They're usually stamped on the headstock or on a plate on the headstock, scratched on a rear panel, or stamped on a paper label visible inside an f-hole or a control cavity. Serials since 1966 include specific date information. Before that, serials can still offer an indication of the model year, and recently Edward Ball's excellent research published in his two books on Gretsch (see the Books list at the back) has made things much clearer.

Serial numbers 1950–1966 (USA)
Before World War II, Gretsch numbering was haphazard, but around 1947, a new system began for most models, and it remained in use until 1966. Edward Ball helped compile the list here, and it uses his model-year attribution as opposed to calendar-year: the model year reflects an instrument's alignment with annual feature changes, whereas some instruments would have been made in the calendar year before such features were officially introduced. Inevitably there will still be a few overlaps – and also please be aware of the handful of general anomalies noted in the table (above right).

Serial numbers 1966–72 (USA)
In summer 1966, Gretsch replaced the existing system with a new method that incorporated the date of manufacture. The number of digits used varied from three to six: the first or first and second digit(s) indicate(s) production month (from 1 to 12); the next digit indicates the last number of the relevant year (from 1965 to 1972); and any remaining digits indicate the monthly production ranking.

For example:
592 suggests May (5) 1969 (9)
7820 suggests July (7) 1968 (8)
96220 suggests September (9) 1966 (6)
107963 suggests October (10) 1967 (7)

SERIAL NUMBERS 1950–1966 (USA)

Number	Approximate model year
4,000 to 5,599	1950, 1966 *
5,600 to 7,699	1951, 1966 *
7,700 to 9,799	1952, 1966 *
9,800 to 10,999	1953, 1966 *
11,000 to 12,199	1953
12,200 to 13,999 **	1954
15,000 to 15,799 **	1954
15,800 to 17,499	1955
17,500 to 20,999	1956
21,000 to 23,999	1957
24,000 to 24,999	1966 ***
25,000 to 26,099	1957
26,100 to 29,299	1958
29,300 to 33,099	1959
33,100 to 38,099	1960
38,100 to 42,599	1961
42,600 to 47,099	1962
47,100 to 53,299	1963
53,300 to 64,099	1964
64,100 to 74,099	1965
75,000 to 82,399	1966

* 4,000 to 10,999: some numbers used again in 1966.
** 14,000 to 14,999: apparently unused.
*** 24,000 to 24,999: not used in 1957 but used in 1966.

Note, however, that certain combinations can be confusing. Months 10, 11, and 12 (October, November, and December) could also indicate month 1 (January) plus years 0, 1, and 2 (1970, 1971, and 1972). In these instances, you have to use other dating pointers to confirm the guitar's age.

Serial numbers 1972–81 (USA)
Gretsch used the previous numbering scheme through to 1981, but from about 1972 the month digits were frequently separated from the rest of the serial number by a hyphen, or a dot, or a space. This was designed to prevent confusion about the year digit, which otherwise could often apply to both the 1965–72 and 1972–81 production periods. The visible presence of hyphen, dot, or space within the number usually confirms that it relates to 1972–81.

For example:
12-8289 suggests December (12) 1978 (8)
5.5125 suggests May (5) 1975 (5)
4 2126 suggests April (4) 1972 (2)

Serial numbers 1989–2003 (Japan)
When Gretsch began guitar production again in 1989, it used a new scheme, consisting of six digits plus a three-digit suffix. The first part provides the year of manufacture by the first two digits, while the fourth, fifth, and sixth digits (and sometimes a few more) are part of the relevant model number.

For example:
901121-154 suggests 1990 (90), Round Up 6121 (121)
946119-982 suggests 1994 (94), Tennessee Rose 6119 (119)
01311962-1235 suggests 2001 (01), Tennessee Rose 6119-1962 (11962)

MODEL DATING

Serial numbers 2003–14 (Japan)
When Fender started to manufacture Gretsch guitars in 2003, it changed the serial system to an eight-digit number with a two-letter prefix. The first two letters indicate country of origin (usually J for Japan) and factory (usually T for Terada; sometimes D for Dyna Gakki or F for Fujigen Gakki). For the numbers, the first two indicate the last two digits of the year of manufacture, the following two the month, and the last four digits represent the number of the particular instrument among the total guitars built that year.

For example:
JT04075003 suggests July (07) 2004 (04)
JT13083612 suggests August (08) 2013 (13)

Serial numbers 2003–14 (Other Asian)
These follow the system for Fender-era guitars, with an eight-digit number and a two or three-letter prefix. The first two letters indicate country of origin (C for China, I for Indonesia, K for Korea) and factory (P for Peerless, S for SPG/Samick, Y for Yako/Reliance) with sometimes a third letter, G for Gretsch. The first two numbers indicate the last two digits of the year of manufacture, the following two the month, and the last four digits represent the number of the particular instrument among the total guitars built that year. (Other Asian instruments – not Japanese – before 2003 have numbers that do not appear to reveal date information.)

For example:
KS06113267 suggests Korea (K), SPG/Samick (S), November (11) 2006 (06).
CYG13100064 suggests China (C), Yako/Reliance (Y), October (10) 2013 (13).

Serial numbers 2004–14 (USA Custom Shop)
The Gretsch Custom Shop uses the regular Fender-era system: an eight-digit number with a two-letter prefix. The first two letters indicate country of origin (U for United States) and Custom Shop (C). The first two numbers indicate the last two digits of the year of manufacture, the following two the month, and the last four digits represent the number of the particular instrument among the total guitars built that year.

For example:
UC05010020 suggests January (01) 2005 (05).
UC11020643 suggests February (02) 2011 (11).
UC14061091 suggests June (06) 2014 (14).

DATE-RELATED FEATURES
In addition to the serial number, you can sometimes use other features to help in dating a Gretsch guitar – although the company, unlike some manufacturers, made comparatively few changes that affected the majority of models across the line at any given time. Old Gretsches are renowned for a succession of gimmicky features that made their mark on various models at certain times, but some features can still be regarded as dating landmarks, at least for some models, and we've listed a number of potentially helpful ones here.

Position markers
At first, Gretsch gave its electrics the kind of fingerboard position-markers it already used on acoustic models: conventional dots or blocks, or the more distinctive and fancier "hump-top" variation of blocks. Dots continued on cheaper Gretsches, but the unique thumbnail "neo-classic" markers were introduced to the remainder of the line in 1957 and 1958. These were used until 1981, but block markers were revived for some models around 1974. Gretsch used other types, too, but only on certain instruments, so they don't serve as general dating pointers. The current lines feature dots, blocks, hump-top blocks, and thumbnail markers, and in the case of vintage-style instruments they match the form of the original.

Zero fret
This is a fret placed directly in front of the nut to determine string height, relegating the nut's role to that of a string guide. Fancifully described in Gretsch literature as the Action-flow fret nut, the zero fret appeared on many models from around 1959 and remained in use until 1981. On current lines it's used mostly where a vintage-style instrument matches the original feature set.

Truss-rod adjuster
On the majority of Gretsch models the truss-rod adjuster was originally located on the headstock, under a cover, but from about 1972 it was moved behind the neck heel, accessed through the back of the body. This was the visible indication of a new truss-rod system, introduced by Gretsch's new owners, Baldwin, and previously used on guitars made by Burns, a British company that Baldwin acquired in 1965 (Baldwin ceased production of Burns instruments in 1970). The Burns-designed "gear-box"-controlled truss-rod appeared on many Gretsch models until 1981.

Made in USA
Coinciding with Baldwin's takeover of Gretsch in 1967, the company stamped "Made In USA" on the rear of the headstock, alongside the serial number. This continued until about 1973.

Body
Gretsch followed Gibson's lead and introduced double-cutaway styling on various hollowbody and semi-solidbody models from about 1961. Gretsch reverted to single-cut solids around eight years later, reflecting the popularity of Gibson designs. The company used large f-holes on many of its hollowbody models until about 1972, when the f-holes became smaller and of more standard type. "Fake" f-holes (blocked-in or painted-on f-holes) were a unique Gretsch feature introduced on certain models around 1957, but they were replaced by the real thing from about 1972.

Pickups
In 1958, Gretsch introduced a humbucking pickup to replace the single-coil unit made by DeArmond, which until then it had used on all the electrics. The new Filter'Tron pickup was featured on many models, and later it was joined by other humbuckers, such as the Super'Tron, around 1963. In about 1960, Gretsch came up with its own single-coil pickup, the Hi-Lo'Tron, which it used on various cheaper hollowbody and solid instruments. The current lines feature revised versions of most of these classic pickup types.

Controls and circuitry
Partnering the launch of the new Filter'Tron humbucker came revised circuitry. Gretsch abandoned conventional rotary tone controls and instead fitted toggle-type selectors to provide "preset" tone changes. From around 1970, the company returned to regular tone controls, but for some models only; others retained the tone selectors until 1981. The current lines feature both types of control layout, in the case of vintage-style instruments following the form of the original.

SPEC CHANGES

Another date-related control was the standby switch. This addition to many higher-end models, used from about 1961 to 1978, allowed the instrument to be turned off without disconnecting the cable. Again, this appears occasionally in the current lines where a vintage-style instrument is intended to match the original's controls.

Pickguard
From about 1972, a more angular, squared-off style of pickguard replaced the original curvaceous Gretsch design. This was one of the few changes made across virtually all models.

Control pot codes
The metal casings of many US-made control potentiometers (usually called pots) are stamped with code numbers that can include information about the date the pot was manufactured, which can be used to confirm that a vintage instrument was not made before a certain date. Be aware that pots were not always used immediately, and also that they may have been replaced at some time. The code consists of six or seven numbers. Of these the first three identify the manufacturer (for example 137, for the CTS company) and can be disregarded, while the final two indicate the week of the production year and are also unimportant for our purposes. In a six-digit code, it is the fourth digit that indicates the last number of the appropriate year during the 50s: 195X. In a seven-digit code, the fourth and fifth digits signify the last two numbers of a year thereafter.

INDEX

acoustic guitars, 9
Action-flow Fret Nut, 61
Adjustamatic, *see* bridge
Anniversary models, 57, *58–59*, 60, 61, *63*, 69, 73, 80, 81, 88, 97, 99, 100, 104, 108, 109, *111*, 126
Armstrong, Tim, 118, 120
Ash, Sam, 81, 129
Ashman, Matthew, 99
Astro-Jet model, 69, *71*, 80, 126
Atkins Axe model, 93, *94*, 97, 104, 127
Atkins, Chet, 24, 25, 28, 29, *31*, 32, 33, *35*, 45, 46, 48, 49, 53, 54, *55*, 56, 58, 60, 61, 65, 72, *78*, 79, 85, *86*, 88, 89, 93, *94*, 98, 101, 105, 110, 116, *118*, 120, *for* Chet Atkins models *see also* Country Gentleman, Solid Body, Tennessean, 6120
Axe model, 93, 127

Bachman, Randy, 92, 108
Baldwin, D.H., 77, 80, 81, 83, 84, 85, 86, 88, 92, 96, 97, 98, 99, 100, 101, 103
Ball, Edward, 32, 40, 105
banjo, 36
Beast models, 97, 98, *102*, 127
Beatles, The, 69, 72, 73, *75*, 76
Beck, Jeff, 44, 47, 51, 116, 117
Benary, R.H., 9
Benedetto, 112
Bigsby vibrato, 28, 29, 31, 32, 35, 46, 68, 80, 100, 105, 154
Bikini models, 68, 127
"Billy-Bo" model, 48, *111*, 128
Billy Duffy model, 100, *103*, 127
Billy Zoom model, 113, 127
Black Falcon models, 146, 147
Black Hawk model, 99, 128
Black Panther model, *see* Panther models
Black Penguin model, 148
Black Phoenix model, *see* Brian Setzer models

Black Prince model, 130
Blanda, George, 108, 112
Blue Caps, 47
Bo Diddley models, 48, 104, 105, *107*, *111*, 112, 128
body: depth, 64; double-cutaway, 64, 65, 66, 70, 155; Electrotone, 64; ML bracing, 109; plastic covering, 17, 20; plywood, 29; sealed, 35, 56, 64; semi-solid, 17, 19, 29; single-cutaway, 12, 66, 155; thinline, 56, 64; trestle bracing, 53, 56, 108, 109
bolt-on neck, 92
Bono models, 128, 135
Booneville factories, *see* factories & offices
Brian Setzer models, 104, 105, *106–107*, 108, 109, 112, 128–129
bridge: Adjustamatic, 154; Melita, 17, 19, 20, 154; Space Control, 57, 154; Terminator, 154
Britton, Chris, 73
Broadkaster models, 16, 92, 93, *95*, 96, 97, 129
Brooklyn factories, *see* factories & offices
BST models, *see* Beast models
Burns, 68, 77, 80, 88, 155
Burns, Jim, 68
Burns vibrato, 68, 70, 80
Butts, Ray, 35, 48, 49, 52, 53, 54, 56, 60, 62, 92, 93, 121
Byrds, The, 73

Cadillac tailpiece, *see* tailpiece
Caiola, Al, *23*, 24
Capozzi, Jimmy, 41
Carducci, Joe, 121
Carllile, Thumbs, 19
Carrington, Charlie, 85
"Cat's-Eye Custom" model, 81, 129
Center-Block models, 118, 120, 135
Chanute office, *see* factories & offices

Charvel, 112
Chet Atkins Country Gentleman, *see* Country Gentleman
Chet Atkins Hollow Body 6120, *see* 6120
Chet Atkins Solid Body 6121, *see* Solid Body
Chet Atkins Tennessean, *see* Tennessean
Cincinnati office, *see* factories & offices
Ciudad Juarez factory, *see* factories & offices
Clapton, Eric, 73
Clark, Roy, 93
Clipper models, 37, *42–43*, 52, 61, 69, 80, 88, 129
Cochran, Eddie, 44, 45, *50*, 51, 104, 113, 116, *see also* Eddie Cochran models
Cohen, Jennifer, 12, 36, 76
Collins, Edwyn, 99
Committee model, 97, 98, *103*, 129
Constellation model, *42*
control knobs, 32, 52
control layout, 10, 17, 32, 52, 60, 61, 65, 155
Convertible model, 37, 40, *42–43*, 56, 129
Coppola, Carmine, 41
Corona, Antony, 113, *114*
Corvette hollowbody model, *14–15*, 21, 24, 37, 130
Corvette solidbody models, 68, 69, *70–71*, 80, 81, *83*, *94*, 96, *118*, 120, 130, 135, 136
Country Classic models, 101, 104, 112, 116, 131–132
Country Club models, 12, 21, 24, *26–27*, 28, 33, 36, 37, 40, 53, 56, 60, 61, *62–63*, 64, 69, 80, 88, 97, 104, 108, *110*, 112, 120, 130–131
Country Gentleman models, 53, *54–55*, 56, 61, 64, 66, 69, 72, 73, 76, 77, *78–79*, 80, 88, 95, 97, 98,

99, 101, 104, 110, 112, 116, 131–133
Country Roc model, 89, *90*, 97, 139
Country Squire model, 98
Crosby, David, 73
Cuesnon, 92
Custom Shop, 108, 112, 113, 117, 115, 155
CVT, *see* Corvette solidbody models

damper, *see* mute
Danelectro, 101
D'Angelico, 24, 25
D'Aquisto, 112
David Lee model, 133
Davis, Bo, 45
De Queen factory, *see* factories & offices
DeArmond, Harry, 12, 16, *see also* pickup
Deluxe Chet model, 85, *87*, 88, 133
Deluxe Corvette model, 96
Diddley, Bo, 47, 48, 81, 106, 110, *see also* Bo Diddley models
DiDomenico, Vincent, 41
DiRosa, Johnny, 41
Dorado, 92
Double Anniversary, *see* Anniversary models
double-cutaway, *see* body
Double Jet models, 135, 143
double-neck models, 104, *106–107*, 112, 134, 136, 143, 149
drums (Gretsch), 11, 20, 21, 33, 98, 101
Duane Eddy models, 46, 104, *107*, 133
Duffy, Billy, 99, 100, *103*, *see also* Billy Duffy model
Duffy, Dan, 40, 41, 68, 77, 84, 85
Duo Jet models, 17, *18–19*, 20, *23*, 24, 37, 40, 47, *51*, *55*, 64, 69, *70*, *71*, 72, *74–75*, 80, 101, 104, 112, 113, 133–134, 141
Dylan, Bob, 101
Dyna Gakki factory, *see* factories & offices

INDEX

DynaSonic, see pickup/DeArmond

Eagle strings, 11
Eagle Tannery, 9
ebony fingerboard, 57
EchoSonic amp, 48
Eddie Cochran models, 45, 113, 134–135, 149
Eddy, Duane, 45, 46, 47, 50, 51, 107, see also Duane Eddy models
Edge, 99
Edwards, Clyde, 85, 86, 93
Electro II models, 12, 14–15, 17, 21, 23, 24, 27, 135
Electromatic (early) models, 21, 135
Electromatic (later) models, 105, 108, 112, 117, 118, 119, 120, 128, 135, 136, 138
Electromatic Spanish models, 10, 12, 21, 135
Electrotone, see body
Elliot Easton models, 104, 112, 136
Everly Brothers, The, 48

factories & offices: Booneville factories, 84, 85, 86, 88, 92, 93, 96; Brooklyn (Middleton Street) factory/office, 8; Brooklyn (South 4th Street) factory/office, 8, 9; Brooklyn (60 Broadway) factory/office, 9, 15, 40, 76, 77, 84, 100; Chanute office, 97; Chicago office, 10, 11, 77, 84; Cincinnati office, 84; Ciudad Juarez (Mexico) factory, 98; De Queen factory, 98; Dyna Gakki factory, 155; Fujigen Gakki factory, 155; Gallatin office, 98; Peerless (Korea) factory, 155; Ridgeland factory, 112; SPG (Korea) factory, 108, 155; Terada (Japan) factory, 101, 112, 155; Texarkana factory, 98; Yako/Reliance (China) factory, 108, 155
fake f-holes, 53, 56, 64, 155
Febbraio, Sal, 81, see also Sal Febbraio model
feedback, 52
Fender, 16, 17, 21, 37, 77, 92, 96, 97, 101, 108, 110, 112, 116, 117, 155
f-holes, 28, 53, 56, 81, 88, 155
Filter'Tron, see pickup
fingerboard markers, 33, 57, 59, 155
Fleming, Chris, 112, 117, 120, 121
Fliegler, Ritchie, 109
floating pickup, see pickup
Floating Sound Unit, 65, 154
Fred Gretsch Manufacturing Company (Mfg Co), 8, 9
FujiGen Gakki factory, see factories & offices
Fulvery, Jim, 85

G. Love model, 136
Gallatin office, see factories & offices
Gallup, Cliff, 47, 51
Garland, Hank, 19, 24

G-brand, 18, 20, 28, 29, 32, 90
G-cutout tailpiece, see tailpiece
gear-box truss rod, 88, 155
General Motors, 36, 56
George Harrison models, 113, 136
Gibbons, Billy, 48, 110
Gibson, 12, 16, 17, 21, 24, 32, 33, 46, 49, 53, 56, 60, 64, 68, 81, 92, 97, 98, 101, 116, 120
G-indent knobs, 52
"Gold Duke" model, 81, 83, 130
Goody, Sam, 81, see also Sam Goody model
Gore, Martin, 99
Grant, Phil, 11, 20, 24, 28, 36, 39, 80, 81, 85
Gretsch (family): Bill (William Walter), 10, 11, 100; Fred, 99, 100, 101, 103, 105, 108, 112, 121; Fred (Jr), 10, 13, 15, 16, 17, 28, 41, 49, 80, 81, 85, 98, 99, 100; Fred (Sr), 8, 9, 10, 15; Friedrich, 8; Louis, 8; Rosa, 8, 9; Walter, 8, 9
Gretsch-American (brand), 9
Gretsch & Bremner, 8
Gretsch Building, The, 9, 15, 84
Grover Imperial tuners, 33
Guild, 101, 105, 112
Guitar Center, 105
Guitarama, 13

Hagner, Bill, 68, 81, 84, 85, 88, 92, 96, 97
Hagner Musical Instrument Corp, 88, 97
half-moon markers, see fingerboard markers
Harmony, 10, 21, 36
Harrison, Dick, 80, 84, 98, 101
Harrison, George, 69, 72, 73, 75, 76, 79, 101, 113, see also George Harrison models
Haugh, Gene, 88, 96, 98
Hayward, Ivan, 72
Henrichsen, Chad, 113, 114
Heritage, 101
Hicks, Andrew, 113, 114
Higham, Darrel, 44, 45, 115, 116, 117
HiLo'Tron, see pickup
Hi-Roller model, 93, 143
Historic models, 105, 142, 143
Hollow Body (model name), see 6120
horseshoe, 32
Hot Rod models, see Brian Setzer models
Houdlett, Albert, & Son, 8
humbucking, see pickup
Hyatt, Dale, 16

Innis, Louis, 25

Jasper Wood Products, 29
Jet Baritone models, 136, 143
Jet Club models, 136, 143
Jet Fire Bird models, 22–23, 37, 40, 48, 64, 69, 71, 80, 92, 95, 104, 112, 137

Jet Pro models, 136, 143
Jet Sparkle models, 136
Jet II model, 136
Johnson, Ben, 97
Jones, Brian, 73
Jones, Mike, 93, 96
Jones, TV, 104, see also pickup
Junior Jet models, 136, 143
Jupiter Thunderbird, see "Billy-Bo" model

Kay, 10
Keith Scott model, 104, 109, 137
Kimble, Tom, 96
King, B.B., 45
knobs, see control knobs, contro layout
Knotty Pine model, 140
Kramer, Charles "Duke", 11, 36, 49, 80, 81, 85, 93, 101
Kustom, 97

La Tosca, 11
Laiken, Sid, 41
Lee, Ronny, 81, see also Ronny Lee model
Lewis, Mike, 108, 109, 116, 121
logo, 20
Lover, Seth, 49
Lynne, Jeff, 101

Madrigal, Gonzalo, 113, 114
Malcolm Young models, 92, 104, 112, 137
Manchester, Don, 88
Marr, Johnny, 99
Marriott, Steve, 73
Marsden, Gerry, 73
McCarty, Ted, 16, 105
McDonald, Skeets, 44
McGuinn, Roger, 73
Melita, see bridge
Melita, Sebastiano "Johnny", 20
Midco, 105
Mini Diddley, see Bo Diddley models
Miracle Neck, 13
Mitchell Morrison, 24
ML bracing, see body
Monkees model, 73, 138
Monopole, 11
Monsanto, 20
Montgomery Ward, 10
mud switch, 52
muffler, see mute
Mundy, Julie, 44
Mure, Billy, 24, 27
mute, 64, 67, 72, 79

Nash, Phil, 9, 10
Nashville Brian Setzer, Keith Scott, Solid Body, 6120 models, see main model name
Nashville Classic model, 110–111, 132
Nashville Junior models, 149
Nashville Western models, 149–150
Neo-Classic markers, see fingerboard markers

Nesmith, Mike, 73
New Jet models, 138
New Nashville model, 149

Oahu, 10
offices, see factories & offices
O.K. card, 41, 43
Orbison, Roy, 101
Osborne, Mary, 24, 26

padded back, 64, 66
Panther models, 119, 138
Patrick Vaughn Stump model, 118–119, 120, 138
Paul, Les, 24
Peavey, 117
Peerless factory, see factories & offices
Perito, Jerry, 41, 52, 98
Petty, Tom, 101
pickup: DeArmond (DynaSonic), 12, 32, 45, 46, 48, 49, 52, 155; Filter'Tron, 52, 54, 56, 60, 92, 155; floating, 42; HiLo'Tron, 52, 54, 61, 64, 155; humbucking, 49, 52, 53, 153; P-90 (Gibson), 45, 51, 113; stereo, 60, 61; Super'Tron, 69, 87, 99, 155; TV Jones, 104
plastic body covering, see body
plywood, see body
Poison Ivy (Cramps), 99
Porter, Dean, 85, 86
position markers, see fingerboard markers
pot (potentiometer) codes, 156
Power Jet models, 134, 137
Presley, Elvis, 48
Prince model, 130
Princess model, 68, 69, 70, 138
Pro Jet models, 136
Professional Series, 108
Project-o-Sonic, see stereo models
Provet, Felix, 41
P-90, see pickup

Rally model, 80, 81, 82–83, 138, 140
Rambler models, 43, 138
Rancher (electric) model, 139
Randall, Don, 37
Reed, Lou, 73
Reinhardt, Django, 61
relic finish, 112
Reverend Horton Heat model, 109, 139
Rex (brand), 9
Ridgeland factory, see factories & offices
Roc models, 81, 87, 88, 89, 93, 95, 97, 139
Roc Jet models, see Roc models
rockabilly, 99, 104, 117
Rodriquez, Fred, 77
Ronny Lee model, 81, 139
Round Up models, 18–19, 19, 20, 24, 28, 29, 37, 40, 89, 90, 104, 112, 139–140

INDEX

Rowe Industries, 12
Roy, Charlie, 97, 98

Sal Febbraio model, 81, 140
Sal Salvador model, 40, 43, 61, 69, 140
Salvador, Sal, 40, *43*
Sam Goody model, 81, 140
Samick, see factories & offices/SPG
Savona, Charles, 68
Schultz, Bill, 101
script logo, 20
sealed body, see body
Sears, Roebuck, 10
semi-solid body, see body
serial numbers, 29, 40, 57, 113, 154–155
Setzer, Brian, 99, 104, 105, *107*, 108, 109, 121, see also Brian Setzer models
seven-string guitar, 81, 145
Sherman Clay, 81
Sho-Bud, 98
"Silver Duke" model, 81, 83, 130
Silver Falcon models, 146, 147
Silver Jet models, 20, *22–23*, 24, 40, 64, *62*, 69, *70*, 101, 104, 112, 113, 127, 140–141
single-cutaway, see body
slanted frets, 65, 67
Smith, Robert, 99
Solid Body (Atkins) models, 29, *30*, *34*, 40, 64, 65, 69, 73, 108, 109, 112, 116, 141–142
Southern Belle model, 98
Space Control, see bridge
Sparkle Jet models, 112, *115*, 141
Special Jet models, 136, 143
Spectra Sonic models, 104, *106*, 112, 142
SPG factory, see factories & offices
Squire, John, 99
standby switch, 65, 156
Stanley, Ray, 44
steer's head, 18, 20, 28, 32
Stephen Stills model, 92, 104, 112, 142
Stereo Guitar model (name), 150

stereo models, 60, 61, *62–63*, 126, 131, 147–148
stereo pickup, see pickup
Stern, Stephen, 112, 113, *114*, 116, 117
Stills, Stephen, 89, 92, *95*, see also Stephen Stills model
strap, 35
strap buttons, 17, 32
Streamliner models, 21, *23*, 24, *27*, 28, 31, 36, 37, *83*, 88, 89, *90–91*, 108, 142
Strong, Emerson, 9, 28, 76
Stump-o-Matic model, see Patrick Vaughn Stump model
Stump, Patrick, 120, 121, see also Patrick Vaughn Stump model
Super Axe model, 93, *94–95*, 97, 99, 143
Super Chet model, 85, *87*, 88, 104, 143
Super Gretsch model, 88, 143
Super Project-o-Sonic, see stereo models
Super Roc models, 96, 139
Super'Tron, see pickup
Synchromatic models, 9, 11, 105, 108, 128, 136, 143
Sychro-Sonic bridge, see bridge/Melita
Sylvain Sylvain, 99

tailpiece, 21, 33
Tennessee Rose models, 101, 104, 109, 116, 144
Tennessee Special model, 144
Tennessean models, 53, 56, *58–59*, 61, 64, 66, 69, 73, *74–75*, 76, 80, 88, 97, 98, 99, 101, 104, 109, 116, 143–144
tenor guitar, 24
Terada, see factories & offices
Terada, Masao, 109
Terminator, see bridge
Texarkana factory, see factories & offices
thinline body, see body
Thompson, Morley, 80

through-neck, 97
thumbnail markers, see fingerboard markers
Tim Armstrong models, *119*, 120, 144
TK 300 model, 96, 97, *102*, 144
Tone Twister, 65, 70
Touch System, 13, 16
Townshend, Pete, 44, 89, *91*
Traveling Wilburys models, 101, *102–103*, 145
Travis, Merle, 45, 46
treble boost, 80, 88
trestle bracing, see body
T-roof logo, 20
truss rod, 88, 155
tuners, 32, 33, 53
tuning fork, 65
TW, see Traveling Wilburys models
Twist model, 68, 69, 120, 145
Twitty, Conway, 19, 20
T-Zone Tempered Treble, 65, 67

ukulele, 24

Valentine, Hilton, 73
Van Eps, George, 81, see also Van Eps models
Van Eps models, 81, 88, 97, 145
Van Trigt, Vincent, *114*, 116
vibrato, 65, see also Bigsby, Burns
Viking models, 65, 69, *71*, 80, *83*, 88, 145
vintage trend, 89, 90, 91

Walsh, Joe, 89
Waverly tuners, 32
Webster, Jimmie, 11, 12, 13, *15*, 16, 20, 25, 28, 31, 33, 36, 37, *39*, 41, 48, 49, *55*, 56, 60, 62, *63*, 64, 65, 66, 68, 69, 76, 83, 85, 121
Western decoration, 20, 28, 32
White Falcon forces newspaper, 36, 37
White Falcon models, 33, 36, *38–39*, 40, 41, 46, 53, 56, 60, 61, *62–63*, 64, 65, *66–67*, 69, 80, *82–83*, 86, 87, 88, 89, *90*, 95, 97, 99, 103, 104, 108, 112, *114–115*, 115, 117, 118, 142, 145–148
White Panther model, see Panther models
White Penguin models, 37, *38–39*, 65, 104, *110–111*, 112, 113, *115*, 148
Woods, Harold, 53, 68

Yako factory, see factories & offices
Yamaha, 105
Young, George, 92
Young, Malcolm, 92, *95*, see also Malcolm Young models
Young, Neil, 73, 89, *95*

Zappa, Frank, 165
zero fret, 61, 155
Zildjian cymbals, 8, 92
Zoom, Billy, see Billy Zoom model

7/11 Songbird model, 140
10th Anniversary, 134
12-String model (name), 149
12-string models (general), 73, 76, 80, 104, 132, 149
20th Century (brand), 9
120th Anniversary, 126
125th Anniversary, 126, 150
130th Anniversary, 126
400 model, 143
5655 model, 136
6040 model, 143
6120 models, 29, *30–31*, 32, *34–35*, 40, 44, 45, 46, *50–51*, 53, *54*, 56, 60, 61, 64, *67*, 69, *71*, 73, 80, 85, *86–87*, 87, 88, 89, 92, 97, 99, 101, 104, 105, *106–107*, 108, 109, *111*, 112, 115, 116, 117, *118–119*, 120, 128, 133, 134, 149–151

ACKNOWLEDGEMENTS

INSTRUMENT PICTURES
OWNERS KEY
The guitars illustrated in this book came from the collections of the following individuals and organisations, past and present, and we are very grateful for their help. The owners are listed here in the alphabetical order of the code we've used to identify their instruments in the Instruments Key that follows. **AB** Andy Babiuk. **AC** Anonymous collector. **AH** Adrian Hornbrook. **AR** Alan Rogan. **CA** Chet Atkins. **BC** Bill Cochran, Pat Hickey, Ed Julson. **DE** Duane Eddy. **FA** Fretted Americana. **GD** Gary Dick. **GG** Gruhn Guitars. **GH** George Harrison. **GR** Gretsch/Fender. **HA** Heritage Auctions. **JB** Jeff Beck. **JC** Jennifer Cohen. **JR** John Reynolds. **LW** Lew Weston. **MB** Mandolin Brothers. **MG** Music Ground. **MJ** Mike Jones. **MW** Michael Wright. **PD** Paul Day. **PI** Peter Ilowite. **RB** Ray Butts. **SA** Scot Arch. **SC** Scott Chinery.

INSTRUMENTS KEY
This key identifies who owned which guitars at the time they were photographed. After the relevant bold-type page number(s) there is a model identifier, followed by an owner code (see the alphabetical list in the Owners Key above). **Jacket** Country Club, GR. **14–15** Electro II LW;

Corvette MB. **18–19** Duo Jet FA; Round Up FA. **19** Twitty Round Up HA. **22–23** Silver Jet SA; Jet Fire Bird HA. **26–27** Country Club green SC; Country Club grey SC. **27** Streamliner JR. **30–31** Streamliner/6120 CA; 6120 CA. **34** Solid Body FA. **34–35** '55 6120 LW; Experimental Guitar CA. **35** '56 6120 AR. **38–39** Falcon SA; Penguin SC. **42** Constellation AR. **42–43** Convertible SC; Clipper JR. **43** Rambler HA. **50–51** Cochran 6120 BC. **51** Beck's Duo Jet JB; Eddy's 6120 DE. **54** 6120 JR. **54–55** Country Gent AC. **55** Duo Jet AR. **58–59** Anniversary AH; Tennessean GG. **59** Double Anniversary GG. **62** Silver Jet Testbed RB. **62–63** Falcon SA; Country Club AR. **66** '59 Falcon AR. **66–67** '60 Falcon JR. **67** 6120 AR. **70** Duo/Silver Jet SA. **70–71** Corvette HA. **71** Astro Jet MG; 6120 SC. **74–75** Harrison's Duo Jet GH; Tennessean AB. **78–79** '62 Country Gent GH; '64 Country Gent GD. **82–83** Falcon JC; Rally GG. **83** Gold Duke Pl. **86–87** 6120 LW. **87** Super Chet HA; Roc Jet LW. **90** Country Roc PD; Streamliner II MJ. **90–91** Falcon MB. **94** Corvette II MJ. **94–95** Atkins's Super Axe CA. **95** Roc I MJ. **102** Beast MW. **102–103** Wilburys PD; TK 300 MJ. **106–107** all GR. **110–111** all GR. **114–115** Falcon GR. **118–119** all GR.

Guitar photography was by Nigel Bradley, Matthew Chattle, Fretted Americana, Gretsch/Fender, Heritage Auctions, Mike Jones, Rock & Roll Hall of Fame, Miki Slingsby, Callum Teggin (CR2 Studios), and William Taylor.

ARTIST PICTURES
Images are identified by bold-type page number, subject, and photographer and/or collection and agency.
50 Cochran, Balafon Image Bank; Eddy, Duane Eddy. **51** Gallup & Blue Caps, Michael Ochs Archives/Getty Images. **55** Atkins, Merle Atkins. **75** Harrison, CBS Photo Archive/Getty Images. **79** Popperphoto/Getty Images. **91** Townshend, BBC/Redferns. **95** Malcolm Young, Larry Hulst/Michael Ochs Archives/Getty Images; Stills & Young, Gijsbert Hanekroot/Redferns. **103** Duffy, Gretsch/Fender. **107** Setzer, Tony Nelson. **115** Higham, Steve Jennings.

MEMORABILIA
Other items illustrated in this book – including advertisements, catalogues, pamphlets, and photographs – are from the collections of Scot Arch; Tony Bacon; Balafon Image Bank; Jennifer Cohen; Country Music Hall of Fame; Paul Day; Ross Finley; Gretsch/Fender; Martin Kelly; *Music Trade Review*; *The Music Trades*; National Jazz Archive; Alan Rogan; and Vintaxe.com.

INTERVIEWS
Original interviews in this book were conducted by Tony Bacon as follows: Chet Atkins (April 1995, May 1995); Ray Butts (April 1995); Joe Carducci (April 2014); Jennifer Cohen (April 1995); Billy Duffy (April 2014); Dan Duffy (September 1995); Duane Eddy (April 1995); Ross Finley (March 1995); Chris Fleming (June 2014); Phil Grant (August 1995); Fred Gretsch (June 1995, July 2004); Bill Hagner (July 1995); Dick Harrison (July 1995, September 1995); Darrel Higham (April 2014); Dale Hyatt (February 1992); Mike Jones (May 2014, September 2014); T.V. Jones (July 2004); Duke Kramer (March 1995); Mike Lewis (July 2004, April 2014); Ted McCarty (October 1992); Don Randall (February 1992); Brian Setzer (June 2014); Stephen Stern (April 2014, August 2014); Patrick Stump (May 2014); Dean Turner (March 1995); and Paul Yandell (July 2004).

THANKS
Special thanks to Ed Ball, Steve Brown, Jason Farrell, Mike Jones, Mike Lewis, Alan Rogan, and Stephen Stern.
Thanks to everyone already named in these acknowledgements, plus: Dustin Addis (Crush Music); Ed Ball; David Brass & Debra Brass (Fretted Americana); Julie Bowie; Walter Carter (Carter Vintage); Bryan K. Christner; Paul Day; Jason Farrell (Fender); Mike Gowen (MSO); Dave Gregory; Mike Gutierrez (Heritage Auctions); Vincent Hastwell; Gene Haugh; Jim Hilmar; Stan Jay (Mandolin Brothers); Sindee Levin; Christie Lucco (Rock & Roll Hall Of Fame & Museum); Brian Majeski (*The Music Trades*); John McLellan; Mike Newton; Geoff Nicholls; Neil O'Brien; Martina Oliver (Getty Images); Mick Peek; Robert Pratt; Meredith Rutledge-Borger (Rock & Roll Hall Of Fame & Museum); Shoji Shiraki (Terada); Ian Tilton; Vincent Van Trigt (Gretsch Custom Shop); Bob Willocks (Fender); and Michael Wright.

BOOKS
Chet Atkins *Me And My Guitars* (Hal Leonard 2003).
Andy Babiuk *Beatles Gear* (Backbeat 2009).
Tony Bacon *50 Years Of Gretsch Electrics* (Backbeat 2005).
Tony Bacon (ed) *Electric Guitars: The Illustrated Encyclopedia* (Thunder Bay 2000).
Tony Bacon & Paul Day *The Gretsch Book* (Balafon 1996).
Edward Ball *Ball's Manual Of Gretsch Guitars: 1950s* (Schiffer 2014); *Gretsch 6120: The History Of A Legendary Guitar* (Schiffer 2010).
Walter Carter, Michael Cochran, Rich Kienzle, John W Rumble *Chet Atkins: Certified Guitar Player* (Country Music Foundation 2011).
A.R. Duchossoir *Guitar Identification* (Hal Leonard 1990).
Dan Duffy *Inside The Gretsch Guitar Factory From 1957 To 1970* (Trafford 2007).
George Gruhn & Walter Carter *Gruhn's Guide To Vintage Guitars* (Backbeat 2010).
Dave Hunter (ed) *Acoustic Guitars: The Illustrated Encyclopedia* (Thunder Bay 2003).
Mark Lewisohn *The Beatles Tune In* (Little, Brown 2013).
Julie Mundy & Darrel Higham *Don't Forget Me: The Eddie Cochran Story* (Mainstream 2000).
Geoff Nicholls *The Drum Book: A History Of The Rock Drum Kit* (Backbeat 2008).
Jay Scott *Gretsch: The Guitars Of The Fred Gretsch Company* (Centerstream 1992).
Tom Wheeler *American Guitars* (HarperPerennial 1990).

WEBSITES
gretsch.com; gretschguitars.com; gretschpages.com; gretschlostweekend.com; gretsch-talk.com; 6120freak.com.

TRADEMARKS
Throughout this book we've mentioned a number of registered trademark names. Rather than put a trademark or registered symbol next to every occurrence of a trademarked name, we state here that we're using the names only in an editorial fashion and that we don't intend to infringe any trademarks.

UPDATES?
The author and publisher welcome any new information for future editions. Write to: Gretsch, Backbeat & Jawbone, 2A Union Court, 20–22 Union Road, London SW4 6JP, England. Or you can email: gretsch@jawbonepress.com.

"Pick up my guitar and play, just like yesterday."
Pete Townshend and 6120, 'Won't Get Fooled Again', 1971

More Great Books by
TONY BACON

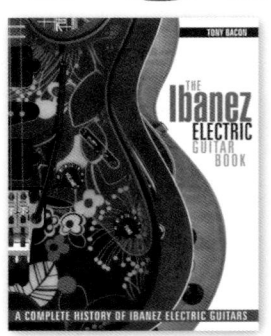

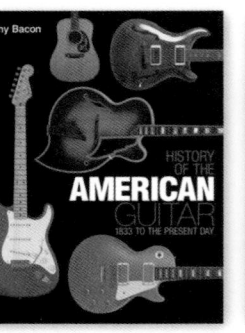

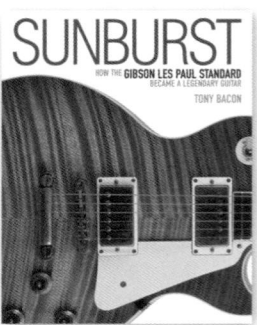

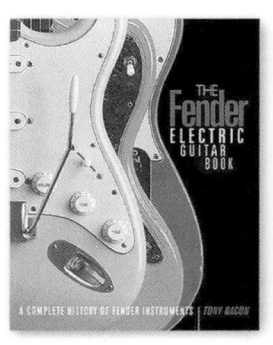

The Ibanez Electric Guitar Book
A Complete History of Ibanez Electric Guitars
by Tony Bacon
978-1-61713-453-1 • $24.99
• 8.5" x 11" • 160 pages •
Softcover • HL00333185

The Les Paul Guitar Book
A Complete History of Gibson Les Paul Guitars
by Tony Bacon
978-0-87930-951-0 • $27.99
• 8.5" x 11" • 176 pages •
Softcover • HL00332752

History of the American Guitar
1833 to the Present Day
by Tony Bacon
978-1-61713-033-5 • $27.99
• 12.5" x 9.75" • 160 pages •
Softcover • HL00333186

The Stratocaster Guitar Book
A Complete History of Fender Stratocaster Guitars
by Tony Bacon
978-0-87930-996-1 • $24.99
• 8.5" x 11" • 160 pages •
Softcover • HL00333046

50 Years of the Gibson Les Paul
Half a Century of the Greatest Electric Guitars
by Tony Bacon
978-0-87930-711-0 • $22.99
• 8.5" x 11" • 160 pages •
Softcover • HL00330951

The Fender Electric Guitar Book – 3rd Edition
A Complete History of Fender Instruments
by Tony Bacon
978-0-87930-897-1 • $24.95
• 8.5" x 11" • 192 pages •
Softcover • HL00331752

The Telecaster Guitar Book
A Complete History of Fender Telecaster Guitars
Revised and Updated
by Tony Bacon
978-1-61713-105-9 • $24.99
• 8.5" x 11" • 160 pages •
Softcover • HL00333189

60 Years of Fender
Six Decades of the Greatest Electric Guitars
by Tony Bacon
978-0-87930-966-4 • $24.99
• 8.5" x 11" • 144 pages •
Softcover • HL00332861

Flying V, Explorer, Firebird
An Odd-Shaped History of Gibson's Weird Electric Guitars
by Tony Bacon
978-1-61713-008-3 • $24.99
• 8.5" x 11" • 144 pages •
Softcover • HL00333076

Rickenbacker Electric 12-String
The Story of the Guitars, the Music, and the Great Players
by Tony Bacon
978-0-87930-988-6 • $24.99
• 8.5" x 11" • 160 pages •
Hardcover • HL00332751

Sunburst
How the Gibson Les Paul Standard Became a Legendary Guitar
by Tony Bacon
978-1-61713-466-1 • $29.99
• 8.5" x 11" • 144 pages •
Softcover • HL00333746

Squier Electrics
30 Years of Fender's Budget Guitar Brand
by Tony Bacon
978-1-61713-022-9 • $24.99
• 8.5" x 11" • 160 pages •
Softcover • HL00333228

Echo and Twang
Classic Guitar Music of the '50s
edited by Tony Bacon
978-0-87930-642-7 • $19.95
• 9.75" x 12.5" • 192 pages •
Softcover • HL00330772

ALSO AVAILABLE IN THIS SERIES:

The Epiphone Guitar Book
A Complete History of Epiphone Guitars
by Walter Carter
978-1-61713-097-7 • $24.99
• 8.5" x 11" • 176 pages •
Softcover • HL00333269

The PRS Electric Guitar Book
A Complete History of Paul Reed Smith Electrics
Revised and Updated Edition
by Dave Burrluck
978-1-4803-8627-3 • $29.99
• 8.5" x 11" • 160 pages •
Softcover • HL00120792

Backbeat Books
AN IMPRINT OF
HAL•LEONARD®

www.halleonardbooks.com

Prices, contents, and availability subject to change without notice.